# PRAISE FOR *DEMOCRACY DENIED*

"This is a must-read for everyone who values our nation's bedrock principles. What Obama is trying to unilaterally impose on the American people is nothing short of regulatory tyranny. Phil Kerpen breaks down the Obama administration's regulatory onslaught and shows those of us who love the Constitution what we can do about it."

—MARK LEVIN, bestselling author
and nationally syndicated radio host

"Phil Kerpen offers both a warning and a lesson about a radical minority and its concerted efforts to control the lives and voices of all Americans. *Democracy Denied* is a literal guidebook on the progressive game plan—now it's up to us to heed the warning."

—GLENN BECK, #1 *New York Times* bestselling author

"*Democracy Denied* demonstrates how President Obama is packing federal agencies with handpicked liberal activists who are rewarding campaign allies, punishing opponents, and pushing the failed Keynesian fiscal policies Americans rejected at the ballot box in 2010. Phil Kerpen's must-read book provides much-needed solutions to the unaccountable bureaucrats who seek to control what cars we drive, the foods we eat, and even the lights we use."

—U.S. Senator JIM DEMINT (R-South Carolina)

"Obama is on a mission—to conceal his socialist record behind a veil of moderation. Phil Kerpen pierces that veil and shows the Obama beneath. He has broken the Obama code."

—DICK MORRIS, Fox News contributor

"President Obama has sought from day one to bypass elected representatives in Congress and impose his liberal agenda by regulatory fiat. This unchecked regulatory assault is draining the lifeblood from our economy and eroding our liberties. Phil Kerpen's book is an excellent tool for anyone seeking to understand the consequences of regulatory tyranny and the story of the REINS Act—the most important reform that, if passed, will restore accountability and balance to the regulatory process."

—U.S. Senator RAND PAUL (R-Kentucky)

"You know Team Obama is up to no good, but you don't even know the half of it. Phil Kerpen takes you inside *all* the back rooms and back doors that these left-wing power-grabbers have used to subvert the will of the people—and trample the rule of law. *Democracy Denied* exposes you to the true size and scope of the Obama regulatory Leviathan. Kerpen's comprehensive research will make your blood boil and stir you to action."

—MICHELLE MALKIN, Fox News contributor
and bestselling author of *Culture of Corruption*

"The American people are the most innovative in the world, but they are being held back by the Obama administration's extreme regulatory agenda. Phil Kerpen cuts to the heart of this problem and shows us the path forward."

—U.S. Representative MIKE PENCE (R-Indiana)

"Federal regulations have the slippery tentacles of an octopus strangling businesses, families, and workers. *Democracy Denied* exposes the threats to economic freedom from Barack Obama's gang of unelected regulatory zealots."

—STEPHEN MOORE, senior economics writer
and editorial board member at *The Wall Street Journal*

"The Obama socialist juggernaut is attempting to ride roughshod over the will of the people, skirt existing laws, and sideswipe the Constitution. In *Democracy Denied*, Phil Kerpen masterfully articulates the challenges we face, and, most importantly, provides common sense solutions and strategies you need to know."

—JERRY DOYLE, nationally syndicated radio host

"As an elected city official, I have seen firsthand how the federal regulatory racket hurts local governments, citizens, and businesses. Phil Kerpen does an excellent job exposing abuses and offering constructive solutions to rein in the autocracy of unelected regulators."

—ERICK ERICKSON, editor of RedState.com

# DEMOCRACY
# DENIED

BenBella Books, Inc.
10300 N. Central Expressway, Suite 400
Dallas, TX 75231
www.benbellabooks.com
Send feedback to feedback@benbellabooks.com

Printed in the United States of America
10 9 8 7 6 5 4 3 2 1

Library of Congress Cataloging-in-Publication Data
Kerpen, Phil. Democracy denied : how Obama is ignoring you and bypassing Congress to radically transform America and how to stop him / by Phil Kerpen.
p. cm. Includes bibliographical references and index. ISBN 978-1-936661-32-9 (alk. paper) 1. United States--Politics and government--2009- 2. Executive power--United States. 3. Legislative power--United States. 4. Obama, Barack--Political and social views. I. Title. E907.K47 2011 973.932--dc23
2011034462

Editing by Debbie Harmsen
Copyediting by Lisa Miller
Proofreading by Sara Cassidy and Michael Fedison
Cover design by Laura Watkins
Text design and composition by Silver Feather Design
Printed by Berryville Graphics

Distributed by Perseus Distribution
(www.perseusdistribution.com)

To place orders through Perseus Distribution:
Tel: 800-343-4499
Fax: 800-351-5073
E-mail: ordentry@perseusbooks.com

# DEDICATION

*For Joanna, the love of my life,
and Lilly, the life of our love.*

# DEMOCRACY DENIED

How Obama Is Ignoring You and Bypassing
Congress to Radically Transform America—
and How to Stop Him

## BY PHIL KERPEN

BenBella Books, Inc.
Dallas, Texas

# TABLE OF CONTENTS

# PREFACE

This book started with a chart scribbled on the white board in my office. It was early 2010, and it was already becoming clear that Democrats were headed for a tea party buzzsaw in the midterm elections. Moreover, with President Barack Obama's limited political capital exhausted by the pushes for ObamaCare and the Dodd-Frank financial regulation bill, any other significant legislation was dead. But Obama's ambitions had not been diminished at all (nor would they be by their utter repudiation in the 2010 elections). I wanted to show how the Obama administration was disregarding Congress and the American people to accomplish its objectives through regulatory back doors.

My original version was developed into what you see on the next page by Americans for Prosperity's graphics whiz Tommy Downs.

As the chart shows, Obama will not take "no" for an answer—from either the American people or from Congress. And the vast regulatory apparatus of the federal government gives him the machinery to disregard the legitimate legislative process and move forward to impose huge "cap-and-trade"-style energy taxes via Environmental Protection Agency regulation, to use his friends at the Federal Communications Commission to regulate the Internet, and to pursue his failed union agenda at the National Labor Relations Board.

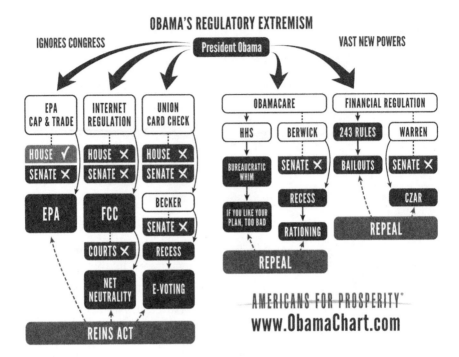

The pattern extends to the two signature pieces of legislation that *did* pass: ObamaCare and Dodd-Frank, which addressed health care and the financial industry, respectively. Both of these sweeping laws included vast expansions of regulatory power that are, even now, being pushed *further* left through abuses of the appointment process and aggressive use of federal regulatory power.

Glenn Beck loves the Obama Chart. The day I sent it to him, he said on his radio program: "This just came in from Phil Kerpen. It is the Obama way of subverting the Constitution."

Beck continued: "He has subverted the process, the legitimate process every step of the way. And nobody seems to have a problem with this. My thanks to Phil Kerpen for this. Phil, I've got to show this on television. It's unbelievable. It's just unbelievable."[1]

That was on March 16, 2010, and he did show an earlier version of the chart on his television program that night. Standing in front of the chart, Beck and his guest, Judge Andrew Napolitano, explained what was happening:

> BECK: Congress, you're out of your mind because you are giving so much power to the president and you've been doing it, as you said, president after president after president. You are going to become irrelevant. Judge, tell me that Congress is not irrelevant.
>
> NAPOLITANO: Congress will become irrelevant when the president can tell the EPA what to do, the FCC what to do, recess appointments, executive orders that the Congress wants to bypass. Look, the Supreme Court has said, power that the Congress has, it can't give to the president. But it has done that and this president is using it in the extreme.[2]

This book is an extended commentary on the chart. In it, I suggest we can seize on the opportunity created by Obama's extremism, and by revealing these power grabs to the public and demanding that Congress stop them, reverse the long-term trend.

# INTRODUCTION

# Crisis and Transformation

*"We are five days away from fundamentally transforming the United States of America."*[1]
—President Barack Obama, October 30, 2008

W hen the American people headed to the voting booth on November 2, 2010, they thought they were putting an end to President Obama's "fundamental transformation" of America. They were wrong.

In the face of an unprecedented wave of public discontent expressed at the ballot box and throughout his time in office, Obama has remained committed to an extreme left-wing agenda. If the separation of powers described by the U.S. Constitution remained intact, Obama's disrespect for the American voters wouldn't matter—he would be unable to move the country further left because he would be unable to pass his agenda through the Republican House.

Unfortunately, for decades Congress has been delegating away its legislative power to bureaucratic agencies that Obama is now using to bypass Congress and the American people to pursue his agenda.

Obama's fundamental transformation agenda, which proceeds apace despite Republican control of the House of Representatives, would turn America into a very different country. A country where:

- the federal government has vastly more control over our jobs, businesses, and families;
- judgments of individuals are supplanted by the judgments of Washington politicians and regulators;
- life-and-death decisions on health care are taken away from patients and doctors and given to regulators;
- every aspect of our financial lives is managed by regulators;
- our energy supply is tightly controlled and regulated;
- government regulators control the Internet; and
- regulators "nudge us" into the paths they choose.

Obama, though usually guarded about his core ideology, has at times given us glimpses into his vision of central economic control. Consider this quote from a 2001 radio interview:

> The Supreme Court never ventured into the issues of redistribution of wealth and more basic issues of political and economic justice in the society and to that extent as radical as I think people try to characterize the Warren Court, it wasn't that radical. It didn't break free from the essential constraints that were placed by the Founding Fathers in the Constitution.[2]

And, of course, his classic comment to Joe the Plumber: "I think when you spread the wealth around, it's good for everybody."[3]

In Obama's transformational shift from our (already compromised) free-market system to a European-style social-democratic "spread the wealth" society, the winners would be the special-interest groups that comprise Obama's base: the extreme environmentalists, union bosses, the so-called "social justice" street organizers (including racial grievance groups), and the trial lawyers who make their livings feeding off of dysfunctional, complex government bureaucracies.

Tragically, Obama failed to learn the central lesson of the 20<sup>th</sup> century: central economic planning is destined to fail. The great Nobel Prize–winning economist F. A. Hayek called the belief that somehow central planners would get it right "the fatal conceit." He explained:

> The market is the only known method of providing information enabling individuals to judge comparative advantages of different uses of resources of which they have knowledge and through whose use, whether they so intend or not, they serve the needs of distant unknown individuals. This dispersed knowledge is *essentially* dispersed, and cannot possibly be gathered together and conveyed to an authority charged with the task of deliberately creating order.[4]

To effect his transformation to a centrally controlled economy, Obama dramatically expanded the scope of regulatory power. Ironically, Obama campaigned against President George W. Bush's executive excesses, promising a return to a constitutionally limited executive branch. Nothing could be further from the truth.

## CRISIS AND BIG GOVERNMENT

Robert Higgs wrote the seminal work on how crises drive permanent increases in the size and intrusiveness of government, substituting centralized control for individual economic freedom. He observed that *regulatory* action is the likely outcome, saying, "the

*A central thrust of the Obama presidency so far has been to seize on the financial crisis as justification for vastly more intrusive federal regulation of nearly every aspect of American economic life.*

concealment of the true costs of governmental action in a crisis offers the most compelling explanation of why the command economy tends to displace the market economy during a national emergency in a democratic society."[5]

Clearly both the terrorist attacks of September 11, 2001, and the financial crisis of 2008 were real crises. But as Higgs warned:

> After the ideological transformation that took place during the Progressive Era, each genuine crisis has been occasion for another ratchet toward Bigger Government. The Progressive ideological imperative that government must "do something," must take responsibility for resolving any perceived crisis, insures new actions. The actions have unavoidable costs, which governments have an incentive to conceal by substituting coercive command-and-control devices for pecuniary fiscal-and-market means of carrying out their chosen policies.[6]

A central thrust of the Obama presidency so far has been to seize on the financial crisis as justification for vastly more intrusive federal regulation of nearly every aspect of American economic life. The administration has done so openly, starting with this explanation from Rahm Emanuel, styling the entire agenda as a crisis response:

> You never want a serious crisis to go to waste. And what I mean by that is an opportunity to do things that you think you could not do before … This is an

opportunity, what used to be long-term problems, be they in the health care area, energy area, education area, fiscal area, tax area, regulatory reform area, things that we have postponed for too long, that were long-term, are now immediate and must be dealt with. This crisis provides the opportunity, for us, as I would say, the opportunity to do things that you could not do before.[7]

One of the mysteries Higgs addresses is the question of why, following periods of crisis (usually a war or an economic depression), government never returns to its pre-crisis levels. One of the likeliest explanations is that most Americans simply do not know what the costs of expanded regulatory power are:

The expansion phase of the ratchet reflects the decisions of a quasi-autonomous government responding to an insistent but ill-defined public demand that the government "do something" about a crisis. Whatever the policy adopted, however, costs must be borne by people outside the government. The greater are the costs, the less willing is the public to tolerate them. When people are burdened too heavily, their resistance jeopardizes not only the policy but, in a normally operating representative democracy, the government itself. Anticipating such reactions, the government takes steps to conceal the true costs of its policies. Most importantly, it substitutes a cost-hiding command-and-control system of resource allocation for the (cost-revealing) market system and its utterly visible measuring rod of money.[8]

Our challenge, then, is as simple—and as difficult—as exposing the astonishing costs of Obama's command-and-control regulatory policies. If we expose them to the public and bring them to bear as election issues, the American public will reject them as intolerable.

The cycle of ratcheting up federal power during a crisis is a common one throughout American history. It is a cycle we must break.

## KING BUSH

One of the most persistent criticisms of Bush from the media, Democrats, and some limited-government conservatives was that he broke the traditional limits on executive power, disregarding Congress to pursue his national security objectives.

Grover Norquist, the stalwart antitax activist who leads Americans for Tax Reform, said: "If you interpret the Constitution's saying that the president is commander-in-chief to mean that the president can do anything he wants and can ignore the laws you don't have a constitution: you have a king."[9]

Elizabeth Drew made the case against Bush's abuse of executive power in a lengthy *New York Review of Books* piece called "Power Grab." She specifically highlighted Bush's use of signing statements (a technique to object to elements of a law while signing it, and refusing to enforce those elements), the detention of foreign combatants at Guantánamo, and warrantless wiretaps. She concluded that Bush was a tyrant:

▶ ▶ ▶

*"If you interpret the Constitution's saying that the president is commander-in-chief to mean that the president can do anything he wants and can ignore the laws you don't have a constitution: you have a king."*

—GROVER NORQUIST, Americans for Tax Reform

James Madison wrote in Federalist Paper No. 47: "The accumulation of all powers legislative, executive and judiciary in the same hands, whether of one, a few or many...may justly be pronounced the very definition of tyranny." That extraordinary powers have, under Bush, been accumulated in the "same hands" is now undeniable. For the first time in more than 30 years, and to a greater extent than even then, our constitutional form of government is in jeopardy.[10]

The left was so angry about Bush's alleged power grabs that they called him everything from a tyrant to a dictator to Hitler.[11]

I am not an expert on national security policy. But I find it curious that most of the people who were aghast at the aggressive use of executive power by Bush in the national security realm (arguably a legitimate sphere of presidential power) are silent as Obama pursues his entire failed legislative agenda, which has already been rejected by Congress and the American people, by regulatory back doors.

Consider this quote:

An executive who arrogates to himself the power to ignore the legitimate legislative directives of the Congress or to act free of the check of the judiciary becomes the central threat that the Founders sought to nullify in the Constitution—an all-powerful executive too reminiscent of the King from whom they had broken free.[12]

Does that sound like a person who would support the EPA pursuing sweeping global warming regulations without the consent of Congress? It was. The person speaking was Al Gore.

Consider Obama's own broken promises regarding Bush policies. He came out in support of warrantless wiretaps even before the election, flip-flopping from his earlier opposition. He promised to close Guantánamo over and over again on the campaign trail, and again after he was elected—but it remains open. He promised to end the Bush administration's enhanced interrogation techniques. He considers them torture, but they continue. *The Wall Street Journal* noted the double standard: "We are relearning that the 'Imperial Presidency' is only imperial when the President is a Republican. Democrats who spent years denouncing George Bush for 'spying on Americans' and 'illegal wiretaps' are now conspicuously silent."[13]

Obama even exceeded Bush on at least one highly controversial security policy—the full-body scanners and intrusive pat downs required by his Transportation Security Administration. A policy he adopted unilaterally, without legislation from Congress.

Even the Bush practice that raised the most ire—the use of signing statements—was embraced by Obama just weeks after he took office, when he said: "it is a legitimate constitutional function, and one that promotes the value of transparency, to indicate when a bill that is presented for presidential signature includes provisions that are subject to well-founded constitutional objections."[14] Contrast that with what Obama had said about signing statements on the campaign trail:

> ▶ ▶ ▶
>
> *"An executive who arrogates to himself the power to ignore the legitimate legislative directives of the Congress or to act free of the check of the judiciary becomes the central threat that the Founders sought to nullify in the Constitution... reminiscent of the King from whom they had broken free."*
> —AL GORE

This is part of the whole theory of George Bush that he can make laws as he is going along. I disagree with that. I taught the Constitution for 10 years. I believe in the Constitution and I will obey the Constitution of the United States. We are not going to use signing statements as a way of doing an end run around Congress.[15]

In April 2011, after a tense showdown that narrowly averted a government shutdown, Obama and House Speaker John Boehner agreed to a compromise spending bill. One of the things Obama agreed to include was language blocking the funding for several of his most controversial policy czars—White House staffers who avoid Senate confirmation, but are given broad powers to direct the federal regulatory apparatus. Even though he had agreed to the language, Obama did precisely what he had promised not to do: he used a signing statement to "do an end run around Congress."

> ▶ ▶ ▶
>
> *With that signing statement, Obama not only embraced what he accused Bush of doing—"making laws as he is going along"—but broke a specific commitment he had made in a negotiated compromise agreement with Congress. Moreover, he did it to keep dangerous, hard-left ideologues in place as czars.*

On April 15, 2011, Obama issued a signing statement on the compromise government funding bill that said: "Section 2262 of the Act would prohibit the use of funds for several positions that involve providing advice directly to the President ... Therefore, the executive branch will construe section 2262 not to abrogate these Presidential prerogatives."[16]

With that signing statement, Obama not only embraced what he accused Bush of doing—"making laws as he is going along"—but broke a specific commitment he had made in a negotiated compromise agreement with Congress. Moreover, he did it to keep dangerous, hard-left ideologues in place as czars.

One of the harshest critics of executive power under Bush, Yale law professor Bruce Ackerman, dismissed the overly simple view of many on the left regarding Obama ending abuse of power. After a warning about an authoritarian takeover, he says:

> This grim prognosis depends on structures, not personalities, permitting us to move beyond knee-jerk reactions to the politics of the day. Most obviously, the election of President Obama has, for many, sufficed to dispatch any serious doubts about the system: Good-bye, imperial presidency; hello, America's first black president, and the nation's remarkable capacity for constitutional renewal![17]

But a paragraph later he falls into the very trap he warned against, absurdly writing of Obama:

> He may be charismatic, but he is no extremist: there is little chance of his running roughshod over congressional prerogative, even those as indefensible as the filibuster. But the next insurgent president may not possess the same sense of constitutional restraint.[18]

Sadly, contrary to the ideologically blinded analysis of most observers from the left, all of the elements of excessive executive power that they feared from Bush have continued—or worsened—under Obama. On top of which he has used the financial crisis as an excuse to seize control—without Congress's approval—of the energy supply, industrial activities, the Internet, and labor policy.

Some of the loudest voices opposing Bush's use of executive power are now cheering for Obama to push things much further. It's different when it's your guy in charge.

# FINANCIAL CRISIS AND THE TARP

Bush laid the foundation for Obama's regulatory agenda when he intensified the financial crisis by warning the country of impending doom, and then proceeded to push for a vast new federal power to intercede in the financial system in the so-called Troubled Asset Relief Program (TARP) legislation.

The initial draft of the bill was little more than a blank check for then-Treasury Secretary Hank Paulson to spend as he saw fit. Some oversight and other minor improvements were added, but the bill still ultimately gave the Treasury a free hand.

Some banks, such as BB&T, were forced to accept TARP money they neither wanted nor needed—even though accepting it subjected them to enormous public backlash and increased regulatory interference. But most of the big banks were happy to accept enormous infusions of taxpayer money, and the special "too big to fail" status it brought, with an implicit government guarantee thereafter supporting all of their operations. The big banks became protectorates of the federal government, subsidizing them at taxpayer expense to the detriment of smaller banks and other financial institutions.

Shortly after the bill was passed, its supposed *raison d'être*, the purchase of troubled assets, was jettisoned in favor of direct equity injections. The Treasury Department seemed to be making it up as it went along.

Obama, for his part, supported the bill. And by appointing Timothy Geithner, who helped shape the bailout as president of the Federal Reserve Bank of New York, as his Treasury secretary, Obama sent a clear signal that extraordinary interventions in the banking sector would continue. (As I discuss in Chapter 6, they would get much worse.)

# Mea Culpa

▶ ▶ ▶

I fell for it—the "do something" desire in a crisis. Credit markets were locking up. The Treasury secretary was forecasting the end of civilization (we later learned that "civilization" meant "Goldman Sachs") if Congress didn't step in with taxpayer dollars, and sweeping new federal authority to bail out the banks. In the Washington puzzle palace, the pressure was intense to support the bill. Moreover, I was genuinely frightened that our financial system would disintegrate.

I hated the bill. It didn't address the root causes of the crisis—most glaringly it did nothing about housing, including Fannie Mae and Freddie Mac. It rewarded imprudent risk-taking. I knew better than to support it. Yet somehow I fell for "do something"— and I regret it.

I regretted it almost immediately. My phone rang seconds after I sent it to Americans for Prosperity's staff list. It was Steve Lonegan, our New Jersey state director and conservative hero with whom I rarely disagree. He was livid.

I left Washington the next day for Wisconsin, where I did a series of town hall meetings around the state with Mark Block, who was then the Wisconsin state director for Americans for Prosperity. At every stop, the rooms were unanimous (or nearly so—there was an occasional lonely dissenter who worked in finance) in opposition to the bailout. It wasn't just the fundamental unfairness of taxpayers being forced to

pick up the tab. It was also the idea that somehow
it was government's role to step in and intervene
when things go wrong in the market. It offended the
sensibility of most Americans. They were right, and
I was wrong. I hope the work I've done advancing
economic freedom since then—and in this book—
makes up for it.

## BUSH'S AUTO BAILOUT AND OBAMA'S SHAKEDOWN

Bush went further. He crossed the line into the kind of domestic
nonsecurity power grabs that would define the Obama presidency
when he ignored the clear will of Congress on bailing out the auto
companies. The auto bailout bill foundered in the U.S. Senate on
December 10, 2008. Senate Republican Leader Mitch McConnell
(R-Ky.) summarized the concern that stopped the bill: "In the end
its greatest single flaw is that it promises taxpayer money today for
reforms that may or may not come tomorrow."[19]

Bush refused to take "no" for an answer. Repurposing funds
that Congress had designated for banks under TARP that had already been repurposed for equity injections, Bush directly disregarded the Senate's rejection of the auto bailout and did it anyway,
to the tune of $17.4 billion. In doing so, he defined a pattern that
the Obama administration has used for its agenda. In short: when
Congress says "No," do it anyway.

Obama repeated this mistake, giving the autos another round
of TARP funds before finally recognizing that there was no alternative to bankruptcy. Worse, the Chrysler bankruptcy was not a

real bankruptcy. It was prenegotiated by the White House based on political considerations and forced on creditors by extra-legal means. It was an egregious abuse of executive power, and did tremendous damage to the rule of law. As Todd Zywicki of George Mason University explained:

> The Obama administration's behavior in the Chrysler bankruptcy is a profound challenge to the rule of law. Secured creditors—entitled to first priority payment under the "absolute priority rule"— have been browbeaten by an American president into accepting only 30 cents on the dollar of their claims. Meanwhile, the United Auto Workers union, holding junior creditor claims, will get about 50 cents on the dollar...
>
> Mr. Obama may have helped save the jobs of thousands of union workers whose dues, in part, engineered his election. But what about the untold number of job losses in the future caused by trampling the sanctity of contracts today?[20]

The message from Obama and his administration was clear: we will accomplish our policy objectives at any cost, and by any means. Indeed that's how they would push two major pieces of legislation they wanted—ObamaCare and Dodd-Frank in the health and financial realms, respectively—and how they would pursue all of their other objectives in the absence of legislation, or even in the face of Congress rejecting their legislation.

## STIMULUS UNITES UNIONS AND GREENS

Obama's first major legislation was an enormous federal spending bill that filled the bank accounts of his special-interest constituencies.

The bill, misleadingly named the American Recovery and Reinvestment Act, was justified as "stimulus."

When the legislation was conceived, the administration thought it would sail through with 75 or 80 votes in the U.S. Senate. Instead, the American people rose up, took to the streets, and protested. It was the birth of the tea party movement, and it forced Obama to go back out on the campaign trail, where he spent a considerable amount of the political capital he had accumulated in his impressive election victory to get his stimulus bill passed.

In the end, the Democratic Congress, aided by three Republicans—Olympia Snowe and Susan Collins of Maine, and Arlen Specter of Pennsylvania (who would later become a Democrat before losing his reelection bid in a primary)—squeaked through a bill hated by the American people.

The idea of government spending making us richer was doomed to fail from the start, even if there hadn't been abuse and incompetence. The simple fact is every dollar the government spends comes from the private sector. Government spending is either financed through higher taxes or higher federal borrowing, or through inflation (printing money). Those are the only possibilities, and they all create greater economic damage than any stimulus effect of new spending.

> ▶ ▶ ▶
>
> *The message from Obama and his administration was clear: we will accomplish our policy objectives at any cost and by any means. Indeed that's how they would push two major pieces of legislation they wanted—ObamaCare and Dodd-Frank in the health and financial realms, respectively.*

When Obama signed the bill, the unemployment rate was at 7.6 percent, and the president promised it would never go above 8 percent. Instead the country spent much of the following year at higher than 10 percent unemployment. Obama and congressional Democrats claimed their bill would save our economy. In truth, it was meant to serve primarily political purposes.

Senate Majority Leader Harry Reid (D-Nev.) specifically credited a little-known group called the Apollo Alliance for developing the stimulus bill.[21] Reid said:

> This legislation is the first step in building a clean energy economy that creates jobs and moves us closer to solving our enormous energy and environmental challenges. The Apollo Alliance has been an important factor in helping us develop and execute a strategy that makes great progress on these goals and in motivating the public to support them.[22]

Historically, the unions and the environmentalists had been on opposite sides of many major public policy fights, with environmentalists largely opposed to the economic development that union workers needed for jobs. The Apollo Alliance's mission—embodied in the stimulus—was to bring these groups together and push for special giveaways from the government so they could prosper together at the expense of taxpayers. The San Francisco-based group's roster includes the American Federation of Labor-Congress of Industrial Organizations, the Service Employees International Union (SEIU), the United Steelworkers, Greenpeace, the Sierra Club, and the Association of Community Organizations for Reform Now, more commonly known as ACORN.[23]

Apollo's man inside the administration was so-called "green jobs" czar Anthony K. "Van" Jones, a former Apollo board member and its model for a new kind of pro-union environmental leader. John Podesta (who chaired Obama's transition team and hired Jones at the Center for American Progress both before and after he worked for the White House) is on the Apollo board, along with Carl Pope from the Sierra Club and Gerald Hudson, a vice president of the SEIU.[24]

Jones had been radicalized in 1992 after an overnight stay in jail when he was swept up while serving as a legal observer at a San Francisco demonstration following the verdict in the Rodney King case. Jones said:

> I met all these young radical people of color—I mean really radical, communists and anarchists. And it was, like, "This is what I need to be a part of." I spent the next ten years of my life working with a lot of those people I met in jail, trying to be a revolutionary. I was a rowdy nationalist on April 28th, and then the verdicts came down on April 29th. By August, I was a communist.[25]

Since then his beliefs have not changed, although his tactics have. "I'm willing to forgo the cheap satisfaction of the radical pose for the deep satisfaction of radical ends," he said.[26]

Jones resigned in disgrace from the Obama administration over his extreme views on everything from using green jobs as the kernel of capitalism's destruction to his signature on a petition saying that the terrorist attacks of September 11, 2001 may have been a Bush administration inside job. But immediately after his resignation, Jones was heartily embraced by the left. He is now a senior fellow at the Center for American Progress,[27] has a teaching fellowship at Princeton,[28] and received a *National Association for the Advancement of Colored People* Image Award.[29]

> ▶ ▶ ▶
>
> *We'll see in policy area after policy area, rewarding the extreme environmentalists and the union bosses continues to be a key goal of Obama's agenda.*

Jones has been heartily embraced by the left because his views are squarely within the mainstream of Obama's Democratic Party. And as we'll see in policy area after policy area, rewarding the extreme environmentalists and the union bosses continues to be a key goal of Obama's agenda.

## THE PEOPLE FIGHT BACK

On February 19, 2009, just six days after the stimulus bill was passed, Rick Santelli, reporting from the *Chicago Mercantile Exchange* trading floor in Chicago on CNBC, let loose a rant that perfectly captured the public mood:

"This is America! How many of you people want to pay for your neighbor's mortgage that has an extra bathroom and can't pay their bills?" he said. "President Obama, are you listening?"[30]

The trigger for the rant was another proposal to bail out homeowners who couldn't afford their mortgage payments.

"Cuba used to have mansions and a relatively decent economy," Santelli said. "They moved from the individual to the collective. Now, they're driving '54 Chevys, maybe the last great car to come out of Detroit."

▶ ▶ ▶

*Santelli's call to action? A tea party. He said: "We're thinking of having a Chicago tea party in July. All you capitalists that want to show up to Lake Michigan, I'm gonna start organizing."*

Santelli's call to action? A tea party. He said: "We're thinking of having a Chicago tea party in July. All you capitalists that want to show up to Lake Michigan, I'm gonna start organizing."

I was on CNBC that night in a panel discussion with Santelli, and I told him—on the air—to just let me know when and where the big Chicago tea party would be and I would make sure all of Americans for Prosperity's members—hundreds of thousands of whom had just signed a petition opposing the stimulus bill—knew about it.

He never organized that tea party, and he never had to. Instead, something even more remarkable happened. Santelli lit a spark that became a wildfire. Americans all over the country took time away from work and family to become a new generation of political leaders. And these folks were not self-serving leaders with personal ambitions, but patriotic leaders sacrificing their time and money to fight for the American ideals of limited government and personal responsibility.

These tea party leaders—some at the national level, but most especially at the local level, in cities and towns large and small—have done something truly remarkable: they have started a movement from the ground up, uniting millions of Americans in opposition to government control of our economy.

I spoke at the Washington, D.C., tea party on April 15, 2009, to thousands of people in the pouring rain. Afterward, I wrote:

> This is the beginning of a new populist revolt, and it's happening all over the country. The top-down, big money, big government forces of [George] Soros, MoveOn.org, and Organizing for America are about to meet a true bottom-up, populist steamroller. Elites will ignore this at their own peril.[31]

All over the country that day—even in New York City, where some of those present had voted for Obama and were saying they had "buyer's remorse"—more than a million people took to the streets to stand for limited government principles. I didn't know if tea party activists could sustain their intensity. Amazingly, not only did they sustain the energy, they increased it. Activists took ownership of the health care debate, and very nearly stopped ObamaCare. Then they turned to political organizing, and became the unstoppable force behind one of the biggest landslide elections in American history.

The 2010 election should have ended Obama's push for a "fundamental transformation" of America, which had been emphatically repudiated. Unfortunately, President Obama has something else in mind. Nothing would stop him. He was going to continue with the strategy, just go to plan B—pursuing his agenda via regulatory back doors.

## RED TAPE NATION

Even before Obama's onslaught of new federal regulations, regulatory compliance costs were placing a crushing burden on job creation and economic growth.

Lafayette College economists Nicole Crain and Mark Crain conducted a study for the U.S. Small Business Administration's Office of Advocacy that quantified the 2008 cost of federal regulations at an astonishing $1.75 trillion.[32] That's nearly twice the amount of total income taxes the federal government collected last year.[33] The compliance costs for small businesses topped $10,500 per employee, per year— 36 percent higher than for their big business competitors. Environmental regulations were the worst culprits, costing small businesses 364 percent more than their competitors.[34]

▶ ▶ ▶

*I didn't know if tea party activists could sustain their intensity. Amazingly, not only did they sustain the energy, they increased it ... They turned to political organizing, and became the unstoppable force behind one of the biggest landslide elections in American history.*

Those 2008 costs were before the enormous new compliance costs associated with all of Obama's new regulations in his first two years, and the even more extreme regulatory agenda he is currently pursuing.

In 2010 alone, federal regulators adopted a record 43 major rules—defined as having costs in excess of $100 million each—with a total cost officially estimated at $26.5 billion.[35] That estimate doesn't include 12 economically significant rules whose costs were considered unquantifiable, and hundreds of minor rules that add up to real money—and government always underestimates regulatory compliance costs.

Wayne Crews of the Competitive Enterprise Institute writes an annual report on federal regulations called *10,000 Commandments*. In the 2011 edition, he reported that the *Federal Register*, which is where regulations are published, now stands at a record 81,405 pages. There were 3,573 new final rules published in 2010, a 20 percent increase from 2009. Another 4,225 rules are in the pipeline, with 224 expected to each have an economic impact of more than $100 million.[36]

A groundbreaking report from the Phoenix Center used econometric modeling to look at the negative economic impact of funding federal regulatory agencies. The results were stunning: each federal regulator destroys 98 private sector jobs and $6.2 million worth of gross domestic product. The researchers found that even a 5 percent cut in spending on regulation would create about 1.2 million jobs annually.[37]

We can't afford even the current level of federal regulation, yet Obama and his cadre of regulatory extremists are eager to go much further, and in the process ignore the American people's message in the 2010 election, bypass Congress, and complete a "fundamental transformation" of America that will wreak havoc on the U.S. economy and the U.S. Constitution. They must be stopped.

## CHAPTER 1

# The REINS Act: How Three Kentuckians Could Save America

*"All legislative Powers herein granted shall be vested in a Congress of the United States, which shall consist of a Senate and House of Representatives."*[1]
—United States Constitution, Article I, Section 1

T he most important idea to stop regulatory tyranny didn't come from a think tank or a university. It didn't come from Washington. It didn't come from a so-called expert. It came from a 78-year-old former county judge in Alexandria, Kentucky, named Lloyd Rogers. In 2009 he handed his congressman, U.S. Rep. Geoff Davis (R-Ky.), a piece of paper with a powerful idea.

Davis understood it immediately, and in record time this big idea went from one paragraph on a piece of paper to a serious legislative proposal that was included in the official House Republicans' 2010 platform document, the Pledge to America. It is one of Speaker John Boehner's top priorities.

> ▶ ▶ ▶
>
> *The REINS Act cuts to the heart of regulatory power abuse by requiring any major regulatory action to receive the approval of the House and Senate as well as the signature of the president before it can take effect.*

The bill is called the Regulations from the Executive In Need of Scrutiny (REINS) Act, known in the House as H.R. 10 and in the Senate as S. 299. The REINS Act cuts to the heart of regulatory power abuse by requiring any major regulatory action to receive the approval of the House and Senate as well as the signature of the president *before* it can take effect. It's an idea so simple and so powerful that it seems obvious. The best ideas always do.

Indeed the idea is a modern, workable way to restore a basic principle that goes back to 1690, when John Locke wrote:

> The legislative cannot transfer the power of making laws to any other hands: for it being but a delegated power from the people, they who have it cannot pass it over to others... The power of the legislative, being derived from the people by a positive voluntary grant and institution, can be no other than what that positive grant conveyed, which being only to make laws, and not to make legislators, the legislative can have no power to transfer their authority of making laws, and place it in other hands.[2]

Locke was widely influential on our founders. John Adams expressed the principle clearly in Article XXX of the Massachusetts Constitution: "The executive shall never exercise the legislative and judicial powers, or either of them ... to the end that it may be a government of laws, and not of men."[3]

Similarly, the founders included this concept as the very first thing (after the preamble) in the U.S. Constitution. Article I, Section

1 states clearly that legislative power—the power to make laws—resides with Congress. In Federalist 47, James Madison explained that the U.S. Constitution was written to avoid the danger of legislative and executive power being fused by prohibiting the executive from making laws:

> From these facts, by which Montesquieu was guided, it may clearly be inferred that, in saying "There can be no liberty where the legislative and executive powers are united in the same person, or body of magistrates,"…where the whole power of one department is exercised by the same hands which possess the whole power of another department, the fundamental principles of a free constitution are subverted…This, however, is not among the vices of that constitution. The magistrate in whom the whole executive power resides cannot of himself make a law.[4]

Yet we now have precisely the situation that Madison and the other framers wanted to avoid. We have regulators who are effectively writing and executing their own laws. The major policy decisions that affect every aspect of our economic lives are moving forward without consent of the people's legitimately elected legislative branch.

The REINS Act is a powerful remedy to restore the legislature to its legitimate role.

I talked to the three Kentucky men who are leading the fight for the REINS Act: Rogers, who originated

> ▶ ▶ ▶
>
> *We have regulators who are effectively writing and executing their own laws. The major policy decisions that affect every aspect of our economic lives are moving forward without consent of the people's legitimately elected legislative branch.*

the idea; Davis, who turned it into legislation and is its leading advocate; and U.S. Sen. Rand Paul (R-Ky.), the bill's current lead sponsor in the Senate. Heeding the wisdom of these three Kentuckians and passing the REINS Act may be the country's best hope to end regulatory tyranny and restore accountability and transparency to our federal government. Here is an overview of my discussions with each of them.

## LLOYD ROGERS AND THE IDEA

Lloyd Rogers is 78 years old, and his is a great American story. "I grew up in an orphan's home," he told me. "My dad died when I was young, and I was raised in a home here in this county," referring to Campbell County, Kentucky. "I never had any college, but I had an ambition. I took speed-reading, I took public speaking, and I took things like that."[5]

A wounded four-year Navy veteran, Rogers was a Disabled American Veterans commander and a Veterans of Foreign Wars commander. His political hero is Thomas Jefferson.

Throughout his life, Rogers has been guided by integrity, which he learned at a very young age. I sensed a hesitance to talk about himself. He is far more concerned with stopping President Obama's regulatory agenda, but it's important to understand where his core principles come from. He revealed:

> The man who was in charge of the orphanage, he used to be in there when he was a kid. He came back and he ran it, and he was a very conservative fellow. And he used to teach us: if there's nothing else anybody can ever say about you when you die, they can write on your tombstone that you were honest.

Inspiring words, and nearly the opposite of the fundamental deception employed when the elected branches of government defer to unelected bureaucrats to make the real decisions.

Rogers came to politics relatively late in life, focusing on his career as a supervisor and an engineer with Cincinnati Bell after his military service. He retired in 1982 after 31 years at the company.[6] "I never voted until I was 40. I never cared. I was interested in other things," he said. "I never get mad at people who say, 'Hey, I didn't vote,' because I went there at one time. So I understood what I should have done. And since then, I have been an activist, trying to reinstitute what our forefathers meant this government to be."

"I became very well versed, and took courses in the Constitution," he continued. "The more I read about what government was doing—and I didn't read fiction—I got so interested in what was happening in government. And I had been so blind all these years, and I didn't pay any attention to it. I just figured it was my responsibility to do it, so I did it."

Rogers went on to become Campbell County Judge Executive from 1982 to 1985 and a member of a military review board, appointed by then-Congressman Larry Hopkins (R-Ky.). "In other words, if you wanted to go to Annapolis or West Point, you came before this board and we interviewed you."[7] (His key collaborator, Geoff Davis, happens to be a West Point graduate.) Still in Campbell County, Rogers was recently a city councilman in Alexandria.

Rogers first tangled with the federal Environmental Protection Agency (EPA) in 1983, when he mobilized 25 local elected officials to go to Washington to push back against new EPA tailpipe emissions testing requirements. U.S. Sen. Wendell Ford (D-Ky.) set up a meeting for the group with Bill Ruckelshaus.

Ruckelshaus was the founding administrator of the EPA when it was created during the Nixon administration. Reagan brought him back in early 1983, when the EPA established tailpipe emissions testing in 64 cities.

Rogers confronted Ruckelshaus:

> I asked him where he got his constitutional author-
> ity—he didn't say. And he didn't know he didn't
> have it. His lawyer didn't know it. And the people
> acquiesce to things like that. They hand these regula-
> tions down to the state, and the state hands them on
> down to the county, and we're going through the pro-
> cess of obeying laws that aren't even on the books.[8]

Rogers organized three counties in Kentucky and one in Ohio
that were hit by the new tailpipe testing and brought an entourage
of public officials to Washington. They successfully got the new requirements put on hold. The EPA kept pushing and Rogers kept
pushing back:

> I was in office two more years, and after I left office
> they got a new guy in charge of EPA and they came
> back with it again. The second time I got a group
> of people together, we went down to the state of
> Kentucky, and we met with our legislators. And this
> time, we got rid of it, and we also sold the building
> so they could never come back again.[9]

It was a small victory, but Rogers took on the EPA and won.
Now he has his sights set even higher—stopping abuse of regulatory power throughout the federal government. His more recent
activism was spurred by another abusive EPA regulation: its tax on
rainwater.

Rogers was outraged by the EPA's sweeping imposition of a
stormwater consent decree that imposed enormous costs on his
county and two neighboring counties in northern Kentucky. It was
part of a growing trend of EPA stormwater regulations that are forcing cities and counties around the country to increase taxes.[10] He

said: "Now they're raising rates, so heavily and so advanced on sewer and on water because of mandates from the EPA. And you know, recently the EPA says if Congress doesn't pass cap-and-tax, then they'll do it."[11]

The stormwater consent decree inspired Rogers to take his one-paragraph idea to Davis, who turned it into the REINS Act. As Rogers describes it: "The REINS Act really reins in the costly overreach of the federal agencies that stifles job creation and hinders economic growth. And this law will restore authority to those who are accountable to the voters, their elected representatives in Congress."[12]

While Rogers continues to build grassroots support for the bill from local governments and tea party groups in Kentucky, Davis is championing the bill in Congress.

## GEOFF DAVIS AND THE FIX FOR OUT-OF-CONTROL REGULATIONS

U.S. Rep. Geoff Davis is the Republican congressman from Kentucky's fourth congressional district in northern Kentucky, along the Ohio River. Davis had a tough childhood in Pittsburgh, Pa., where he worked as a janitor in high school to help support his family, leaving after high school to join the Army. Accepted into West Point, Davis had a distinguished 11-year military career commanding assault helicopters before embarking on a successful career leading his own consulting firm specializing in lean manufacturing.[13]

Davis, elected to Congress in 2004, is a member of the House Committee on Ways and Means and a Deputy Republican Whip. He brings a business-like approach to government and has a keen understanding of regulatory issues. In short, he is a rising star—and the sponsor of the most important process reform bill in Congress.

Davis, like his constituent Lloyd Rogers, had long been concerned about the regulatory process, and was spurred to action by the stormwater consent decree. "Everybody's taxes were doubled as a result of it," Davis told me. "There was no commensurate improvement in service whatsoever." He pointed out the money could have been much better spent on replacing the I-75 Brent Spence Bridge, which carries 3.8 percent of the country's GDP every year. "I took a very strong position against the consent decree from day one, based on the fact that I saw it as taxing and legislating by regulation," Davis said. "I was constantly on a mantra about this, about the growth of the executive branch. It affects every area."[14]

Then, the answer came to him from Rogers. It happened in late August 2009, when Rogers called Davis and requested a meeting. Rogers talked about one of their favorite topics—the consent decree and the enormous impact it was having on fees. And then Rogers, according to Davis, laid out a very simple—profound, really—proposition.

Rogers said: "How come you guys can't vote on these things?"[15] and he handed Davis a piece of paper with a paragraph of text. It was the big idea, the idea that would become the REINS Act. This is, verbatim, what the piece of paper said:

Proposed legislation:
In adherence to the U.S. Constitution, Article 1, section 1 ... "All legislative Powers herein granted shall be vested in a Congress of the United States, which shall consist of a Senate and House of Representatives." All rules, regulations, or mandates that require citizens, state or local governments financial expenditures must first be approved by the U.S. Congress before they can become effective.[16]

Davis took the idea back to Washington and huddled with his key advisers to develop the simple idea into a robust, workable piece of legislation. He analyzed it the way he used to analyze manufacturing processes. He agreed with Rogers that the key element missing from the regulatory process is accountability. Davis explained:

> One of the folks at AEI [the American Enterprise Institute] described this bill, particularly the way that we had presented it, as truly revolutionary, because it changes the entire mindset of the "detached experts," many of whom have never even worked in the fields they're regulating. To bring back accountability to the people, with transparency, accountability, and a true check and balance.
>
> My biggest concern is the unchecked growth of the executive branch, where the Congress becomes less and less relevant as each decade goes by.[17]

Davis's real-world business experience was critical to developing the bill. He said:

> You want to have a constant check and a process. The Toyota production system is a perfect example of this. If something is not right, or if there's an exception to a standard, the process stops. Lights go on, and everybody converges on the issue to bring attention to it.
>
> And I always had this rolling around in the back of my mind as a way to approach this. That conversation became the genesis for the REINS Act. Here really was the question. We needed to create that kind of a stop that forced a vote on the bill.[18]

To make the bill more workable, Davis began by limiting it to major rules with an economic impact above $100 million. And he worked through the technical legal issues with his counsel to make sure the bill would maintain a constitutional balance and meet the requirements for bicameralism and presentment, of which the Supreme Court ruled earlier "legislative vetoes" of executive action had run afoul.[19]

Bicameralism and presentment mean that for a bill to become a law, both the House and Senate must pass it, and it must be presented to the president for signature or veto. That's precisely the procedure that the REINS Act requires for major regulations, as constitutional scholar Jonathan Adler has pointed out.[20]

To prevent procedural maneuvers in Congress to stall as a way to derail regulations, REINS requires a vote to take place within 70 legislative days of when a new rule is submitted to Congress, with timelines for committee action and a streamlined process to provide for consideration without amendments or procedural motions. There is a narrowly crafted exception for temporary emergency rules to take effect for no more than 90 days. Davis and his team anticipated the objections to the bill and found solutions to make it airtight.

Once the bill was drafted, it was immediately embraced by Republican House leadership and attracted a large number of cosponsors:

> Well, I basically had 50 cosponsors in probably two hours. And I would just explain this to most members. And John Boehner … in fact, I approached him on the issue, explained it to him. And he signed on immediately. And so did Eric Cantor and Kevin McCarthy. They all embraced it from early on.
>
> And we were doing quite a bit of media on the bill, on the concept, through the spring, in the

summer, pointing out all rules. And just as you've rightly pointed out in your writings with Dodd-Frank, with the health care bill, the EPA move on cap-and-trade, Lord Julius [Genachowski] with the FCC issue—and frankly this backdoor issue on card check has huge implications for the business community if they can put this in place.[21]

McCarthy (R-Calif.), Peter Roskam (R-Ill.), and Boehner (R-Ohio) not only decided to include the REINS Act in the Pledge to America, but they also all specifically touted the bill in speeches starting in the summer of 2010. "I was very humbled, frankly, when it got picked up in the Pledge to America," Davis said.[22]

Davis explained that the REINS concept is not antiregulation. It is simply for regulation that is transparent and has a built-in political accountability mechanism. The hope is that by improving the process, Congress can stop unnecessary regulations and make necessary regulations less costly. Davis told me his approach even attracted the support of an EPA official, with whom Davis spoke at an AEI event:

▶ ▶ ▶

*The REINS concept is not antiregulation. It is simply for regulation that is transparent and has a built-in political accountability mechanism.*

He said what he liked about the concept was that it was not antiregulation, but it tightens communication between the Congress and the executive branch and the agency community. Typically, and you have seen legions of bills through your time studying these, very generic legislation will be cobbled together to get the votes to pass something, and then it's thrown over the wall to the administration.

And oftentimes you'll come back with regulations, think HIPAA [the Health Insurance Portability and Accountability Act], that don't even remotely resemble the intent of Congress.[23]

That's especially critical when you consider that some of the major authorizing legislation that regulations flow from is decades old, and passed by members of Congress who are now long gone. Davis stresses that the accountability mechanism created by REINS ensures that major regulatory actions have the support of the most recently elected Congress.

Davis also understands that fixing our regulatory process is, in a competitive world, an economic imperative if we want to have jobs in America. And explaining that to the public is the key to advancing reform:

> As these regulations were growing, we were the 900-pound gorilla in the world. We could always increase salaries, and we could always increase prices, when those costs were there. Now we've hit a point in global competition and we don't have that economic flexibility anymore. And we're going to have to take—in the way that we look at government and managing these outcomes—an approach similar to what we had to do in the manufacturing world to stay competitive, with lean manufacturing.

> Toyota came in and changed the entire game, because they chose to introduce a different set of rules by which they were going to compete. And the Big Three are still damaged because of assumptions prior to that introduction.

> I'd say those kinds of competitive practices must come in, but people will not support these

kinds of changes until they see it in a way that hits their pocketbooks.[24]

Stopping these astonishing regulatory power grabs is all about jobs. It's about bringing accountability for the economic impacts to bear on our elected officials.

## RAND PAUL TAKES THE SENATE LEAD

On the Senate side, U.S. Rep. Geoff Davis found a partner in U.S. Sen. Jim DeMint (R-S.C.), who picked the bill up in September 2010 and introduced it with 13 cosponsors. DeMint has been a hero on every free-market fight since he joined the Senate in 2004 and a standout in fighting to stop the Obama administration's regulatory power grabs.

This Congress, DeMint handed off REINS to U.S. Sen. Rand Paul, making it a Kentucky-led effort on the Senate side as well as the House side. Paul talked about the REINS Act as one of his major campaign themes and is committed to it as a top legislative priority.

Lloyd Rogers was a tireless campaigner for Paul, organizing DAV and VFW units around the state and putting up more than 140 Rand Paul signs. Rogers was the Campbell County chairman for the Paul campaign, and it was through the campaign that he connected with the tea party.

Paul met Rogers in the summer of 2009, when he was a long-shot, outsider candidate for the U.S. Senate. Paul told me that he and Rogers seemed to "hit it right off."[25] Paul noted that Rogers "is known for being independent-minded, also a gentleman with an incredible amount of energy to have done all this in his midseventies."[26]

One of the toughest things to do on a campaign is to get businesses to take sides. They are generally concerned about angering part of their customer bases. But Paul told me that Rogers persuaded hundreds of Campbell County businesses to put up campaign signs, saying: "I'd go up and down the main highway up there and he'd have them up at business after business. It takes some incredible convincing."[27]

Paul had long been concerned with unelected bureaucrats writing laws, and it was a campaign theme from the beginning. As he explained: "Congress has abdicated its role. Congress has let power devolve away to the president but also to regulatory agencies that really don't have oversight."[28]

Paul saw it as a perfect issue for tea party activists because it speaks to their desire for good, accountable government. He learned about the REINS Act by hearing Davis talk about it and he quickly adopted it as a central part of his campaign platform.

Paul explained why the REINS Act is such a critical tea party priority:

> I think it's an amazingly good government issue. I tell even the liberals on the floor: "Don't you at least want to have some say in what regulations are passed? You might think the regulation is a good idea, I might think it's a bad idea, but don't you think we ought to vote and not unelected bureaucrats?" And some of them nod their heads. It's a good government, nonpartisan issue.[29]

While he pushes for the REINS Act, Paul is also committed to fighting Obama's regulatory abuses "tooth and nail" using existing legislative tools, especially the Congressional Review Act (CRA), which can overturn regulations with 51 votes in the Senate—but requires a presidential signature. Paul believes stopping the regulatory agenda was a major impetus of the 2010 election, and the new Congress has a mandate to follow through on it. While Obama may or may not veto CRA actions, Paul correctly observes it is "a useful tool" because it shows Obama "that we will fight him if he tries to evade Congress."[30]

# REINING IN REGULATORY ABUSE

In the end, success will depend not on the House and Senate but on us—American citizens and voters. Davis put us to the test, telling me:

> We're in an economic place and a constitutional place where that activism is necessary.
>
> I'll put this into context. The guy that was the founder of Sam Adams beer said he would know he'd been successful when he was walking in a strange city and he found his bottle cap on the ground. And there's this anecdotal story about how that happened some years ago. And to me, I think the real excitement about the REINS Act is when it's well beyond anything that we do as an office. The key is not us, here; the key is it's an idea that can restore constitutional balance.[31]

He's right and that's our challenge. Tell your local civic, cultural, political, and religious groups about the REINS Act. Write to your local newspapers. Call talk radio shows. Talk to your family, friends, and neighbors.

President Obama has given us an opportunity. As Paul said during our interview: "This particular president is an advocate of just about every form of regulation of business you can think of, and he's also said, fairly explicitly, that if he can't get things through Congress he'll simply write regulations."[32] That should get the attention of the public, and—with an educational push—move them to action.

▶ ▶ ▶

*Tell your local civic, cultural, political, and religious groups about the REINS Act. Write to your local newspapers. Call talk radio shows. Talk to your family, friends, and neighbors.*

Support for the REINS Act needs to be a basic litmus test for candidates for the House of Representatives, Senate, and president of the United States. Candidates who refuse to promise to restore accountability for legislative decisions to Congress are not worthy of support. Especially for presidential candidates, it's critical to get them on the record in support now—before they become president—because unless there is enormous public pressure, almost every president will want unchecked regulatory power.

We have a tool that can help us solve one of the basic structural problems destroying jobs and economic freedom. As we work to restore the U.S. Constitution, the very best place to start is at the beginning, with Article I, Section 1.

## CHAPTER 2

# The Heat Is On: Global Warming and the EPA (Extreme Power Abuse)

*"Under my plan of a cap-and-trade system, electricity rates would necessarily skyrocket."*

—PRESIDENT BARACK OBAMA[1]

*"We put nothing in writing, ever."*

—MARY NICHOLS, chairman, California Air Resources Board describing the secret deal with then-White House Energy Czar Carol Browner to impose the first national carbon dioxide regulations.[2]

F or decades, environmental extremists have been stymied when their doomsaying predictions collide with the reality of an ever-improving environment, driven by the enormous wealth created by our market economy. The "problem" they describe is always something different, but the "solution" is always the same: draconian restrictions on economic activity, vastly expanded government power (usually internationally), and greatly diminished individual freedom.

In the 1960s, the doomsayers wrung their hands about overpopulation and predicted widespread famines before better technology drove an enormous increase in crop yields. In the 1970s, resource shortages were predicted that would cripple the global economy, with everyone from the Club of Rome to President Jimmy Carter convinced that we were up against meaningful resource constraints to growth. Yet prices plummeted for every significant natural resource as technology drove production and substitution. In the 1980s, the scare story was biodiversity, focused on the idea that the loss of so-called keystone species would cause a cascading effect that would kill us all. That turned out not to be true. So in the 1990s, the environmental extremists settled on a new doomsday scenario: global warming.

Global warming is different because its doomsday predictions can't be tested by reality. They depend on computer models that predict disaster many decades, or even centuries, into the future. The environmental extremists no longer need a new scare story every decade.

Carbon dioxide—a colorless, odorless gas with no direct adverse health effects—is at the heart of the global warming debate because it is the greenhouse gas that is most directly connected to human activity. The Obama administration is intent on having its way with carbon dioxide emissions at any cost, and by any means. In fact, President Obama's relentless pursuit of extreme global warming regulations is perhaps the clearest example of his disregard for our constitutional system of separation of powers and democratic accountability. There was fierce public debate over Obama's 2009 plan for draconian emissions cuts. The public opposed it, Congress rejected it, and the electorate, via the polls, clearly said "no." Yet Obama pushes forward.

These regulations will cost every American household thousands of dollars a year without any environmental benefit to show for it—except a nice, green feeling for our political elites. And to what end? The regulations would have *no* discernible impact on global levels of greenhouse gases or on global average temperature, even if you believe the most dire predictions about global warming. In fact, the 83 percent reduction in emissions Obama supports would prevent a ridiculously insignificant 0.09 degrees Fahrenheit of warming.[3]

These regulations are not being worked up on the House or Senate floor. They're being discussed behind closed doors. A secret effort has quietly moved forward to implement cap-and-trade—and even more extreme forms of regulation—by backdoor administrative means at the Environmental Protection Agency (EPA), an abbreviation that might better be reinterpreted as "Extreme Power Abuse."

*The Obama administration is intent on having its way with carbon dioxide emissions at any cost, and by any means. In fact, President Obama's relentless pursuit of extreme global warming regulations is perhaps the clearest example of his disregard for our constitutional system of separation of powers and democratic accountability.*

## CAP-AND-TRADE: A TAXING SITUATION

One of Obama's top priorities after taking office was to impose a national cap-and-trade scheme to ration energy use. Obama explained how the system would work in a meeting with the *San Francisco Chronicle* editorial board during the 2008 campaign:

> Under my plan of a cap-and-trade system, electricity rates would necessarily skyrocket. Even regardless of

what I say about whether coal is good or bad. Because I'm capping greenhouse gases, coal power plants, you know, natural gas, you name it—whatever the plants were, whatever the industry was, they would have to retrofit their operations. That will cost money. They will pass that money on to consumers.[4]

In other words, cap-and-trade is a way to impose a massive energy tax—and pretend it's not a tax. Once elected, Obama stopped honestly describing cap-and-trade; instead he launched a deceptive campaign to convince the American public that cap-and-trade would magically cause Americans to use much less energy without noticeably raising prices. Whether this campaign was borne from a deep sense of denial or outright malfeasance remains to be seen.

> ▶ ▶ ▶
>
> *Cap-and-trade is a way to impose a massive energy tax—and pretend it's not a tax.*

Al Gore himself explained the origins of cap-and-trade in describing the lesson he learned from an attempt to pass a straightforward energy tax in 1993:

I worked as vice president to enact a carbon tax. Clinton indulged me against the advice of his economic team…One House of Congress passed it, the other defeated it by one vote then watered it down and what remained was a pitiful 5 cent per gallon gasoline tax. That contributed to our losing Congress two years later to Newt Gingrich.[5]

Enter cap-and-trade. The political "innovation" of the cap-and-trade scheme is that instead of levying a tax directly, it puts a cap on overall greenhouse gas emissions, and establishes a market for companies to buy and sell emission permits. The overall effect is the same—if a company wants to emit more carbon dioxide, it must pay more. So it's a tax with the added uncertainty of a rate that's unknown and set at auction. Despite these efforts at obfuscation, the so-called American Clean Energy and Security Act of 2009, known as Waxman-Markey, collapsed after its chief sponsors, U.S. Reps. Henry Waxman (D-Calif.) and Edward Markey (D-Mass.), could not hide its true tab. The Congressional Budget Office scored that cap-and-trade bill—a whopping 1,200-page tome, plus a 300-page amendment that was added at three in the morning on the day of the House vote—as an $873 billion tax hike.[6]

The budget office also agreed, in its official analysis, with what Obama told the *San Francisco Chronicle*—that the costs would be passed on to consumers in the form of higher prices. CBO Director Doug Elmendorf explained in his Senate testimony, "Under a cap-and-trade program, consumers would ultimately bear most of the costs of emission reductions."[7]

I don't often agree with MoveOn.org, but on April 17, 2009, the organization sent out an urgent fund-raising alert to try to save cap-and-trade that got it exactly right. MoveOn.org's Adam Ruben said in the e-mail: "If Republicans convince voters that clean energy legislation amounts to a new tax, Obama's plan is toast."

Of course, it *was* a tax. And it was toast. Enough Americans broke the code, with the help of those of us who weren't going to let the Obama administration impose a nearly $1 trillion stealth tax on an already overburdened economy. Obama's failure wasn't a failure of communication, it was a failure of obfuscation. Cap-and-trade is a huge tax hike, and the American people don't want it.

While Waxman-Markey squeaked through the House in June 2009, it stalled in the Senate. Energy-state Democrats balked at the wildly unpopular bill, which was a bridge too far with the American people, already erupting in anger over health care takeover legislation.

Not even Senate Majority Leader Harry Reid (D-Nev.) and Obama could twist enough arms to force every Senate Democrat to walk the political plank on cap-and-trade, and only one Republican, U.S. Sen. Lindsey Graham (R-S.C.), continued to publicly support the bill. Eventually he pulled the plug, too, and the American people went to the ballot box in 2010 to, among other things, decide the future of cap-and-trade.

## THE PEOPLE SPEAK:
## CAP-AND-TRADE IS TOXIC

Cap-and-trade was utterly buried in the 2010 election, most visibly in southwest Virginia, where coal-country Congressman Rick Boucher (D-Va.)—who had not only voted for cap-and-trade but cut the key deal to try to buy off opposition from some energy companies—was soundly defeated on the issue. Just a few days before the election, Boucher gave an explanation to the *Roanoke Times*: "It puts the burden on me to provide a complicated explanation to a complex issue and go through about a four-step logical process to persuade people that what I did was the right thing for coal."[8]

It wasn't, of course. And it was the wrong thing for the country. The people of his district had too much sense to listen to his excuses. Boucher, after 28 years, is no longer a congressman.

In nearby West Virginia, Democrat Joe Manchin was trailing in the polls until a game-changing television ad, "Dead Aim," showed him shooting a bullet through the House-passed cap-and-trade bill with a rifle. According to *The Washington Post*'s Chris Cilizza, "It was a high-risk, high-reward move that clearly helped turn the race back in Manchin's favor."[9] Manchin is now a U.S. senator.

It was the same story all over the country. Cap-and-trade supporters in competitive races lost. Notable losers who provided Nancy Pelosi with the key votes to get cap-and-trade past the finish line in the House included: Betsy Markey (D-Colo.), Alan Grayson

(D-Fla.), Suzanne Kosmas (D-Fla.), Debbie Halvorson (D-Fla.), Baron Hill (D-Ind.), Frank Kratovil (D-Md.), Ike Skelton (D-Mo.), Harry Teague (D-N.M.), Steve Driehaus (D-Ohio), Mary Jo Kilroy (D-Ohio), John Boccieri (D-Ohio), Zach Space (D-Ohio), Paul Kanjorski (D-Pa.), Tom Perriello (D-Va.), Rick Boucher (D-Va.), and Steve Kagen (D-Wis.).

That's a pretty thorough rejection of cap-and-trade. One would think that the administration would get the hint and focus its attention elsewhere. But, incredibly, Obama and his EPA are attempting to revive this nefarious scheme, this time trying to hide it even further from taxpayers' eyes and the democratic process by using an administrative agency to impose the regime, instead of following the legislative process described by the Constitution.

## REWRITING THE CLEAN AIR ACT OF 1970: A BACK DOOR TO SOARING ENERGY PRICES

Just to show you how unfazed the Obama administration was by the political defeat of cap-and-trade, consider what's on page 146 of Obama's 2012 budget: "The administration continues to support greenhouse gas emissions reductions in the United States in the range of 17 percent below 2005 levels by 2020 and 83 percent by 2050."[10] Those just happen to be the same levels required by the failed Waxman-Markey cap-and-trade bill. Obama is telling the EPA to just pretend the bill passed and regulate away.

In fact, Obama's EPA was already moving full-steam ahead to implement a global warming regulatory scheme that could be even *more* costly than cap-and-trade—without the approval of the American people and without so much as a vote in Congress. On December 7, 2009—

> ▶ ▶ ▶
>
> *Obama is telling the EPA to just pretend the bill passed and regulate away.*

right in the middle of the media firestorm over the Climategate scandal, which leaked e-mails from leading global warming alarmists that called some of the basic science into question—the EPA issued a so-called "endangerment finding" for greenhouse gases, paving the way for onerous greenhouse gas regulations to be shoehorned into the 1970 Clean Air Act, despite the fact that Congress had considered—and decisively rejected—adding such regulations in 1990, when the Clean Air Act was amended.[11] It is such an ill-fitting vehicle to address greenhouse gases that in order for this strategy to succeed, the EPA must, illegally, rewrite the law to suit its purposes.

The EPA wants to handpick which industries and carbon emitters it will regulate, because applying the law as written to greenhouse gases would by the EPA's own admission create "absurd results."[12] Not only is such a discriminatory approach patently illegal, but it will also fail to stop a regulatory cascade that will paralyze the American economy.

The Supreme Court opened the door for the misuse of the 1970 Clean Air Act with its decision in *Massachusetts v. EPA* in 2007. That five-to-four decision instructed the EPA to decide whether or not to pursue global warming regulation based on the language of the statute.

Applying the Clean Air Act to carbon dioxide means regulating millions and millions of facilities across the United States never before subject to federal permitting, all the way down to some single-family homes. Even the EPA isn't that crazy, but instead of simply responding to the Supreme Court by concluding the Clean Air Act cannot be used for this purpose, the EPA has promoted itself to super-legislature of the United States, attempting to arbitrarily rewrite the law to apply only to larger facilities and moving forward.

The organization is doing this despite the fact that one of the 1970 Clean Air Act's original authors, U.S. Rep. John Dingell (D-Mich.), who supports cap-and-trade, by the way, admitted that the Obama administration's move is a recipe for disaster. He said:

We are also looking at the possibility of a glorious mess being visited upon this country...

In last year's Supreme Court decision in *Massachusetts v. EPA*, the court stated that it believed that greenhouse gases are air pollutants under the Clean Air Act. This is not what was intended by the Congress and by those of who wrote that legislation...

So we are beginning to look at a wonderfully complex world which has the potential for shutting down or slowing down virtually all industry and all economic activity and growth...

Now, I am certain that the legal profession will enjoy this mightily and I am satisfied that this will be a full employment situation for lawyers, of whom I happen to be one, and maybe if I leave the Congress I will return to the practice of law so that I can enjoy this kind of luxurious emolument for creating complexity for our society and a significant downturn in economic activity.[13]

Through his mandate to the EPA, Obama himself has confirmed that, from his perspective, the resounding wishes of the American people on this issue are irrelevant. Furthermore, in the president's postelection press conference, he hid behind the Supreme Court decision, misinterpreting it as a "court order" (a legal term of art that as a former law school instructor Obama surely understands) for regulation. This is what he said about the EPA, underscoring that he still very much intends to make energy prices skyrocket, if not by cap-and-trade then by other means:

The EPA is under a court order that says greenhouse gases are a pollutant that fall under their [sic] jurisdiction... Cap-and-trade was just one way of skinning the cat; it was not the only way. It was a means, not an end. And I'm going to be looking for other means to address this problem.[14]

The following day, former White House green jobs czar Van Jones let the plan slip in even franker terms, saying:

> Those are your only three options. Regulate them hard. Tax them hard. Make them buy permits. Make 'em buy permits, that's called cap-and-trade. Unfortunately, the minute we did that, the cap-and-trade proposal got called "cap and tax" and everything else and "socialism," and now we are without an option...So the only thing left for you, young folks, next year is to go back to the EPA and say, "Listen, we tried *to pretend* that what was going on was a market failure, i.e., we had the price wrong for carbon. The price being zero. And that didn't work, so now we're going to have *to pretend* it is a regulatory failure."[15]

Jones often says openly what his friends and allies on the left believe but are usually more guarded about.

## THE TRAIN WRECK: THE EPA'S MANY WAYS TO 'SKIN THE CAT'

Two weeks after the 2010 election and Obama's "skin the cat" comment, a leading D.C.-based, left-wing advocacy group, the Center for American Progress, published a 53-page report called *The Power of the President: Recommendations to Advance Progressive Change*, detailing a sweeping far-left agenda that flies directly in the face of what voters made clear they wanted.[16] The report was coauthored by the president of the Center for American Progress, John Podesta, who was the chairman of Obama's transition team, and who has direct influence over the president and his key advisers.

The Podesta report does not comment on the EPA's efforts to regulate greenhouse gases directly under the Clean Air Act. It urges other less direct, but no less devastating, regulatory moves to accomplish the same goal.

Many of the EPA actions urged by the Podesta report are already under way at the EPA and are referred to in the energy industry as the "train wreck" because they seek to massively burden the coal industry with enough regulations to bankrupt it.[17]

> ▶ ▶ ▶
>
> *"If somebody wants to build a coal plant, they can—it's just that it will bankrupt them."*
> —PRESIDENT BARACK OBAMA

Obama, during the same 2008 interview when he said his plan would make electricity prices "necessarily skyrocket," also explained the impact of his cap-and-trade plan on coal: "So, if somebody wants to build a coal plant, they can—it's just that it will bankrupt them."[18]

Not enough? The following rules are other ways to "skin the cat" and bankrupt the coal industry.

- A rule that would classify coal ash as hazardous waste, which the Center for American Progress notes would "spur the retirement of coal-fired power plants."[19]

- An enormously expensive so-called Maximum Achievable Control Technology rule for industrial boilers, with exceptions for politically favored biomass facilities. While the rule is ostensibly targeted at mercury, dioxins, and particulate matter, the Center for American Progress includes it in the section on greenhouse gases because the real goal is, of course, to cripple coal. Jon Basil Utley recently summarized the impact of this rule in *Reason*:

> The EPA wants new, more stringent limits on soot emissions from industrial and factory boilers. This would cost $9.5 billion according to the EPA, or over $20 billion according to the American Chemistry Council. A study released by the Council of Industrial Boiler Owners says the new rules would put 300,000 to 800,000 jobs at risk as industries opted to close plants rather than pay the expensive new costs. The ruling includes boilers used in manufacturing, processing, mining, and refining, as well as shopping malls, laundromats, apartments, restaurants, and hotels.[20]

- A Power Plant Air Toxics rule, which the Center for American Progress urged the EPA to adopt by November 2011. This rule would require very expensive new technology at coal plants. As they explain: "Despite the rule being directed at toxics—and not greenhouse gas emissions—the new pollution control requirements could lead to many old inefficient plants being shut down rather than attempt to achieve compliance."[21] On March 16, 2011, the EPA announced precisely this rule, with a targeted date of November 2011.[22]

- The EPA's proposed tightening of ground-level ozone (smog) rules—a problem that most Americans thought was already solved. A study by the Manufacturers Alliance found that the EPA's new proposed ozone rules would knock a jaw-dropping 5.4 percent off of GDP by 2020, destroying 7.3 million jobs.[23] Because these regulations fall heavily on refiners, they will bring a big jump in prices for gasoline and home heating fuel—along with a major hit to manufacturing and to coal.

Taken together, these regulations represent an all-out war on the coal industry and affordable electricity even above and beyond what the EPA is doing on the direct greenhouse gas regulation front.

## THE CZAR BEHIND THE CURTAIN

Driving the implementation of the EPA's massive power grabs and circumvention of the legislative branch was a key White House official who avoided Senate confirmation by being installed as White House Energy Czar: Carol Browner.

The potential Senate confirmation fight Obama sidestepped by creating a czar position for Browner would have likely centered on her membership on the board of the Socialist International Commission for a Sustainable World Society.[24] Browner was listed as one of 14 members of the commission on its website as recently as January 5, 2009—the day she was named Obama's White House energy czar.[25] This commission pursues an openly socialist agenda of centralized control under a regime of global governance that would enforce extreme environmental political correctness globally. The commission's views on global warming are, to say the least, extreme. Commission statements from the time Browner served include:

- "Global governance is no longer a concept but an urgent necessity."[26]
- "A global system for monitoring and forecasting climate change, an international rescue service, an international center to design new industrial constructions ecologically, should be set up."[27]
- "Measures against climate change in every country will inevitably have to include a change in life style

and a substantial reduction of greenhouse gases. The use of flexible mechanisms should be limited."[28]

Browner is a longtime Washington insider who previously served as Al Gore's legislative director and as the administrator of the EPA for all eight years of Bill Clinton's presidency.[29] Browner was on the board of Podesta's Center for American Progress.[30] She also worked for Podesta on the Obama transition team, chairing the energy and environment policy working group.[31] Her ideas—the ideas of the Socialist International Commission on a Sustainable World Society—are likely shared by President Obama, who appointed her.

In 1998, long before *Massachusetts v. EPA*, Browner, as Bill Clinton's EPA administrator, had her general counsel, Jonathan Z. Cannon, prepare a now-infamous memorandum arguing—for the first time—that the EPA possessed the power to adopt sweeping economy-wide global warming regulations without an act of Congress.[32] At the time it was dismissed as a wild-eyed overreach that Congress would never allow. Now it's happening. We have national greenhouse gas regulations under the Clean Air Act for cars and light trucks. And it was Browner, an unconfirmed White House czar, who made it happen.

Mary Nichols, the chair of the California Air Resources Board, told *The New York Times* that Browner was the lead White House negotiator in establishing new automobile emissions standards. California had been threatening to adopt its own, more expensive standards, and the EPA had previously denied the state's requests. Now the White House was playing ball, secretly adopting expensive, California-style regulations nationally

> *"Global governance is no longer a concept but an urgent necessity."*
> —Socialist International Commission for a Sustainable World Society, of which former White House Energy Czar Carol Browner was a member up to the day of her Obama appointment

via the Congress-sidestepping legal theory Cannon had argued for a decade before.

But unlike previous vehicle mileage requirements (legally, but at a great cost to consumers) enacted by Congress under the Corporate Average Fuel Economy law, these standards were created administratively, relying on the EPA's asserted authority to regulate greenhouse gases under the 1970 Clean Air Act.

Nichols told *The New York Times* that Browner "quietly orchestrated" the secret negotiations between the White House, regulators, and auto industry officials. "We put nothing in writing, ever," Nichols said.[33]

To make matters worse, the already costly new automobile regulations, negotiated in secret by Browner and Nichols, are now set to be ratcheted up to absurd levels. In October 2010 the EPA issued a "Notice of Intent" to adopt new standards on automakers to ensure that, fleetwide, their cars get 62 miles per gallon by 2025, up dramatically from the current mandate of 35.5 mpg by 2016. No cars on the road are anywhere close to 62 mpg. As Pat Michaels of the Cato Institute, a leading libertarian think tank, has pointed out, even the highest mileage vehicle now on the market, the third-generation Prius, gets no more than 50 mpg, and its vehicle weight is too high to ever get much more than that.[34]

> ▶ ▶ ▶
>
> *The White House was playing ball, secretly adopting expensive, California-style regulations nationally via the Congress-sidestepping legal theory Cannon had argued for a decade before.*

The only vehicles that could ever meet this hypothetical 62 mpg standard would be tiny, underpowered, electric vehicles that consumers don't want. And if some larger vehicles were still available for families and workers that need them, that would force small passenger cars to get even *higher* mileage to average out to 62 mpg. They might as well just shutter the auto industry.

Left unchecked, Browner's unconstitutional plan will move beyond automobiles to regulate everything that moves—light-duty trucks, heavy-duty trucks, buses, motorcycles, planes, trains, ships, boats, tractors, mining equipment, RVs, lawn mowers, forklifts, and just about every other piece of equipment that has a motor, and lots of things that don't. Any building over 100,000 square feet could be pulled in, along with smaller carbon dioxide emitters, like restaurants, schools, and hospitals that have commercial kitchens with gas burners.[35] Because there is no control technology for greenhouse gases, the EPA would require complete redesigns and operational changes. This is all part of the EPA's staggering 18,000-page blueprint for regulating the U.S. economy.[36]

# MEET THE NEW ENERGY CZAR

▶ ▶ ▶

After the 2010 election, Carol Browner pushed for a promotion to deputy White House chief of staff—and even, apparently, the chief of staff job itself.[37] Given her controversial past, the White House decided, sensibly, not to promote her and she resigned as czar. Curiously, the announcement was made not by Browner herself or by official White House staff, but by Podesta, who said: "There was a feeling it was time to move on...It's a loss. I hate to see her go."[38] Podesta's lead global warming strategist at the Center for American Progress, Dan Weiss, said the White House was losing the "all-star quarterback of President Obama's green dream team."[39]

The Obama administration moved quickly to allay their concerns, promoting Browner's top deputy, Heather Zichal, to the climate czar role. Zichal, a former John Kerry staffer, holds the same extreme views and is committed to continuing the same extreme agenda. She said: "We're maintaining staff, the same focus and mission that this office has had since the first day of the administration."[40] To paraphrase The Who, meet the new czar, same as the old czar.

Browner's handpicked administrator, Lisa Jackson, remains at the helm of the EPA. The Jackson/Zichal team is without question moving forward on Browner's Socialist International agenda—and Browner herself, like Podesta, will continue to exert enormous influence even after officially leaving the administration.

Browner, predictably following in the footsteps of former green jobs czar Van Jones, announced her return to Podesta's Center for American Progress on April 19, 2011.[41]

The first regulations for large industrial facilities came into effect at the beginning of 2011 for major modifications. They are set to expand to include new construction later in the year, and will be expanded over time until, eventually, they could paralyze the

American economy.[42] One of the first effects, of course, will be the skyrocketing energy prices that President Obama desires.

One EPA official, Anna Marie Wood, has let slip that the EPA intends to adopt cap-and-trade itself as part of its Clean Air Act regulations.[43] My Americans for Prosperity colleague James Valvo analyzed precisely how the EPA intends to implement cap-and-trade, mainly by adopting emissions trading requirements as a control technology and forcing states to amend the Clean Air Act State Implementation Plans to include cap-and-trade. Valvo concluded:

> The idea of turning to the agency state to accomplish the same goals that the people's congressional representatives refused to make law runs afoul of the nation's democratic principles. Unfortunately, it appears that cap-and-trade advocates are less concerned with preserving these institutional checks-and-balances than they are with pushing hard to get the scheme enacted.[44]

Hold on to your wallet.

## THE VIEW FROM COPENHAGEN: OBAMA AS THE WORLD'S PRESIDENT

The full scope of what Obama, Browner, and the EPA intend to do without any congressional authorization was on display at the United Nations climate conference I attended in Copenhagen in December 2009.

At a side event hosted by Greenpeace called "Yes, he can! How Obama can deliver stronger emissions reductions," the Center for Biological Diversity presented a paper titled: "Yes, He Can: President Obama's Power to Make an International Climate Commitment Without Waiting for Congress."[45] The center laid out a frightening blueprint for precisely how the president could negotiate and enforce an agreement with just a simple majority of Congress instead of the 67 Senate votes our founding fathers required for treaty ratification, or, if he so chooses, he can instead bypass Congress and the Constitution entirely and simply rely on EPA action under the Clean Air Act for enforcement. If the administration is allowed to get away with this reprehensible tactic, it would set an ominous precedent for international promises and bypassing Congress to enforce them in other policy areas.

▶ ▶ ▶

*The Center for Biological Diversity... laid out a frightening blueprint for precisely how the president could negotiate and enforce an agreement with just a simple majority of Congress instead of the 67 Senate votes our founding fathers required for treaty ratification.*

The remarkable disrespect for our democratic system was driven by a sense that Obama really worked for a global society, rather than for the American people. This was made especially clear by Marcelo Furtado, the executive director of Greenpeace Brazil, who said:

> I know the U.S. public elected Obama, but as you know he was voted around the world as a leader. He was elected as a moral leader from the global society. It was not a U.S. election only. It was a global leadership election.[46]

He got an enthusiastic reaction from the room, and his sentiments were echoed by others. Clearly, Obama was the great hope for the Copenhagen crowd, though these fans were disappointed at his inability to force an intransigent Senate to accept cap-and-trade. They held out hope, however, that Obama would disregard the American people and instead serve the global society that had, in their view, elected him. That meant moving forward with unilateral executive action on the EPA track.

During the question-and-answer session I asked Kassie Siegel, one of the authors of the "Yes, He Can!" report, about the apparent illegality of the EPA's sleight of hand in the so-called Tailoring Rule, which requires permitting only for sources emitting more than 25,000 tons (the EPA would later raise this threshold to 75,000 tons), even though the Clean Air Act—which was written for toxic air pollution, not carbon dioxide (which, as one of the normal components of air is much more abundant)—sets the threshold at 100 or 250 tons, depending on the type of facility. As I noted earlier, the EPA did this because applying the law as it is actually written would create "absurd results." Instead of using that absurdity to conclude the Clean Air Act shouldn't be used for greenhouse gases, the EPA is attempting to arbitrarily rewrite the law.

Siegel's response? She made it clear that at least one environmental group with a history of aggressive litigation is unconcerned about (or perhaps supportive of) the bureaucratic nightmare of millions of homes and business ultimately being subject to EPA permitting requirements. She said:

> The political argument that's been made by the Chamber of Commerce and many polluters is that, "Hey, we couldn't do this. It would be unworkable because so many things emit carbon dioxide that if you went all the way down to the 250-ton threshold you would have to issue thousands and thousands of permits a year. And it would be a big problem and it would be a big mess, so let's not do it."
>
> I think that's wrong...
>
> I don't think it would actually be such a big problem. We need to reduce emissions. I think way too much is being made of having to issue these permits. I think it's completely workable... It is a

reasonable proposal to start with big sources first
and get to the smaller ones later.[47]

Siegel's group, the Center for Biological Diversity, has a
multimillion-dollar litigation war chest to find judges sympathetic
to their views, which means—despite the EPA's efforts to rewrite the
law—judges may eventually apply the full force of the Clean Air Act
to greenhouse gases. You might need a federal permit if you have
too many fireplaces.

## CONGRESS? WHAT'S THAT?

Unfortunately, the strategy of bypassing Congress is not simply a
pipe dream of groups like Greenpeace and the Center for Biological
Diversity. As the secret Browner/Nichols deal on automobile emissions made clear, this way of thinking is now driving administration policy. That was confirmed by a
pamphlet from the EPA given out at
the United States pavilion in Copenhagen titled: "Working Domestically
to Drive Innovation and Greenhouse
Gas Reductions." It outlined many of
the EPA actions covered in this chapter, promising the "EPA will continue
to work with international partners,
states, and localities, *as well as Congress*, to put climate solutions into ac-
tion" (emphasis added). It appears that Congress, and the American
people who elect them, are an afterthought, and the bureaucrats are
committed to moving forward with or without them.

> ▶ ▶ ▶
>
> *EPA administrator Lisa
> Jackson...promised the
> EPA was moving forward
> with or without Congress.*

That was confirmed by another briefing I attended in
Copenhagen by Jackson, where she promised the EPA was moving
forward with or without Congress. When she was asked whether
cap-and-trade legislation would be helpful to avoid lawsuits slowing

down the EPA, she responded that lawsuits were inevitable. Then she volunteered something surprisingly frank:

> The main reason for legislation is that it's economy-wide and that it's a very clear signal and that it allows for the give-and-take that happens in the legislative process so that people buy in and really buy in.[48]

That's the real reason for the big push for cap-and-trade legislation—for broader political buy-in—not because she needs, in her view, *any* new statutory authority to pursue sweeping regulations of the whole U.S. economy.

## FIGHTING BACK: THINK GLOBALLY, ACT LOCALLY

▶ ▶ ▶

*In order to implement its vision ... the EPA must coerce state legislatures to amend their state laws to conform to the new definitions the EPA has created. It takes executive power to new and unprecedented levels ...*
*If they can get away with it now, the next step will be to force states to adopt cap-and-trade programs.*

While the Obama administration is eagerly trying to use the EPA to disregard the wishes of American voters to please its friends in the "global society," one solution to the globally driven EPA attack on American democracy is local: state governments can and must fight back.

In order to implement its vision of regulating the U.S. economy by shoehorning greenhouse gases into the Clean Air Act, the EPA must coerce state legislatures to amend their state laws to conform to the new definitions the EPA has created. It takes executive power to new and unprecedented levels, because we now have unelected, unaccountable federal bureaucrats dictating to the elected legislatures of the states that they must change state laws to conform to the new bureaucratic paradigm. Moreover, if they can get away with it now, the next step will be to force states to adopt cap-and-trade programs.

But the good news is that the states are fighting back. At least 15 states have filed federal lawsuits challenging the EPA's greenhouse gas regulations.[49] The lawsuits challenge such issues as the basic science of global warming, whether warming would on balance endanger human health, the way the EPA handled proprietary data, and the EPA's failure to conduct the appropriate economic analysis required by law. Unfortunately, most of the states are also bringing their laws into compliance at great human and economic cost in case they lose in court.

The exception is Texas, which is taking a defiant stand with the commonsense position that federal bureaucrats, acting contrary to Congress's wishes, do not have the right to demand changes to state laws. Texas Attorney General Greg Abbott and Texas Commission on Environmental Quality Chairman Bryan W. Shaw sent a letter to the EPA explaining their decision not to comply. They said:

> In order to deter challenges to your plan for centralized control of industrial development through the issuance of permits for greenhouse gases, you have called upon each state to declare its allegiance to the Environmental Protection Agency's recently enacted greenhouse gas regulations—regulations that are plainly contrary to U.S. laws... To encourage acquiescence with your unsupported findings you threaten to usurp state enforcement authority and to federalize the permitting program of any state that fails to pledge their fealty to the Environmental Protection Agency. On behalf of the State of Texas, we write to inform you that Texas has neither the

authority nor the intention of interpreting, ignoring or amending its laws in order to compel the permitting of greenhouse gas emissions.[50]

With this bold statement, Texas has made clear that it will not proceed with the new EPA greenhouse gas rules pending litigation over their legality. Other states would be wise to follow Texas's lead, because the administrative burden on state permitting agencies will be crippling.

The backlogs created by the flood of new permit applications will not only shut down economic activity, most notably new construction, but will also cripple state environmental agencies, which will be unable to deal with the crush of new paperwork. Thus the EPA's global warming power grab may actually undermine environmental enforcement at the state and local levels. (That's okay, evidently, since it will increase the power of the Obama administration and people like Zichal and Jackson.)

> > >

*Other states would be wise to follow Texas's lead, because the administrative burden on state permitting agencies will be crippling.*

In America, as our founders intended, the states are where the rubber meets the road, and at least one big state is simply refusing to go along with what the EPA is doing. It's a fight worth having, even if the courts ultimately do not agree, because in the meantime it will protect Texans and help educate the rest of the country about what the EPA is trying to do and the need for Congress to step in and stand up for itself and the American people.

# WILL CONGRESS STOP THE EPA?

As with all executive power grabs, the EPA ultimately can only do what Congress allows. Voters must constantly remind their elected representatives that they expect them not only to oppose bad laws but to step in and stop the executive branch when it oversteps its bounds.

The U.S. Senate had its first opportunity to stop the EPA's global warming regulations on June 10, 2010. On that day, U.S. Sen. Lisa Murkowski (R-Alaska) forced a vote on overturning the EPA's finding that greenhouse gases endanger public health and welfare. Because all of its subsequent global warming regulations (though not the indirect threats, which must be stopped separately) legally depend on the endangerment finding, it would have effectively closed the door on the direct regulatory threat. Vehicle emissions standards would exist only under the Department of Transportation as authorized by the CAFE law.

It usually takes 60 votes to get things done in the U.S. Senate, but overturning regulations can be done with a simple majority of 51. That's because of a special procedure passed as part of the 1994 Contract with America called the Congressional Review Act. It created a special process where it takes only 30 senators signing a petition to force an up-or-down, filibuster-proof vote on overturning a federal regulation on the Senate floor. It can only be done within 60 legislative days of a regulation going final, though, so it's a one-shot deal.

The process has two principal weaknesses. First, unlike Kentucky Republican Congressman Geoff Davis's REINS Act, it fails to place an affirmative burden on Congress to approve new regulations. Instead, even enormously consequential regulations like the endangerment finding can move forward by default unless Congress decides to intercede. While REINS is proactive, the Congressional Review Act is reactive. Second, there is no expedited procedure on the House side, which means Congressional Review Act actions can typically only be voted on if House majority leadership wants them to be.

Nonetheless, the use of the Congressional Review Act put every senator on the record as to whether or not he or she wanted to stop the EPA. It was more than symbolic. If it had passed the Senate, the House would have been under tremendous pressure to consider it. If it passed the House, Obama would have had to either stand the EPA down or veto the resolution, taking full personal credit for what the agency is doing.

That's why the White House intervened in an enormous way to turn the tide when it looked like Murkowski's resolution would pass. The White House issued a veto threat and dispatched top officials, including Carol Browner, to the Hill to pressure Democratic senators.

When every other tactic had failed, and the resolution still appeared headed for passage, Harry Reid promised a group of terrified coal-state Senate Democrats a political cover vote on *delaying* the EPA regulations if they would agree to vote against *stopping* them. Even so, all 41 Republicans and six Democrats voted to stop the EPA. The 47 votes were just four shy of the 51 needed for passage. The six Democrats who did the right thing were Blanche Lincoln (D-Ark.), Mary Landrieu (D-La.), Ben Nelson (D-Neb.) (those three were cosponsors and most in need of some redemption after their health care votes), Evan Bayh (D-Ind.), Mark Pryor (D-Ark.), and Jay Rockefeller (D-W.Va.).

When the Senate had its first chance to stop the EPA, it failed to do so, and all the Democrats who voted "no" bear responsibility. Senators like Bill Nelson (D-Fla.), Claire McCaskill (D-Mo.), Jon Tester (D-Mont.), Kent Conrad (D-N.D.), Sherrod Brown (D-Ohio), Robert Casey (D-Pa.), and Herb Kohl (D-Wis.) were convinced that even though the regulations at stake were disastrous for their states, they could survive politically because the issue of regulation is not well understood. They deserve to be shown otherwise.

Another senator whose term is up in 2012 gave one of the most bizarre floor speeches I've ever seen in the debate over Murkowski's resolution: Jim Webb (D-Va.). For months Webb had quietly worked to build support for the resolution among Democrats. He comes from the coal country of southwest Virginia, the same area that dumped Rick Boucher for advancing cap-and-trade. He has a strong populist streak that bristled at the idea of bureaucrats setting policy instead of Congress. But when the chips were down and Obama and Reid applied pressure, Webb folded.

The strangest thing, though, is that his floor speech made quite clear he knew he was doing the wrong thing and betraying his constituents. He said that day:

> ▶ ▶ ▶
>
> *"I do not believe that Congress should cede its authority over an issue as important as climate change to unelected officials of the Executive Branch...Congress—and not the EPA—should make important policies, and be accountable to the American people for them."*
>
> —JIM WEBB (D-Va.), who then voted not to stop the EPA

I do not believe that Congress should cede its authority over an issue as important as climate change to unelected officials of the Executive Branch. Without proper boundaries, this finding could be the first step in a long and expensive regulatory process that could lead to overly stringent and very costly controls on carbon dioxide and other greenhouse gas emissions. Congress—and not the EPA—should make important policies, and be accountable to the American people for them.[51]

Webb went on to specifically debunk all of the Democratic arguments against the resolution. He argued passionately that Congress must stop the EPA.[52] Then he voted not to. His decision not to run for reelection in 2012 is almost certainly motivated, at least in part, by his inability to explain away this betrayal of his state's coal industry.

Contrast what Webb ended up doing with left-wing stalwart U.S. Sen. Jay Rockefeller of West Virginia, who made clear that he, unlike Webb and most other Democrats, would not allow the EPA to destroy his state's economic future. This is what he said:

> I have long maintained that the Congress—not the unelected EPA—must decide major economic and energy policy. EPA regulation will have an enormous impact on the economic security of West Virginia and our energy future. I intend to vote for Senator Murkowski's Resolution of Disapproval because I believe we must send a strong message that the fate of West Virginia's economy, our manufacturing industries, and our workers should not be solely in the hands of EPA.[53]

His statement was as true for the national economy as for the West Virginia economy.

The vote was fundamentally about one thing: who decides our economic future?

In our constitutional republic, the Congress of the United States is the legitimate legislative branch of government, charged with making the laws. A decision to adopt any national global warming program is an enormous one, with hundreds of billions of dollars and personal liberties at stake. This is simply not something that ought to be done through the back door via an unelected, unaccountable agency like the EPA.

The Senate had its first chance to do the right thing and it failed. Then came the watershed 2010 elections. Confronting the EPA waited as a key challenge for the new Congress.

# THE NEW CONGRESS IS PUT TO THE TEST

On April 7, 2011, the U.S. House voted resoundingly, 255 to 172, to stop the EPA backdoor energy taxes via Clean Air Act regulation of greenhouse gases. Every Republican and 19 Democrats voted for H.R. 910, the Energy Tax Prevention Act of 2011.[54] While the bill wouldn't have stopped all of the other ways the EPA is trying to "skin the cat," it would have stopped the biggest and most outrageous effort to accomplish the goals of cap-and-trade through regulation.

Unfortunately, the very same day, it was a different story in the Senate, where only 50 senators voted for the Energy Tax Prevention Act, which was offered as an amendment to a small business bill by Senate Republican Leader Mitch McConnell. Those 50 included Democrats Joe Manchin (W.Va.), Mary Landrieu, Mark Pryor, and Ben Nelson, along with all but one Republican—Susan Collins from Maine.[55]

Fourteen senators who voted not to stop the EPA—including Rockefeller, who had so eloquently stood up for his state of West Virginia the previous June—sought political cover by voting for sham amendments that only pretended to address the problem, while 36—all Democrats—openly endorsed the EPA's power grab.

The Baucus amendment, a rubber stamp for the EPA codifying the so-called Tailoring Rule, was touted as a way to help small businesses and farms but was opposed by the National Federation of Independent Business and the American Farm Bureau.[56] It got seven votes: Max Baucus (D-Mont.), Mark Begich (D-Alaska), Conrad, Kay Hagan (D-N.C.), Tim Johnson (D-S.D.), Amy Klobuchar (D-Minn.), and Carl Levin (D-Mich.).

The Rockefeller amendment, which purported to delay some of the EPA regulations for two years, but was written in a largely ineffective way, got 12 votes: three Republicans—Scott Brown (R-Mass.), Collins, and Graham; and nine Democrats—Conrad, Johnson, Landrieu, Manchin, McCaskill, Ben Nelson, Pryor, Rockefeller, and Webb.

The Stabenow amendment, a zero-plus-zero combination of the Baucus and Rockefeller amendments, got seven votes: Sherrod Brown, Casey, Conrad, Johnson, Klobuchar, Pryor, and Debbie Stabenow (D-Mich.).

All told, 64 senators voted against some aspect of the EPA's energy taxes, a broad bipartisan consensus that something must be done. Unfortunately, 14 of the senators who recognized the *political* need to stand up to the EPA chose not to provide the real *economic* relief that would come from actually stopping the rogue agency.

The result was a green light for sweeping regulations that will cost millions of jobs, based on the support of a minority in the House and just half of the Senate. It's our constitutional process turned upside down.

Fortunately, Congress will have more chances to do the right thing—not just on greenhouse gases but on the EPA's whole job-crushing agenda. What happens now is in our hands. We can acquiesce to the bureaucratic tyranny of an Environmental Protection Agency that wants to regulate every aspect of American life, eviscerate our manufacturing base, and destroy millions of jobs. Or we can stand and fight. We can demand accountability from our elected officials, and we must.

As citizens we are responsible for changing the political dynamic. Structural reforms can improve the system, but ultimately it is up to voters to change the politics of executive power by making it clear to Congress that failure to stop the executive branch will have serious political repercussions. We must have a constant drumbeat, a unified message to

*We must have a constant drumbeat, a unified message to each member of Congress: your job is to stop these outrageous EPA power grabs that threaten to destroy the U.S. economy and millions of jobs; if you are unable or unwilling to do that, we will elect someone who will.*

each member of Congress: your job is to stop these outrageous EPA power grabs that threaten to destroy the U.S. economy and millions of jobs; if you are unable or unwilling to do that, we will elect someone who will.

We need to make good on that promise, repeatedly, until this threat has been neutralized.

## CHAPTER 3

# Hacking Our Online Rights: The FCC's Internet Takeover

*"I will take a back seat to no one in my commitment to net neutrality."*[1]

—President BARACK OBAMA

*"At the moment, the battle over network neutrality is not to completely eliminate the telephone and cable companies. We are not at that point yet. But the ultimate goal is to get rid of the media capitalists in the phone and cable companies and to divest them from control."*[2]

—ROBERT MCCHESNEY, founder of Free Press

On December 21, 2010, President Obama's Federal Communications Commission (FCC) fittingly chose the darkest day in 372 years to impose potentially devastating regulations on the previously free-market Internet.

Early that morning, for the first time since 1638, the moon was eclipsed, blocking out the sun on the day of the winter solstice, already the darkest day of the year. And just as the moon was eclipsed that day, Congress, the American people, and our constitutional system of government will be eclipsed if the FCC's regulatory *coup d'état*—orchestrated by the White House—is allowed to stand.

On a party-line vote, three Democrats at the FCC decided to substitute their own judgment for the legitimate democratic process.

Those three FCC commissioners ordered that the Internet be regulated in the name of network neutrality, despite the fact that such regulations have almost no support in Congress, where U.S. Rep. Ed Markey's legislation, which aimed to do by legitimate means what the FCC is doing surreptitiously, had just 27 cosponsors. (It takes 218 votes to pass a bill in the House, so he was fully 12 percent of the way there.)

The Internet will be regulated, the FCC ordered, despite the fact that:

- America had just seen a shockwave election in which people overwhelmingly demanded smaller, less intrusive government.

- Ninety-five candidates who signed the Progressive Change Campaign Committee's pledge to promote Internet regulation lost. That's zero for 95. Total repudiation.[3]

- The D.C. Circuit Court of Appeals ruled unanimously in *Comcast v. FCC* just eight months prior to this order that such regulations have no legitimate basis in law.[4]

- The public overwhelmingly opposed regulation. A Rasmussen poll conducted at the time of the order found that only 21 percent of Americans supported Internet regulation, with 54 percent opposed. The poll also found that 56 percent of Americans thought the FCC would use its newly created powers to pursue a political agenda.[5]

How did we get to the point that the FCC would ignore all of that and regulate the Internet? It took a remarkable political effort from the far left and a breakdown in our constitutional system that allowed regulators to bypass Congress. That breakdown must be corrected.

## THE LEFT'S RELENTLESS—AND ILLOGICAL—PUSH

The big money pushing these regulations comes from Silicon Valley companies like Google and IAC/InterActiveCorp that run websites and want to make sure they will never be charged for sending content to end users—a business model that might or might not make sense, but should be determined by the market. They want government to guarantee that only consumers pay. Since at least 2002, voices on the political left have aligned with these companies seeking a regulatory free ride to tell a seductive scare story about the Internet. Unless government steps in immediately and regulates, the big bad phone and cable companies, they say, will block what websites you can go to, disrupt traffic, and generally destroy the network.

> ▶ ▶ ▶
>
> *Markets work and competition is a remarkably effective way to discipline anti-consumer behavior...If the phone company ever blocked or redirected access to a website, it would lose its customers to the cable company in droves...The idea that government has to step in and protect us seems sillier and sillier.*

Of course, it never happened. It never will happen, because markets work and competition is a remarkably effective way to discipline anti-consumer behavior. In brief, if the phone company ever blocked or redirected access to a website, it would lose its customers to the cable company in droves. Moreover, broadband Internet markets are getting much more competitive, as fourth-generation wireless offers a viable substitute for home broadband connections. People will increasingly consider cutting the cord for Internet service as many already have for voice service. With even more competition, the idea that government has to step in and protect us seems sillier and sillier.

Moreover, given that the original scare story started in 2002 and has been proven wrong continuously since then, common sense would dictate that we could finally dispense with these concerns as empirically denied. But in Washington, unfortunately, bad left-wing ideas never seem to die, and with Obama's election, advocates of regulating the Internet in the name of "net neutrality" had an ally all the way at the top. He would not disappoint them.

Obama and his transition team chairman John Podesta hired Michigan law professor Susan Crawford—who has openly called for reducing the Internet to a public utility—to oversee the transition at the FCC.

Crawford oversaw Obama's selection of his close friend from Harvard Law School, and former executive of IAC/InterActiveCorp, Julius Genachowski, as the FCC's chairman. Obama then hired Crawford as a White House staffer and a member of his National Economic Council. She was the point person in the White House on Internet regulation—his Internet czar.

The team was in place and the marching orders from the top were clear: disregard public opinion, common sense, and the intentions of Congress—and find some way to regulate the Internet in the name of net neutrality.

## WHAT IS NET NEUTRALITY?

Network neutrality, or net neutrality, is the beneficent-sounding name for sweeping new government regulatory power that would prohibit Internet service providers (ISPs) from innovating in their own networks. This would lead to much less broadband investment by private companies and could potentially force government subsidization, control, and outright nationalization of the Internet.

In its strictest form, such a regime would require every bit that travels over a network to be treated the same way. That might sound fair in theory, but it means big problems in practice. If broadband providers can't manage their network traffic, they can't offer high-quality, high-value services that are free from the degradation of bandwidth hogs—like teenagers who download huge amounts of bootleg movies, music, and games from file-sharing networks.

▶ ▶ ▶

*Network neutrality ... would lead to much less broadband investment by private companies and could potentially force government subsidization, control, and outright nationalization of the Internet.*

Robert Kahn, the engineer best known as the father of the Internet, has been highly critical of network neutrality mandates. "I am totally opposed to mandating that nothing interesting can happen inside the net," he said. Kahn has pointed out that to incentivize innovation, network operators must be allowed to develop new technologies within their own networks first—something that network neutrality mandates could prevent.[6]

Similarly, David Farber, the former FCC chief technologist known as the grandfather of the Internet, warned:

> I think the most important thing is that we have to create an environment where innovation is possible, where experimentation is possible, and where constraints are not imposed on the field from any regulatory authority. Let the marketplace determine what's

acceptable or not. That's gotten us a long way. I'm not a true believer that the marketplace will always decide right, but after being in Washington for a year, I'm semi-convinced that I'd rather take a chance on that than many of the regulatory environments.[7]

Without the flexibility to develop technologies that can most efficiently serve customers while generating revenue, there will be less private investment in upgrading the capacity of the Internet. Larry Lessig of Stanford University, a leading proponent of net neutrality, says openly that it will lead to less private investment in the Internet and therefore will require the government to step in with the investment of tax dollars. Lessig's rationale is that "broadband is infrastructure—like highways, if not railroads."[8]

▶ ▶ ▶

*"I'm not a true believer that the marketplace will always decide right, but after being in Washington for a year, I'm semi-convinced that I'd rather take a chance on that than many of the regulatory environments."*

—DAVID FARBER, former FCC chief technologist

Vint Cerf, Google's chief net neutrality propagandist, agrees. Cerf calls for the effective nationalization of the Internet, arguing that "incentives could be provided that would render the Internet more like the public road system ... not owned by the private sector," with its use "essentially open to all."[9]

Not only does the Internet in its current form work much better, and improve much more quickly, than government-run highways and railroads, but anyone who knows anything about highway and railroad contracts knows that large-scale infrastructure management by the government invites politically motivated deal-making, as well as rampant fraud and abuse.

Regulations will freeze in place the network as it exists now, preventing the remarkable innovations that have defined the Internet era from continuing. It is a failure of imagination on the part of regulators to see freezing the network in place and running it like a utility as a triumph. The tragedy is we may never know what innovations would have occurred because they were instead prevented.

The push for these regulations comes from both the ideological left that genuinely believes government control of the network would be a good thing—groups like Free Press and MoveOn.org—as well as self-interested content companies like Google and Barry Diller's IAC/InterActiveCorp (the FCC chairman's former employer) who want a free ride at the expense of consumers. Those content companies are worried that in a free market, we may see business arrangements in which the content company helps pay part of the cost of the broadband transmission to end users, which they would recover from advertising or sales revenue. Such business model experimentation could be necessary to avoid the full cost of home Internet service falling directly on consumers, which in a world of high-definition video could be prohibitively expensive.

> ▶ ▶ ▶
>
> *Companies like Google ... want net neutrality regulation that will guarantee they never have to pay to access consumers ... They want government to intervene in the market to make sure they pay less and you pay more.*

So companies like Google, which has such extensive ties to the Obama administration that my colleague Erik Telford has aptly described the search giant as the "Halliburton of the Obama administration," want net neutrality regulation that will guarantee they never have to pay to access consumers—a big deal considering that Google owns YouTube, which generates an enormous amount of traffic. They want government to intervene in the market to make sure they pay less and you pay more.

## REGULATION WILL LEAD TO CONTENT CONTROL

It's not, as Free Press's Megan Tady has asserted, "a crackpot conspiracy" to be concerned that economic regulation could lead to content regulation.[10] It is easy to envision a scenario in which the Internet, transformed into a piece of public utility infrastructure, tightly regulated, and subsidized with billions of taxpayer dollars, would be subject to content restrictions.

Consider the words of Michael Copps, one of the three Democratic FCC commissioners who forced net neutrality regulation on us. He said:

> Can you tell me that minority and women's voices on the Internet are getting through to major audiences—really being heard—like the big corporate sites? Should we just take it for granted that the small "d" democratic potential of new information technologies will somehow be magically realized without questions being raised about how they are designed and managed?[11]

That's really the central question. Do we think the Internet should be designed and managed by central economic planners to make sure certain voices are heard? By Washington bureaucrats? Or do we want to continue the remarkably successful experiment with a free-market, privately owned, competitive Internet? Copps, an advocate of the old Fairness Doctrine, which effectively blocked conservative talk radio by requiring equal airtime for liberal talk radio that didn't have an audience and couldn't make money, wants to apply something very similar to the Internet.

Groups like Free Press and people like Obama genuinely believe that they can design and manage the Internet in some centralized fashion sure to achieve their political objectives and desires. I would rather take my chances with a free market, robust competition, innovation, and investment, driven not by government design or management but by individual freedom.

Consider this. An Australian professor at the University of Sunderland, Alex Lockwood, supports U.S. nationalization of the Internet as a way to get a handle on the problem, in his view, of scientists skeptical of global warming who use the Internet to disseminate their research. His reasoning—that politically undesirable ideas should be filtered out like computer viruses—shows how easily the rationale for regulation can creep from network structure control to content control:

> ► ► ►
>
> *Do we think the Internet should be designed and managed by central economic planners to make sure certain voices are heard? By Washington bureaucrats? Or do we want to continue the remarkably successful experiment with a free-market, privately owned, competitive Internet?*

There is clearly a need for research into the ways in which climate scepticism online is free to contest scientific fact...Vint Cerf...lead for Google's Internet for Everyone project, made a recent suggestion that the Internet should be nationalised as a public utility...I would argue that climate disinformation online is a form of cultural and political malware every bit as threatening to our new media freedoms, used not to foster a forum for open politics but to create, in Nancy Fraser's term, a "multiplicity of fragmented publics" that harms not only our democracy, but our planet.[12]

Just like that, pluralism is dismissed as fragmentation, while free speech gives way to political correctness—and the censorship of dissenting opinions. Whatever you think about the global warming debate, a similar case can be constructed for any controversial issue, making a government-run or government-controlled Internet subject to political manipulation that, even if well intentioned, would serve to shut down our greatest forum for free speech.

Once we accept that it's the role of government to regulate the economics of the Internet and the way traffic is managed on the network, we'll start down a path in which government not only designs and manages but also builds and owns. As taxpayers, we'll pick up the tab for the enormous costs of building broadband networks that are regulated so strictly they can't earn a market return. And the government-owned and -controlled network will almost certainly be subject, eventually, to pervasive content restriction as well.

Just what, exactly, is the problem we are supposedly trying to fix, anyway?

## THE ABSURDLY NAMED 'FREE PRESS'

The driving force behind manufacturing net neutrality as an issue—as well as pushing similar heavy-handed government takeovers of the rest of our communications system like television, radio, and print journalism—is the left-wing pressure group Free Press. The name can only be understood in the great left-wing tradition of calling things the opposite of what they are, because in every area Free Press's agenda is to displace the freedom offered by private ownership and competition, and replace it with government control.

Free Press was founded by Robert McChesney in 2002. McChesney is an avowed socialist and the longtime editor of the *Monthly Review*, which, according to McChesney "is one of the most important Marxist publications in the world, let alone the United

States."[13] McChesney told *The Wall Street Journal* he was "hesitant to say I'm not a Marxist."[14]

To understand Free Press's mission, we need to take seriously McChesney's revolutionary socialist agenda. Start with his explanation of Free Press's push for net neutrality:

> At the moment, the battle over network neutrality is not to completely eliminate the telephone and cable companies. We are not at that point yet. But the ultimate goal is to get rid of the media capitalists in the phone and cable companies and to divest them from control.[15]

So-called media reform—the government takeover of the Internet, television, radio, and print journalism—is, to McChesney, an instrument of socialist revolution. As he explained: "Instead of waiting for the revolution to happen, we learned that unless you make significant changes in the media, it will be vastly more difficult to have a revolution."[16]

And McChesney's broader agenda? His ultimate endgame? As he explained: "In the end, there is no real answer but to remove brick by brick the capitalist system itself, rebuilding the entire society on socialist principles."[17]

This is a man who, two weeks after the September 11, 2001, terrorist attacks, said: "The United States is, I think, by any honest account, the leading terrorist institution in the world today."[18]

Simply exposing Free Press's ideological roots provokes the organization to call its critics McCarthyites. They can't stand having their own words quoted—just like they claimed

▶ ▶ ▶

*"In the end, there is no real answer but to remove brick by brick the capitalist system itself, rebuilding the entire society on socialist principles."*

—Robert McChesney, founder of Free Press

former Free Press board member Van Jones was "smeared" by having video and audio clips of his own statements played on television.[19]

Free Press wants the American people to ignore that McChesney is still on its board of directors and that its whole purpose is to promote his policy ideas.

The organization can't defend what McChesney has said, so Free Press President Josh Silver attacks critics, including me, for quoting his own founder:

> McCarthy-esque allegations against our organization, painting our efforts to protect consumers and promote critical journalism as part of a "Marxist" government takeover of the Internet.
>
> Because nothing Free Press actually says or does remotely reflects their rhetoric, they recycle out-of-context quotes from one of our cofounders. Or they draw up elaborate conspiracy theories. It is the province of liars and scoundrels.[20]

But it's not a lie. Free Press is the leading advocate for undoing a decade of free-market Internet policy that has driven economic growth, innovation, creativity, and the creation of remarkable spaces for democratic organizing across the political spectrum.

To Free Press, private ownership is a problem. Its solution is onerous federal regulation, and ultimately, "rebuilding the entire society on socialist principles." So when the organization talks about freedom, it means freedom from "corporate control," relinquishing everything to the government.

The vast majority of Americans understand freedom differently and would rather take their chances with private competition than government control. Which is why just 21 percent of Americans support net neutrality regulation.[21]

As John Fund has explained, Free Press and its allies were funded by major left-wing foundations to weave out of whole cloth the net neutrality issue as a pretext for government regulation. It was a follow-up to the left's manufactured campaign finance reform effort, recycling many of the same operatives and the same tactics to create the appearance of a grassroots uprising—where, in fact, none existed. The funders were also the same. Fund wrote:

> Of the eight major foundations that provided the vast bulk of money for campaign-finance reform, six became major funders of the media-reform movement. (They are the Pew Charitable Trusts, Bill Moyers's Schumann Center for Media and Democracy, the Joyce Foundation, George Soros's Open Society Institute, the Ford Foundation, and the John D. and Catherine T. MacArthur Foundation.) Free Press today has 40 staffers and an annual budget of $4 million.[22]

The idea that there is something terribly wrong with the Internet that requires dramatic government intervention just doesn't make sense to the vast majority of Americans, who are quite happy with the Internet and look forward to it continuing to get even better.

Nonetheless, Obama's FCC is tightly connected to Free Press. The FCC transition team was led by Free Press ally Crawford, who brought over Free Press's communications director Jen Howard, to be the FCC's press secretary. The FCC also brought on board Mark Lloyd as its chief diversity officer. Lloyd, best known for his praise of Hugo Chavez, had co-authored a Free Press study calling

> ▶ ▶ ▶
>
> *The idea that there is something terribly wrong with the Internet that requires dramatic government intervention just doesn't make sense to the vast majority of Americans, who are quite happy with the Internet and look forward to it continuing to get even better.*

for strict regulation of talk radio, going beyond the old Fairness Doctrine with draconian licensing rules, taxes, and diversity requirements designed to regulate commercial broadcasting out of existence while expanding public broadcasting.

Howard in particular deserves scrutiny because there are indications she continued to work for Free Press even after she became an official employee of the FCC. On October 20, 2009, reporters received a Free Press e-mail invitation to a conference call that said "Jen Howard" in the "From" line. The subject line was "Open Internet Coalition to Discuss FCC Net Neutrality Rulemaking." As I said in a press release at the time, "Now that Howard is running the press office for FCC Chairman Julius Genachowski, it is shocking that she would still be a soldier for a left-wing advocacy group. Today's revelation that it is sharing employees with a group that is dedicated to destroying our free market system is unacceptable."[23]

## CRAWFORD AND THE 'OPEN INTERNET' RULE

The subject of that Howard conference call was the FCC's first Obama-era effort to impose crippling regulations on the Internet, the so-called "Open Internet" rulemaking in October 2009. At that time the Obama administration had apparently directed the FCC simply to pretend Congress had given it authority to regulate and move forward.

▶ ▶ ▶

*At that time the Obama administration had apparently directed the FCC simply to pretend Congress had given it authority to regulate and move forward.*

The initial effort was led by the eager, ideologically committed Crawford. Officially, she was Obama's special assistant for science, technology, and innovation policy. *Wired Magazine* called her "the most powerful geek close to the president."[24]

Bloggers and online activists, led by Bill Collier at Freedomist.com, aptly dubbed her the "Internet Czar."[25]

Crawford had ties to a wide array of radical, left-wing groups, including the Association of Community Organizations for Reform Now (ACORN), which is one of the participating organizations of her "OneWebDay" project.[26] Crawford modeled OneWebDay on Earth Day and the radical environmental agenda that it propelled forward, saying:

> Earth Day was the model when I founded OneWebDay in 2006. In 1969, one man asked the people to do what their elected representatives would not: take the future of the environment into their own hands...People's lives now are as dependent on the Internet as they are on the basics like roads, energy supplies, and running water. We can no longer take that for granted, and we must advocate for the Internet politically and support its vitality personally.[27]

Earth Day, of course, is celebrated each year on Vladimir Lenin's birthday, April 22, and has become a rallying point not for celebrating the remarkable record of environmental improvement that has been driven by economic growth and free markets, but for calling for ever stricter government controls. Crawford picked her model well.

In other words, her agenda—which informed her selection of FCC staffers when she was on the Obama transition team, as well as her work in the White House—was to transform access to the Internet into a government entitlement project, with all the necessary government intrusion and control in order to guarantee it to everyone—in the world. Not surprisingly, Free Press is listed on the OneWebDay participating organizations list.[28]

Genachowski, Obama and Crawford's pick for FCC chairman, has a reason to aggressively pursue the net neutrality agenda, beyond his political ties to the White House—the president himself had told Google employees in a campaign stop, "I will take a back seat to no one in my commitment to net neutrality."[29]

Genachowski was also advancing the interests of his former employer, IAC/InterActiveCorp, where he was chief of business operations, reporting to Diller. IAC/InterActiveCorp is probably second only to Google in corporate lobbying for net neutrality regulations because the company operates numerous websites, ranging from video site Vimeo to dating site Match.com to left-wing magazine site *Daily Beast*. According to its company website: "Visited over 870 million times monthly, IAC's sites offer an array of content in categories that make daily life easier for millions of consumers... from search and shopping to dating and home repair."[30] Regulations preventing content companies like IAC from ever paying for part of the cost of broadband networks—putting the full cost onto consumers—had obvious bottom-line appeal to them.

Free Press, of course, hailed Genachowski and pledged to work with him to advance Obama's net neutrality agenda, saying: "We greatly look forward to working with Mr. Genachowski to put the president-elect's plan into action."[31]

It's of no apparent concern to Obama, Crawford, and Genachowski that net neutrality regulations—which would require network operators to treat every bit of traffic the same way, regardless of whether that makes sense from an engineering or business standpoint—will result in a collapse of private investment in Internet infrastructure, because they regard private investment as unnecessary within their vision of government ownership and control. Taxpayers are always there to pick up the tab, starting with Obama's stimulus bill, which included $7.2 billion for broadband Internet. As *The Wall Street Journal* reported:

Crawford stressed that the stimulus money is a down payment on future government investments in the Internet. "We should do a better job as a nation of making sure fast, affordable broadband is as ubiquitous as electricity, water, snail mail, or any other public utility," she said.[32]

The key to that eventual public utility world was strict regulations in the name of net neutrality, or a so-called "open Internet." The left-wing outfits like Free Press and MoveOn.org so thoroughly expected to dominate the public comment process that Howard, their inside woman, stooped to lying about the number of comments that were filed. As I wrote at the time, free-market activists filed far more comments than Free Press and its allies, but Howard simply asserted—and a pliant mainstream media accepted—that 90 percent of the comments supported the regulations.[33]

As the business community and public became aware of how extreme the proposal was, the backlash spread to the White House. Point person Crawford was forced to resign. As *The American Spectator* reported:

> White House senior adviser Susan Crawford resigned last week to little fanfare, but some White House insiders say her leaving may reveal growing tensions inside the Obama Administration about just how radical the administration has become in developing policies...
>
> White House sources say that she ran afoul of senior White House economics adviser Larry Summers, who claimed he and other senior Obama officials were unaware of how radical the draft Net Neutrality regulations were.[34]

After leaving the White House, Crawford was even more up front about the goals of the net neutrality push. Speaking at an April 2011 Free Press conference, she said of the communications companies: "the world where regulating these guys into an inch of their life is exactly what needs to happen."[35]

The FCC's initial regulatory effort proceeded with only slight moderation until March 2010, when it suffered a seemingly final blow. The D.C. Circuit Court of Appeals emphatically smacked down the FCC's regulatory proposals in Comcast v. FCC. At issue was the FCC's attempt to regulate how Comcast had handled BitTorrent traffic (an issue that was settled amicably without regulation). The court ruled unanimously, in a 36-page stinging rebuke to the FCC, that the commission lacked any jurisdiction to regulate broadband Internet access and therefore could not issue net neutrality regulations.[36]

# A REVISED PAST AND NUCLEAR ESCALATION

Immediately after the FCC got smacked down in *Comcast v. FCC*, Free Press and its allies started pressuring the commission not to back down, but to double down—to escalate the attack on the free-market Internet to the regulatory equivalent of a nuclear war. Specifically, they proposed reclassifying the Internet from an unregulated information service under Title I of the Telecom Act into a regulated monopoly telecommunications service under Title II of the Act.

Free Press, in urging the move, insisted that its support was intended to advance a "free market," saying:

> The Federal Communications Commission is simply pursuing a path that will ensure that the free market works for the American public, something that prior FCCs failed to do.[37]

Perhaps reading the public mood, a socialist organization decided it needed to pretend to be in favor of free markets. Absurd.

Contrary to Free Press's analysis of the "free market," Wall Street analyst Craig Moffett of Bernstein Research coined the term "nuclear option" to describe the reclassification proposal because of the total devastation it would have on investment and growth in the industry. He explained that Title II "would have sweeping implications, far, far beyond net neutrality," including "a raft of regulatory obligations from the days of monopoly telecommunications regulation, potentially including price regulation." He went on to say that Title II "would broadly throw into question capital investment plans for all broadband carriers, potentially for years, while the issue was adjudicated."[38]

The case for the nuclear option was seemingly based on the party slogan from George Orwell's novel on a totalitarian, Big Brother state, *Nineteen Eighty-Four*: "Who controls the past, controls the future." Advocates of regulation began to advance a deeply flawed revisionist history of the Internet.

According to this revised history pushed by Free Press and Democrats at the FCC, the government used to regulate the Internet until the last administration turned it over to corporate controllers. But the truth is nearly precisely the opposite.

Broadband Internet service has never been regulated like old-fashioned telephone lines. The FCC settled the matter definitively in 1998, when Clinton-appointed FCC Chairman William Kennard demolished the arguments for Title II that are being made today in that year's report to Congress:

> Our findings in this regard are reinforced by the negative policy consequences of a conclusion that Internet access services should be classed as "telecommunications" … Classifying Internet access services as telecommunications services could have significant consequences for the global development

of the Internet. We recognize the unique qualities of the Internet, and do not presume that legacy regulatory frameworks are appropriately applied to it.[39]

Even that 1998 statement did not represent a departure from earlier policy with respect to the nonregulation of Internet services, because the 1996 act had left in place the framework created in the Carter era. The agency went on to affirm the treatment of broadband Internet as an unregulated information service at every opportunity—including in regard to cable modem service in 2002, DSL in 2005, and mobile broadband in 2007.

There are few more successful policies in the history of the country. The free-market, unregulated Internet became the engine of American economic growth, innovation, competition, and free expression. Such triumph makes a compelling argument for continuing existing policies.

The FCC had two basic choices after getting rebuked by the U.S. Court of Appeals in *Comcast v. FCC*. The straightforward, honest, constitutionally valid option would have been to ask Congress to consider legislation aimed at regulating broadband. Of course, even in the wildly Democratic 111th Congress, that path was unlikely to succeed because members of Congress can be held accountable by their constituents, who would repel at the idea of Internet regulation.

Unfortunately, under the direction of Obama, who infamously said, "I will take a back seat to no one in my commitment to network neutrality," the lack of legal and public support was seen not as a reason to back down, but as a reason to escalate. The FCC decided to pursue the nuclear option, skipping the congressional step of net neutrality regulation and moving directly to the end goal of transforming the Internet into a public utility.

Orwell's Big Brother would be proud.

Free Press, on the other hand, offered only guarded support. Free Press President Silver said: "This is extremely welcome news. We reserve judgment, however, on whether the FCC has gone far enough."[40] Of course, nothing will be enough for Free Press, short of McChesney's plan to "remove brick by brick the capitalist system itself."[41]

Ultimately, the FCC was not brazen enough to actually deploy the nuclear option. But they used the nuclear threat of Title II reclassification to take the Internet service providers hostage. In a mad rush to impose regulations before the new Congress was sworn in, negotiations reached a fever pitch and, ultimately, a very unfortunate resolution.

Through a series of secretive, closed-door, so-called stakeholder meetings, the FCC made it clear that the only options on the table would be bad and worse. The Internet service providers could accept unlawful net neutrality regulations that had never been enacted by Congress and had already been rejected by the courts, or they could be immediately reclassified as public utilities and subjected to onerous monopoly-style regulation from the Ma Bell era that gave regulators complete control of every aspect of their business.

It was a classic Chicago-style, extralegal Obama administration tactic. Most of the ISPs (though not all—Verizon and MetroPCS have thus far challenged the regulations in federal court) decided that accepting net neutrality regulations was the only way to prevent the nuclear option.

It's worth noting, however, that the Title II docket remains open, and the threat of a total takeover is still out there (and Free Press and others are busily promoting it). Also worth remembering, of course, is that net neutrality regulations are a step toward the same end goal of reducing the Internet to a government-controlled utility.

# WORSE THAN OBAMACARE?

Christmas Eve 2010 was an eerie, sad *déjà vu* of the health care take-over on Christmas Eve 2009. Despite the fact that the free-market movement had just led a resounding triumph at the polls, another takeover was coming, this one engulfing about a sixth of the economy. But the Obama administration had learned from its health care mistake. The pre-Christmas 2010 takeover happened without one of those pesky votes of Congress.

On December 21, 2010, the FCC voted on a three-to-two par-ty-line vote to regulate the Internet. Among those voting against it was FCC Commissioner Robert McDowell, a stalwart free-market champion President Bush had appointed, and President Obama re-appointed. It was McDowell who first observed that the vote took place, fittingly, on the year's darkest day.

In following through with the regulations approved by its vote, the FCC did not go for the nuclear option, but it did for the first time impose net neutrality regulations, which are likely to eventu-ally lead us down the same path of a government-regulated network with much less innovation and much less private investment (to be made up with taxpayers' dollars, of course).

My friend Seton Motley, president of Less Government, made a compelling case that given the widespread opposition, this move by the FCC was actually a worse power grab than ObamaCare. He noted:

> It was done without authority from the People's representatives. In fact, 302 of them (including more than 80 Democrats) told the FCC not to do it. Then there was the D.C. Circuit Court, which ruled unanimously that the FCC doesn't have the author-ity. More than 150 organizations, state legislators, and bloggers gave them the anti-Nike "Don't do it." So too did seventeen minority groups (that are usu-

ally almost always in Democrat lockstep) and many additional normally Democrat paragons—including several large unions, several racial grievance groups and an anti-free market environmentalist group.[42]

While the FCC is supposed to be an independent regulatory agency, under Mr. Genachowski it has become a clear political extension of the White House, which endorsed the regulatory power grab. At the time the order was issued, official White House visitor logs show 78 visits by Genachowski, including at least 11 personal meetings with the president.[43]

Obama's statement on that darkest day in centuries concluded: "I congratulate the FCC, its chairman, Julius Genachowski, and Congressman Henry Waxman for their work achieving this important goal today."[44]

Praising Waxman was odd considering Congress was out of the loop completely on the regulatory move. It was as if the president felt some need to pretend the process had been more legitimate than it was.

> ► ► ►
>
> *Praising Waxman was odd considering Congress was out of the loop completely on the regulatory move. It was as if the president felt some need to pretend the process had been more legitimate than it was.*

The Obama FCC's regulations had already been pre-rejected by Congress and the American people. Yet they are now in full force—unless and until we can compel Congress to step in and act.

(It should be noted that Jen Howard moved from Free Press to the FCC to pilot the public relations effort on the net neutrality rules, declared victory, and then moved on—to the new Consumer Financial Protection Bureau. More on that in Chapter 6.)

## GLOBAL IMPLICATIONS

The implications of the FCC's decision to begin regulating the Internet reverberate far beyond the borders of the United States. Ambassador Philip Verveer, assistant secretary of State and U.S. coordinator for international communications and information policy, raised the very practical concern that regulating the Internet domestically would undermine our diplomatic efforts to prevent other countries from regulating and censoring the Internet.

In March of 2010 Verveer said:

> I can tell you from my travels around the world and my discussions with figures in various governments around the world there is a very significant preoccupation with respect to what we are proposing with respect to broadband and especially with respect to the net neutrality.[45]

Verveer went on to argue that American net neutrality regulations "could be employed by regimes that don't agree with our perspectives about essentially avoiding regulation of the Internet and trying to be sure not to do anything to damage its dynamism and its organic development. It could be employed as a pretext or as an excuse for undertaking public policy activities that we would disagree with pretty profoundly."[46]

Shortly after Verveer made his comments, he had a new colleague. Ben Scott, the policy director for Free Press, joined the State Department in May 2010 as a "policy adviser for innovation."[47] Ben Scott is a doctrinaire proponent of government control—once saying on C-SPAN: "The Internet is no longer a commercial service, it's an infrastructure."[48] We can imagine what kind of policy advice Scott is giving at the State Department.

FCC Commissioner Robert McDowell has argued that regulating the Internet could also accidentally trigger United Nations jurisdiction. He wrote in *The Wall Street Journal*:

> At two meetings of the U.N.'s World Summit on the Information Society in 2003 and 2005, the U.S. found itself in the lonely position of fending off efforts by other governments to exert U.N. or other multilateral control over the Internet. ITU member states have attempted to expand their control over Internet governance, Web address registries, and cybersecurity. These nations will likely be encouraged by talk of more U.S. Web regulation.[49]

Early indications are that these fears were well founded. Within weeks of the new United States net neutrality rules and using them for cover, Venezuela passed a new law giving the executive the authority to regulate all Internet service providers to block content that, among other things, "refuses to recognize the government's authority." The Institute for Policy Innovation put it well:

▶ ▶ ▶

*FCC Commissioner Robert McDowell has argued that regulating the Internet could also accidentally trigger United Nations jurisdiction.*

> The result is an oppressive government seizing control of the Internet and using new U.S. regulations as at least partial cover for their own bad behavior. Oh sure, Venezuela needed little provocation for its continued oppression, especially from the U.S., but now Chavez has the comfort of knowing that the U.S. has joined Venezuela in the company of governments who regulate the Internet.[50]

Of course some of the things said by Free Press founder McChesney are enough to call into question whether this outcome may have been intentional. For example, consider this statement by him: "Aggressive unqualified political dissent is alive and well in the Venezuelan mainstream media, in a manner few other democratic nations have ever known, including our own."[51]

## FIGHTING BACK: CONGRESS MUST MAKE THINGS RIGHT

The FCC responded to the 2010 election by passing its final net neutrality order using the same shakedown tactics we saw with the Chrysler bondholders, using the threat of a more extreme measure (reclassification) to force acquiescence to an extralegal power grab.

This sets up a crystal-clear test case of whether the Obama administration can get away with ignoring the election, Congress, the legitimate legislative process, and the American people to force a big-government power grab through a regulatory back door.

To pass the test, Congress must step up and overturn the network neutrality order, either using Congressional Review Act action, an appropriations rider, or stand-alone preemption legislation of the type proposed by U.S. Rep. Marsha Blackburn (R-Tenn.).

The new leadership in the House of Representatives stepped up early to meet the challenge. Speaker John Boehner has made overturning the net neutrality order a priority, as has Energy and Commerce Committee Chairman Fred Upton (R-Mich.) and Communications and Technology Subcommittee Chairman Greg Walden (R-Ore.). On April 8, 2011—the same week the House stood up to the EPA—they used the Congressional Review Act to pass a resolution that would overturn the net neutrality order. It was a solid 240 to 179 vote, with just six Democrats voting to overturn the order and just two Republicans voting not to.[52] It passed despite the fact that President Obama promised to veto it. That veto threat will be put to the test if 51 senators agree with the House majority.

Nancy Pelosi missed the vote. She was busy attending a Free Press conference with McChesney, Crawford, and two Democratic FCC commissioners in Boston. "I don't think this bill is going anyplace," she assured the Free Press crowd.[53]

If Pelosi is wrong and the resolution, or any other legislative vehicle to stop the order, succeeds, Obama will be forced to either back down from his veto threat and suffer a political loss as Congress asserts its rightful authority, or veto it and take full ownership of completely disregarding the Constitution and this last election to keep pushing left with ever more government control. Either way, it would be a huge statement from Congress that regulatory power grabs will not go unnoticed.

Congress must assert itself now before the Obama administration uses similar regulatory back doors to thwart the electorate and continue shoving the country hard to the left. Given the complete lack of support for this agenda in Congress or among the American people, this radical FCC power grab may stand as the ultimate test for Obama. If he can get away with this, he can get away with almost anything.

> > > *This radical FCC power grab may stand as the ultimate test for Obama. If he can get away with this, he can get away with almost anything.*

Of course, if the REINS Act had been in effect at the time of the order, the order would have gone down in flames in Congress. We simply must fix the regulatory process to put a check on these sorts of power grabs. Judge Lloyd Rogers, whose idea inspired the REINS Act, understands, as most voters do, that the federal government should not regulate the Internet:

> It's terrible. And I don't want it to happen. Did the government ever do anything right? Every time they've gotten into something, they've screwed it

up. And I don't want them getting their hands on
the Internet.[54]

Yet the Obama administration is only intensifying its ties to
the radicals at Free Press and their visions of control. On February
8, 2011, the government welcomed Free Press's board chairman
Tim Wu into the fold as a special adviser on Internet and wireless policy at the Federal Trade Commission (FTC). *The Wall Street
Journal* noted:

> Silicon Valley has a new fear factor. Columbia Law
> School professor Tim Wu, an influential academic
> and author who popularized the term "net neutrali-
> ty," has been appointed senior advisor to the Federal
> Trade Commission.[55]

The appointment shows the administration is not putting all its net
neutrality eggs in the FCC basket,
and Congress will have to exercise
scrutiny on the FTC as well.

We simply must restore Congress
to its legitimate constitutional role as
the legislative branch. Our elected
representatives must stand up and
take responsibility for major policy
changes like net neutrality. There
aren't enough "sixths of the economy" left for us to lose.

▶ ▶ ▶

*We simply must restore
Congress to its legitimate
constitutional role as the
legislative branch. Our
elected representatives
must stand up and take
responsibility for major
policy changes like net
neutrality. There aren't
enough "sixths of the
economy" left for us
to lose.*

CHAPTER 4

# On the Waterfront: The Secret Plan to Force You into a Union

*"I've spent my entire adult life working with SEIU. I'm not a newcomer to this. I didn't suddenly discover SEIU on the campaign trail."*[1]

—President Barack Obama

*"Employers should be stripped of any legally cognizable interest in their employees' election of representatives."*[2]

—Craig Becker, the former SEIU lawyer Obama put on the National Labor Relations Board without Senate approval

Nobody did more to make Barack Obama the president of the United States than labor unions, most significantly the Service Employees International Union (SEIU). Now they want their payback, and it doesn't matter to them—or their handpicked president—that Congress and the American people have rejected their agenda.

SEIU is largely responsible for Obama's remarkable primary upset over Hillary Clinton, spending more than $9 million supporting Obama through the critical three-month stretch that determined the nomination.[3] In Obama's own words: "I've spent my entire adult life working with SEIU. I'm not a newcomer to this. I didn't suddenly discover SEIU on the campaign trail."[4]

And that primary support was just the beginning, as then-SEIU President Andy Stern said: "We spent a fortune to elect Barack Obama—$60.7 million to be exact—and we're proud of it."[5] How proud? SEIU even gave its blessing—and funding—to a 2009 documentary film highlighting the pivotal role the union played in getting Obama into the White House.[6]

> ▶ ▶ ▶
>
> *"We spent a fortune to elect Barack Obama—$60.7 million to be exact—and we're proud of it."*
>
> —Former SEIU President ANDY STERN

SEIU and its affiliates, including the Association of Community Organizations for Reform Now (ACORN), were the shock troops of the Obama campaign. All told, unions like SEIU and the American Federation of Labor-Congress of Industrial Organizations (AFL-CIO) claimed to spend upward of $300 million to elect Obama and fill Congress with friendly, pro-union majorities. The National Right to Work Committee has estimated that, factoring in all of the spending by locals and affiliates in the 2008 election cycle, including internal union communications, it may have been as much as $1 billion.[7]

The unions expected that enormous investment to pay dividends, and Obama did not intend to disappoint them. While the public has mostly focused on the high-profile fights raging in Congress, the key implementer of the union agenda is a relatively obscure federal agency called the National Labor Relations Board (NLRB). Now stacked with SEIU lawyers who are Obama's ideological fellow travelers, the board is poised to grant union bosses vast new powers without so much as a vote in Congress.

# THE UNIONS' DESPERATE CARD-CHECK PLOY

The unions have become obsessively focused on politics and elections—to the tune of hundreds of millions of dollars deducted from the paychecks of workers—because they are in a desperate battle for survival.

As James Sherk of The Heritage Foundation noted:

> Union membership fell by over 600,000 workers in 2010. In the private sector, 93.1 percent of workers are non-union, more than when President Franklin Delano Roosevelt signed the National Labor Relations Act (NLRA) in 1935.[8]

This remarkable chart from Sherk, on the following page, tells the story.

The unions face a nearly insurmountable problem: workers increasingly believe, correctly, that unions either provide little in return for their dues or work against their interests, including driving the companies they work for overseas or out of business.

Unions and their Democratic allies are looking to rig the rules because workers see the industries that unions have destroyed and want no part of them. As Stephen Moore and Arthur Laffer noted:

> States that permit workers to be compelled to join unions have much lower rates of employment growth than states that don't. Many companies say they will not even consider locating a factory in a state that does not have a right-to-work law.[9]

## Union Membership Falling to Historic Lows

Union Membership Percentages

*1945: 35.5%*

Percentage of Non-Agricultural Payroll Employment

Percentage of All Wage and Salary Workers

*1935: 13.2% (year National Labor Relations Act signed into law)*

11.9%

Percentage of Private Sector Wage and Salary Workers

6.9%

**Note:** This chart displays union membership using two separate data sources: assorted union reports filed with the department of labor between 1930 and 1980, and data from the Current Population Survey. Data for 1982 have been interpolated.

**Source:** Data for 1930–1980: U.S. Department of Labor, assorted labor union reports and Haver Analytics; 1977–2010: Heritage Foundation calculations using data from Barry T. Hirsch and David A. Macpherson, "Union Membership and Coverage Database from the Current Population Survey," Unionstats.com, at http://www.unionstats.com, and from the U.S. Department of Labor, Bureau of Labor Statistics.

Chart 1 • WM 3099 ☎ heritage.org

Even onetime left-wing icon and 1972 presidential nominee George McGovern argued in a 2006 *Los Angeles Times* op-ed that unions are no longer necessarily advancing the interests of their workers. In a piece that should be required reading for sincerely pro-worker Democrats, McGovern argued the antibusiness attitude of unions to push for ever more pay and benefits without respect to the consequences is ultimately harmful to workers. After citing the woes of the auto and airline industries, he said:

> "More" has, unfortunately, become "too much" in a global and far more competitive economy.
>
> Many of my friends will consider this view heretical. But it is based on stark reality. Some progressive union leaders, facing this economic reality, have come to the same conclusion. Others are holding fast. Their behavior is partially a function of internal politics—and sheer habit. Not unlike members of Congress, union leaders are in the business of asking for more.[10]

Workers are simply not interested in sending a portion of every paycheck to union leaders who will demand so much from management that they cripple or possibly kill key American industries. Until union leaders deal with that reality and find a way to offer genuine value to workers, their only option for survival is the bare-knuckle strategy of using intimidation tactics to force workers into dues-paying membership.

# THE ORWELLIAN EMPLOYEE FREE CHOICE ACT

Big Labor turned to Obama and an overwhelmingly Democratic Congress they helped elect to rig the game in their favor and allow

▶ ▶ ▶

*Big Labor turned to Obama and an overwhelmingly Democratic Congress they helped elect to rig the game in their favor and allow them to force workers into unions.*

them to force workers into unions. They call this absurd scheme pretty much the opposite of what it is: the Employee Free Choice Act (EFCA).

It might more reasonably be called the Employee Force and Coercion Act. The bill would abolish secret ballot elections for union certification. The bill would allow unions to organize via so-called card-check campaigns, in which union representatives can collect signatures to form a union without any privacy protections for the workers. Union organizers can go to workers' homes, openly pressure them in front of coworkers, and use many other high-pressure techniques to collect signatures. Many workers sign union cards knowing they can safely and privately vote against the union later. Under this bill that would be practically impossible.

Unions know that they can easily pressure workers into signing cards who would not actually vote for the union. This is precisely why union leaders believe they need a supermajority of workers to sign cards before they even have a chance of winning a secret ballot election.[11] Consider this, from the AFL-CIO, in a survey of its organizing: "It is not until the union obtains signatures from 75 percent or more of the unit that the union has more than a 50 percent likelihood of winning the election."[12]

Under existing law, before a union is recognized, an employer has the right to request a federally supervised secret ballot election. This allows both the union and the employer to make their case and lets workers decide on a union without fear of reprisal, in a private voting booth. Considering that a union becomes the exclusive bargaining agent for wages, benefits, hours, working conditions, and just about every other aspect of a worker's professional life, this is a reasonable precaution for such a highly consequential vote.

U.S. Rep. George Miller of California, the point man on this effort for Obama and Nancy Pelosi, and the top Democrat on the House Education and Labor Committee, used to be a strong supporter of secret ballot elections. In 2001 Miller and 15 other House Democrats—including Barney Frank (D-Mass.), Bernie Sanders (I-Vt.), Dennis Kucinich (D-Ohio), and other reliable leftists—wrote to a local government official in Mexico: "the secret ballot is absolutely necessary in order to ensure that workers are not intimidated into voting for a union they might not otherwise choose."[13]

Perhaps most notable among the signers of the letter was Hilda Solis, then a Democratic congresswoman from California and now Obama's secretary of Labor. Solis has a history of supporting the secret ballot, including her lead sponsorship of a 1997 bill in the California legislature that required a secret ballot vote for changes to overtime schedules.[14]

They have all since done a 180-degree turn, and Miller was the lead sponsor of EFCA, along with 228 Democratic members of the House last Congress and two New Jersey Republicans: Chris Smith and Frank LoBiondo.

While they would take away the secret ballot from workers, many EFCA supporters cherish their own secret ballot rights in representation elections. Consider that in November 2008, during a difficult vote that ended with U.S. Rep. Henry Waxman replacing U.S. Rep. John Dingell as the chairman of the House Energy and Commerce Committee for the upcoming 111th Congress, Democratic members used the secret ballot process to vote with their conscience rather than vote in the open as they would force workers to do.[15] EFCA cosponsor Louise Slaughter (D-N.Y.) even said, "It's a secret ballot. Thank the Lord."[16]

Why would Democrats push for such an undemocratic, unpopular measure? Because they need the unions to reverse their decline and to keep the big political donations flowing. They need to somehow force more workers to pay union dues that they can then feed back into Democratic campaign coffers.

> ▶ ▶ ▶
>
> *Under Obama's promised bill, workers would be effectively stripped of private ballot rights. Unions might even be able to use violence to achieve their objectives.*

In August 2009 the left-wing Netroots Nation convention hosted a panel titled, "The Secret Plan to Defeat the Right Forever," featuring panelists from SEIU, the American Federation of State, County and Municipal Employees, AFL-CIO, and ACORN.[17] They were openly plotting to use EFCA to force millions of Americans to pay union dues that would, in turn, be used to fund left-wing political activities.

That's probably why Obama made EFCA a top priority, saying on the campaign trail:

> We need to stand up to the business lobby that's been getting their friends in Congress and in the White House to block card check. That's why I was one of the leaders fighting to pass the Employee Free Choice Act. That's why I'm fighting for it in the Senate. And that's why we'll make it the law of the land when I'm president.[18]

Under Obama's promised bill, workers would be effectively stripped of private ballot rights. Unions might even be able to use violence to achieve their objectives—the Supreme Court has exempted labor unions from the provisions of the Hobbs Act, which is meant to curb extortion, as long as the union members are using violence to advance "legitimate union objectives."[19]

## CARD CHECK COLLAPSES

Obama made a serious push for EFCA, as promised, in the early months of 2009, with a full-court press on wavering Democratic senators and soon-to-be-Democrat Arlen Specter of Pennsylvania, who had voted for an earlier version of the bill. Obama needed to hold all the Democrats and Specter and have Al Franken win the contested Minnesota race to get to 60 votes to break the filibuster and move forward with the bill. And it looked like he might succeed—until the public learned that the private ballot was at stake and put pressure on the Senate.

Once the public learned what was in it, the bill became wildly unpopular because the public was dead set against eliminating the secret ballot for union elections. A 2009 McLaughlin poll found that 82 percent of the public preferred the current process to the card-check procedure, and among union householders, support was even higher, at 85 percent.[20] Union members are apparently even more aware than the general public how workers can be pressured into signing cards. A Zogby poll specifically found that 78 percent of union members prefer the current process to one with less privacy protection.[21]

In April 2009, U.S. Sen. Blanche Lincoln came out against EFCA. She was followed by Specter, who was then still a Republican but had voted for the bill in the previous Congress. Both did it because they feared the voters of their states more than the union special interests that had the ability to steer financial support to them or their opponents. Lincoln was increasingly feeling a political backlash from a state that is heavily dependent economically on nonunion employers that would have been devastated by the bill— most notably because Walmart is headquartered in the state. Specter made his announcement one day before a poll was released showing him trailing his primary opponent Pat Toomey by 14 points.[22]

By summer the legislative effort appeared stalled, but Obama called major union leaders, including then-SEIU President Andy Stern and AFL-CIO President John Sweeney, into the White House on July 13, 2009, to reassure them he remained committed to passing EFCA.[23]

Just days later, a new strategy was announced by a group of Senate Democrats: they would remove the card-check provisions in favor of "quickie elections" that would retain the private ballot but be scheduled at a moment's notice, based on the union's strategic considerations, before the employer has an opportunity to make its case to workers. An improvement, but still a disastrously anti-worker giveaway to the union bosses.

Moreover, card check was never the only problem with EFCA. The bill also included—and would continue to include—provisions for mandatory binding interest arbitration.

Less noticed but possibly even worse for the U.S. economy than the card-check provisions, binding arbitration would take the "bargaining" out of collective bargaining by empowering a federal bureaucrat to set contract terms for wages, benefits, and working conditions without so much as a vote of the workers. Calling that "free choice" would be funny if it weren't deadly serious for our already reeling national economy.

The current National Labor Relations Act attempts to strike a balance between the workers' desire for collective bargaining and the employer's right to actually bargain and come to mutually acceptable terms. Once a union has been certified, the employer is obligated to negotiate in good faith. The National Labor Relations Board has powers to encourage employers to meet the good-faith obligation (including the ability to order back pay), and the union has the option of calling a strike to increase its leverage. Once a deal is done, the workers vote on whether or not to accept the contract.

Under EFCA, the bargaining process could still occur, but the union would have an enormous incentive to stall through a 120-day mediation process and then go to binding arbitration. In theory, the arbitrators should be evenhanded, but there is nothing in the past of Obama or Solis to suggest that arbitrators under their direction wouldn't be politically motivated. Such arbitrators would be likely to impose terms, including forced union dues, that advance the interests of the union bosses (who provide the legwork and funding for the left) rather than the interests of workers, who depend on economically viable companies for jobs. Absurdly, this so-called "free choice" bill would not even allow workers to vote on the arbitrator-imposed contract, and there would be no way to exit the contract or to decertify the union for two years—a very destructive prospect for employer and employee rights.

Several small business owners have told me that while card check gets most of the attention, mandatory arbitration is an even worse economic killer in EFCA. In a card-check campaign, the employer still has some voice during the negotiation of a collective bargaining agreement. Employers may be able to negotiate agreements with unions that their businesses can survive. In a regime of contracts imposed by left-leaning government arbitrators, by contrast, workers have little say and employers have none at all. In an already fragile economy, that could be the public policy weapon of mass destruction that sends us spiraling further downward.

> ▶ ▶ ▶
>
> *In a regime of contracts imposed by left-leaning government arbitrators, by contrast, workers have little say and employers have none at all. In an already fragile economy, that could be the public policy weapon of mass destruction that sends us spiraling further downward.*

Unfortunately, while the EFCA legislation collapsed after being exposed to the public, the radical objectives of the unions and their allies in the Obama administration are being pursued by other means as payback for their political support.

## UNIONS SCORNED:
## THE ARKANSAS SENATE PRIMARY

Nobody was a bigger target for the unions in the 2010 election cycle than Lincoln, for her apostasy of opposing the EFCA legislation. For that she was subjected to the most intense primary challenge in the country, by Arkansas Attorney General Bill Halter, who enjoyed the backing of the union bosses and their ideological allies like MoveOn.org. The venomous attacks on Lincoln and the enormous union spending in the race made clear that the top priority for the progressive left remained the EFCA legislation, not other purported priorities, such as the ObamaCare bill for which Lincoln had cast the crucial deciding vote to help it pass. It was EFCA, and with it the ability to force more workers into unions and into paying union dues, that was the ultimate loyalty test for the key power brokers on the Democratic left.

Even in a Democratic primary with unified union and progressive opposition, Lincoln was able to survive, however, suggesting that the radical union agenda is so at odds with the beliefs of most Americans that it's impossible to force rigid discipline on the issue, even in a Democratic primary, and even with record political spending.

> ▶ ▶ ▶
>
> *Thumbing your nose at union bosses can be a smart political move, whether it's on their top priority of undermining private ballot rights or their number-two priority of creating a vast, new, unionized health care bureaucracy ... Big Labor's agenda is a big loser with the public.*

As one anonymous White House aide pointedly put it the day after the election: "Organized labor just flushed $10 million of their members' money down the toilet."[24]

Lincoln went on to lose in a landslide general election to now-U.S. Sen. John Boozman (R-Ark.), whose campaign stressed Lincoln's vote for ObamaCare.

The twin lessons of Arkansas in 2010 were that thumbing your nose at union bosses can be a smart political move, whether it's on their top priority of undermining private ballot rights or their number-two priority of creating a vast, new, unionized health care bureaucracy. Lincoln stood up to the unions on their top priority; if she had done the same on their second she might still be a United States senator. Bottom line: Big Labor's agenda is a big loser with the public.

## GASPARD AND BECKER: ACORN'S INSIDE MEN

When then-SEIU President Stern was asked whether the failure of EFCA meant the enormous amount of SEIU-member dues he spent on electing Obama were wasted, he pointed to appointments as the reason the investment was worthwhile, saying:

> Clearly there have been a number of appointments that have been enormously important to labor and more are coming. Patrick Gaspard, for one, is White House political director. He comes from SEIU.[25]

Gaspard, a former lead SEIU organizer in New York City, was the Obama White House's first political director—successor to Karl Rove—and ran the Obama campaign's much-touted field operation. Based on his SEIU work, New York Mayor Michael Bloomberg's political consultant called Gaspard the "best political mind of his generation in New York and maybe the nation," and David Axelrod said, "I wouldn't dispute that."[26]

Gaspard is the radical left's inside man, epitomized by a comment Al Sharpton made to a White House official about Gaspard: "It's hard for me to march against you if I ever get mad, because you've got our best organizer."[27]

Gaspard serves as the Obama administration's connection to SEIU and its more radical affiliate ACORN, which were described in a compelling investigative report by the House Oversight Committee Republican staff report as a "criminal conspiracy."[28] Matthew Vadum of the Capital Research Center, the leading investigator of ACORN, dubbed Gaspard "ACORN's Man in the White House," based on his past contributions to ACORN and his previous position serving as its top political adviser in New York.[29]

With Gaspard making the political decisions (he has since left the White House to become executive director of the Democratic National Committee for the 2012 election), Stern could be sure his union interests would be a top White House priority.

Therefore, it is not surprising that the White House would select Craig Becker, who served as the associate general counsel of both the SEIU and the AFL-CIO, as a nominee to the National Labor Relations Board. Becker is an ultraradical union lawyer whose views are at odds with both the law and any commonsense notion of balance between the interests of unions and employers, as well as the rights of workers to make informed decisions without being subject to union intimidation.

In addition to his publicly acknowledged ties to SEIU—and notwithstanding his denials—Becker has clear ties to ACORN. In fact, Becker worked directly for SEIU Local 880 in Chicago, which was "part and parcel of ACORN," according to Vadum.[30] When Obama first nominated Becker, ACORN founder Wade Rathke said, "Here's a big win no matter how you shake and bake it," and, "Thanks for a solid, President Obama!"[31]

Union lawyer William Forbath openly argued that Becker's nomination was labor's hard-earned reward for its campaign contributions to Obama, writing:

> The Becker nomination offers President Barack
> Obama a more important opportunity, what he likes

to call a teachable moment…Unions spent $300 million for Obama and the Democrats in 2008. Unions are a key reason there remain substantial numbers of working-class white Americans who vote Democratic…If the Democrats won't even go this far to halt the battering unions have been taking…soon, we won't have any institutional player to do the heavy lifting, to provide the serious money the Democrats need.[32]

Unions had already explained that the NLRB was the Plan B after EFCA failed. As longtime SEIU and AFL-CIO organizer Stewart Acuff put it:

It [sic] we aren't able to pass the Employee Free Choice Act, we will work with President Obama and Vice President Biden and their appointees to the National Labor Relations Board to change the rules governing forming a union through administrative action.[33]

Becker was the ideal NLRB nominee for that task, having once written a stunning 46,000-word law review defending this conclusion:

Challenging the logic of rules shaped by a simple political analogy, this Article illuminates fundamental differences between the systems of political and labor representation. In light of these differences, it concludes that employers should be stripped of any legally cognizable interest in their employees' election of representatives.[34]

Becker has long been the leading proponent of the NLRB contriving to change the rules to adopt elements of the EFCA legislation. In that infamous law review article, he said his plan to strip employers of rights "could be achieved with almost no alteration of the statutory framework."[35]

He even argued that employers should be barred from complaining about illegal union activities during organizing drives: "Employers should have no right to raise questions concerning voter eligibility or campaign conduct."[36]

Obama saw Becker as the man to use backdoor means to advance his extreme union agenda that Congress had already rejected.

The resulting Senate fight over Becker's nomination was widely understood to be an indirect fight over many of the same ideas that had already been rejected by the American people and Congress when the EFCA legislation failed. It therefore initially appeared unlikely that Becker could attract the 60 votes needed to break a Republican filibuster and be confirmed to the board.

By January 2010, however, union desperation had reached a new peak in the aftermath of the shocking defeat of their preferred candidate, Martha Coakley, in the Massachusetts special election to fill the Senate seat previously held by the late U.S. Sen. Ted Kennedy (D-Mass.).

## SCOTT BROWN TO THE RESCUE?

The White House, Senate Democratic leadership, and the union bosses decided to ram through Becker's nomination before Scott Brown could be seated as a United States senator. This was, in effect, a consolation prize when it appeared that Brown's election would stop the union-backed ObamaCare legislation (as we'll see in Chapter 5, that legislation would later be revived by procedural trickery developed by the union-led front group Health Care for America Now).

Senate Republicans and grassroots activists held firm that the newly elected U.S. Sen. Scott Brown (R-Mass.) be seated prior to any consequential Senate votes. The Becker nomination was seen as highly consequential because it was widely understood that Becker intended to reshape the NLRB in an activist fashion to obliterate the rights of employers and enact elements of the card-check legislation.

Ultimately Brown was seated and the possibility of Democrats jamming Becker through with 60 Democratic votes was thwarted. Moreover, U.S. Sen. Ben Nelson also voted against Becker, saying: "Mr. Becker's previous statements strongly indicate that he would take an aggressive personal agenda to the NLRB, and that he would pursue a personal agenda there."[37]

Lincoln also voted "No," and four Democratic senators chose not to vote, trying to avoid angering either the union bosses or the business community when the matter had already been decided. Becker's nomination had been derailed, it seemed.

Yet Obama had no intention of abiding by the twice-expressed will of the United States Senate on the issue of card check. Despite the fact his legislation has been rejected based on overwhelming public opposition, and despite the fact that his attempt to appoint Becker to the NLRB was exposed as a backdoor effort to accomplish card check by extralegal means and stopped cold in the Senate, Obama abused the recess appointment power of the president to install Becker and another union lawyer, Mark Pearce, on the NLRB on March 27, 2010.[38]

This was a curious use of the recess appointment power given the strenuous objection Obama had offered as a senator when President Bush installed John Bolton as UN ambassador. Bolton was a controversial pick whose nomination was stalled in the Senate. Bush simply insisted on having Bolton represent the United States at the United Nations. At the time, Obama was skeptical of recess appointments, signing a letter to President Bush that said: "Sending someone to the United Nations who has not been confirmed by the United States Senate … is going to set our efforts back in many ways."[39]

Yet when Obama became president, he found the presidential powers that offended his democratic sensibilities when he was a senator were now his necessary prerogative—because Becker had faced a firestorm every bit as contentious as Bolton's. As he has often done, Obama pushed a Bush action he had opposed to a greater extreme, installing a man far more radical—and far more dangerous—than Bolton in a position of power, without Senate confirmation.

## THE NLRB FINDS BACK DOORS TO CARD CHECK

It didn't take long for the Becker-led NLRB to move forward on an agenda to accomplish the goals of card check by other means.[40] The most significant proposal is called "electronic voting," and it entails the obliteration of private ballot protections for union organizing elections in favor of a system of voting over the Internet. The problems here are obvious, given the reality of rampant union abuses and coercive tactics to force workers to sign union cards.

The union guys can show up at your house and say it's time to go online and vote for the union. Just as surely as the card-check law, this proposal removes any meaningful privacy protection for the most important vote many Americans will cast—the vote for who can negotiate their wages, hours, working conditions, and every other aspect of their working life.

As I've explained, many workers sign union cards under duress even though they have no intention of voting for the union. They know they have the backstop of the private ballot booth to express their true preferences without fear of reprisal. The electronic voting proposal would strip them of that fallback, allowing organizers to walk around with laptops or iPads and pressure workers to vote for unions electronically on the spot.[41] There is also the potential for online security breaches to falsify the results of elections conducted in this manner.

Mark Mix, president of the National Right to Work Foundation, has pointed out that "much like card check organizing, electronic voting leaves the door open to coercion and identity theft, and will be used by aggressive union organizers to impose forced unionism on more workers."[42]

Making matters worse, the Becker-led NLRB is moving forward on a separate track to give union organizers nearly unfettered access to the workplace to harass and intimidate workers while they are on the job. With many workers seeing no other way to get organizers to stop disrupting their work, they may sign union cards or click "yes" on an electronic voting screen just to be left alone.

The NLRB's workplace access mandate is moving forward under *Roundy's v. Milwaukee Building and Construction Trades*, which seeks to reverse 54 years of settled law to require that any employer that allows access to any nonprofit or charitable organizations must also allow union organizers into the workplace. Employers have pointed out that this standard will force them to choose between allowing Girl Scouts to sell cookies and keeping out SEIU and other extremely aggressive union organizers, whose goal is to disrupt and harass companies until they succumb to union pressure and allow in a union that may well undermine the interests of workers.

> ▶ ▶ ▶
>
> *"Much like card check organizing, electronic voting leaves the door open to coercion and identity theft, and will be used by aggressive union organizers to impose forced unionism on more workers."*
>
> —MARK MIX, President of the National Right to Work Foundation

As Brett McMahon of Miller & Long Concrete Construction explained:

> If this new request by union leaders is allowed to become law, its effect will be for many business operators like myself to have no choice but to close doors to any outside groups…Sorry, Girl Scouts. Sorry, Boy Scouts. Sorry, Red Cross. And the local soup kitchen. This is not hyperbole…Any business owner worth their salt would immediately shut their workplace to all outside organizations because it's economic suicide to welcome those whose stated purpose is to drive up your costs and in many cases are there to seek consumer boycotts or other damaging actions.[43]

The clear intention of these proposals is, as we expected from radical Becker, an attempt to "discover" the provisions of EFCA inside current laws.

Another far-reaching Becker idea that could advance at the NLRB is called "micro-unionization," which is the creation of very small unions of just a handful of workers. This would allow the creation of unions for, say, just poker dealers at a casino (a real proposal Becker supports) or just busboys at a restaurant. As former Department of Labor official Glenn Spencer explained:

> They'd still need to win an election or prove that they had a majority through card-check, but what it would enable them to do is not have to worry about organizing, say 100 people, they could just go in and find five and have the appropriate job classification and say, "Well, this is all we want, right here." Instead of having to win an election amongst 100 people, you only have to win an election amongst five.[44]

Breaking workplaces down into unions based on very narrow job classifications would give them a foot in the door where they can persuade only a small number of workers to join them. It would also be a bureaucratic disaster for employers to manage. It's just another example of the many ways Becker is changing the rules to benefit union bosses.

The NLRB is also pursuing the "quickie elections" concept that emerged as a key element of later versions of EFCA as its own regulatory proposal. Peter Schaumber, a former NLRB chairman during the Bush administration, explained how the new proposed procedure would work:

> Without the employer's knowledge, the union will secretly collect employee signatures on a petition, covertly telling the employees they solicit what the union can do for them. After achieving the requisite number of signatures, the union will file the petition, catching the employer and the remaining employees by surprise. The employer will be faced with election only days away with little opportunity to inform itself about the union or the issues involved, and without the ability to express itself on the issue of unionization to its employees…
>
> Over the last thirty years or more, board law has changed when political control of the board changed. But what we are witnessing today from the Obama board goes far beyond what has occurred in the past. The board majority readily ignores statute language and congressional intent and trashes decades of board law and procedure with the sole goal of augmenting union power, even at the expense of workers' rights.[45]

The NLRB is even intervening in decisions of individual companies to block them from locating in right-to-work states where workers cannot be forced to join a union. In a chilling April 20, 2011, complaint written by *Acting* (not Senate-confirmed) General Counsel Lafe Solomon, the NLRB ordered Boeing to move the second production facility of its 787 Dreamliner—already mostly built in South Carolina, at a multibillion-dollar cost—to more union-friendly Washington.[46] That decision is being challenged in court and in Congress. If it survives, it portends almost unlimited power for federal bureaucrats to commandeer businesses to provide payback to union bosses.

> ▶ ▶ ▶
>
> *One of the concerns about Becker as a nominee was that he would be forced to recuse himself from many of the cases before the board. His solution to that problem was simple: ignore the conflict of interest and unethically rule on cases brought by his former longtime employer.*

## ETHICS LAPSE

Not only is Becker radical, he is also unethical. Given his lengthy and extensive work for the SEIU, one of the concerns about Becker as a nominee was that he would be forced to recuse himself from many of the cases before the board. His solution to that problem was simple: ignore the conflict of interest and unethically rule on cases brought by his former longtime employer.

The National Right to Work Committee explained:

> Becker argues that he may participate in cases involving SEIU affiliates because the national and local unions are "separate and distinct legal entit[ies]." The SEIU's own constitution, however,

considers local affiliates "constituent subordinate bodies" of the national union. Moreover, in 2009 over 85 percent of the SEIU's receipts came from a per capita tax on the locals' membership dues and fees. The national union even has the power to assume control over its locals if they do not conform to International policies.[47]

Becker, of course, signed the Obama administration's highly touted ethics pledge, including the so-called "revolving door ban" committing him not to participate in any matter involving his former employer.[48] But abiding by the ethics pledge would have defeated the purpose of putting a union hand like Becker on the board—to rule in favor of his former employers.

## THE STATES FIGHT BACK

In the face of ongoing concerns about both the EFCA legislation and the possibility of worker rights being eroded by backdoor efforts of the Obama administration, the Goldwater Institute, located in Arizona, launched an ambitious project called Save Our Secret Ballot, or SOS Ballot, to enact state constitutional amendments guaranteeing a private ballot right in any representation election, including union organizing elections.

Their efforts culminated in four states enacting such constitutional protections via votes of the people in the 2010 election: Arizona, South Carolina, South Dakota, and Utah. Voter support ranged from 60 percent in Arizona and Utah to 79 percent in South Dakota to a stunning 86 percent in South Carolina.[49]

These stunning election results were the last nail in the coffin of Democratic efforts to jam through the EFCA legislation in the lame-duck session following the election, as U.S. Sen. Tom Harkin (D-Iowa) floated in June 2010.[50] In the face of overwhelming public opposition—reflected not just in the states where the secret ballot was upheld, but nationally in a Republican landslide—unions shelved EFCA in the lame duck, instead pushing a far less ambitious piece of legislation to force unionization of public safety workers. Even that bill failed by five votes, attracting only 55 of the 60 votes required.[51]

Nonetheless, the NLRB announced on January 14, 2011, that it would sue the four states that enacted constitutional amendments to protect the secret ballot. It is an attempt by the NLRB to keep the path clear for its efforts to undermine private ballot rights through its electronic voting proposal and other legally dubious efforts to sidestep Congress.[52]

The lawsuits, which have moved forward, display the stark contrast between state governments following proper legal procedures, with a mandate of the people, to protect rights and an Obama administration that disregards all of the democratic safeguards of our federal constitutional system to reward unions and other special-interest groups.

The four states leading this effort deserve enormous credit for standing up to the federal government and powerful union interests. As South Carolina Attorney General Alan Wilson put it: "South Carolina voters spoke overwhelmingly to ensure that their ballot votes are kept between them and their Maker—not to be influenced by union bosses."[53]

The state protections are valuable even if the NLRB wins, because there are many industries that are not subject to federal regulation, including state and local government, agricultural, and domestic employees. Government employees, in particular, are critical because there are now more government employees in unions (51.8 percent as of 2010) than there are private-sector workers.[54]

The NLRB's aggressive action to undermine state protections for private ballot voting rights in union organizing elections shows how determined the board is to accomplish card check by backdoor means—against the wishes of the American people and Congress.

Voters in the other 46 states would do well to contact their state legislators and demand they enact a similar protection in their own state constitutions. When the union thugs come organizing someday, those state-law protections could prove vital.

It is an open question, however, whether these protections, applied to workers covered by the NLRB's jurisdiction, will survive the NLRB's legal challenge. Ultimately, Congress must step up and take responsibility.

## THE UNIONS' OTHER CAPTIVE FEDERAL BOARD

There are two industries whose union elections are not supervised by the National Labor Relations Board. A second, more obscure board called the National Mediation Board (NMB) was created by the 1934 Railway Labor Act. The NMB has jurisdiction over railroads and airlines, which have always been treated differently from other companies because their operations are inherently national, and thus allowing them to be organized as local unions would give extraordinary power to small groups of local workers to shut down national transportation networks with widespread impacts.

Congress established the NMB with its own rules to oversee the unionization of those industries only on a national basis. For 75 years, from the NMB's inception until a 2009 letter from the AFL-CIO to the board suggested otherwise, elections under the NMB required a majority of the workers in a craft or class to vote for a union. That meant workers who failed to vote would be considered not to support the union. Given the far-flung, national footprint of the railroad and airline industries, this was a sensible rule to ensure a relatively small number of workers could not vote to unionize the whole

▶ ▶ ▶

*On May 10, 2010, the National Mediation Board changed its rule and unilaterally overturned 75 years of precedent. It ruled that a union could be certified with a majority of those voting, rather than a majority of workers, which is what the Railway Labor Act requires.*

workforce without the awareness and support of workers throughout the company.

Moreover, this was a straightforward interpretation of the statute, and any effort to change it should have gone through Congress. Nonetheless, on May 10, 2010, the National Mediation Board changed its rule and unilaterally overturned 75 years of precedent. It ruled that a union could be certified with a majority of those voting, rather than a majority of workers, which is what the Railway Labor Act requires.

NMB Chairman Elizabeth Dougherty issued a blistering dissent in the two-to-one decision, writing:

> The rule in question has been applied consistently for 75 years—including by Boards appointed by Presidents Roosevelt, Truman, Johnson, Carter, and Clinton. Making this change would be an unprecedented event in the history of the NMB, which has always followed a policy of making major rule changes with consensus and only when required by statutory amendments or essential to reduce administrative burdens on the agency...
>
> Assuring that a representative certified by the NMB enjoys true majority support is even more important given that union certifications under the RLA must cover an entire transportation system— often over enormously wide geographic areas with large numbers of people. I also note that there is no process for decertifying a union under the Railway

Labor Act. These unique aspects of the RLA do not
exist under the National Labor Relations Act or elsewhere, and they render irrelevant comparisons between the RLA and other election procedures...

The Majority has not articulated a sufficient
rationale for making the change. Moreover, the request from the Transportation Trades Division of
the AFL-CIO that prompted this rule change was
made in an informal, two-page letter with no legal
analysis, no mention of changed conditions, and no
discussion of our statutory authority.[55]

Nonetheless, she was outvoted. Regulators had—even more
clearly than the ongoing efforts at the NLRB—disregarded the law,
bypassed Congress, and stacked the deck in favor of the unions.

U.S. Sen. Johnny Isakson (R-Ga.) was outraged, saying:

The National Mediation Board simply does not have
the legal authority to make such a radical change
without Congressional authorization. With this rule
change, a union could be permanently recognized
without a majority of employees having ever supported representation. I will not stand by and let
this administration compromise fairness to grant
favors to labor unions. I will do everything in my
power to stop this backdoor attempt to shift the balance between labor and management.[56]

Isakson introduced a resolution of disapproval under the
Congressional Review Act, S.J. Res. 30, which allowed him to force
a Senate floor vote on overturning the NMB's union giveaway. The
vote was on September 23, 2010, and Isakson's resolution got only
43 votes (51 were needed to overturn the rule). The only Democrats
who voted to stand up to the unions and take responsibility as the

legitimate legislative branch of government were Lincoln and Mark Pryor of Arkansas and Ben Nelson of Nebraska.[57] Every other Senate Democrat can and must be held responsible for allowing the NMB power grab to proceed.

Ironically, the immediate motivation for this outrageous move to upend 75 years of established law by a regulatory back door was to make it easier to unionize flight attendants at Delta Air Lines, who had repeatedly voted against the union. Nonetheless, even with the new voting rules, Delta flight attendants voted against the union again. The Obama administration and its union allies won't take no for an answer and have filed a mountain of frivolous complaints against Delta.[58] Given the NMB's absurd bias toward the unions, expect it to somehow contrive to order a new election. Let's hope the Delta flight attendants are smart enough to keep voting against the union.

# FIGHTING BACK: THE CONGRESSIONAL SOLUTION

It is not enough for Congress to reject the card-check bill if the representatives and senators are willing to collectively sit on their hands while union lawyers in the Obama administration undermine worker rights by other means. Congress must pass legislation un-ambiguously guaranteeing workers the right to a secret ballot, free from intimidation, to choose whether they wish to be represented by a union, and if so, which union.

Legislation to that effect has been introduced by U.S. Sen. Jim DeMint as the Secret Ballot Protection Act. The legislation, to date, has no Democratic cosponsors, which exposes the extent to which Democrats are willing to put union payback ahead of the basic prin-ciples in which they claim to believe.

DeMint has also joined with Lindsey Graham (R-S.C.) and Lamar Alexander (R-Tenn.) to introduce legislation called the Job

Protection Act (S. 964) that would overturn the NLRB's attempt to stop Boeing from building in a right-to-work state. The bill would prohibit the NLRB from ordering any company to relocate jobs from one location to another and guarantee employers the right to choose where to do business in the United States. It's sad that such a bill is needed, but it is.

Structural reforms like the REINS Act would also limit the ability of agencies like the NLRB and NMB to perform an illegitimate legislative function, since their major rulings would be subject to a requirement of congressional approval before they could take effect.

Ultimately, all efforts to stop the dangerous union influence on the Obama administration depend on the ability of activists to educate the public and effectively communicate how serious these threats are. On the card-check legislation itself, an enormous public education effort rang the alarm and successfully blocked the legislation by making it politically toxic. It is a much bigger challenge to do the same thing with respect to the decisions of a little-known federal board.

▶ ▶ ▶

*Ultimately, all efforts to stop the dangerous union influence on the Obama administration depend on the ability of activists to educate the public and effectively communicate how serious these threats are.*

Yet we must rise to that challenge. Indeed the outrage of pursuing this agenda that was twice-rejected by Congress is an opportunity to engage the tea parties and grassroots activists across the political spectrum by appealing to their sense of fair play and respect for the legitimate constitutional power of Congress to make the laws.

At the end of the day, we must make it clear to Congress that failing to stop the NLRB and NMB is unacceptable, and amounts to complicity in a conspiracy to deprive workers of their basic rights.

We need to politicize *inaction* in Congress on this issue on a level equivalent to the repugnant *action* of supporting the original EFCA legislation. And we must mobilize and vote accordingly in 2012.

## CHAPTER 5

# Ill-Advised: ObamaCare Keeps Getting Worse

*"We have to pass the bill so that you can find out what is in it, away from the fog of the controversy."*[1]

—NANCY PELOSI

I t was Saturday, the day before the final House passage of ObamaCare, and I was on Capitol Hill around 7:30 a.m. for the last big "Red Alert" rally opposing a heavier government role in health care and the monstrous bill that had become known as ObamaCare. It was the culmination of an unprecedented public wave of discontent that had started the previous summer and had only continued to build through the remarkable upset election of U.S. Sen. Scott Brown in Massachusetts. The heartfelt passion in the crowd was palpable: America hated this bill.

Democrats in Washington, however, had contrived to abuse the legislative process and force the hated legislation through. That day, thousands of activists from across the country who had been to countless tea parties, town hall meetings, and local protests made one more trip to Washington. If even a handful of the supposedly pro-life Democrats, led by Michigan Congressman Bart Stupak, stuck to their word, it would be enough to stop the bill.

The next day, Sunday, March 21, 2010, Congress ignored us and passed ObamaCare. Stupak broke his word and accepted a phony executive order from the White House to sign off on taxpayer funding for abortion and the bill passed (and Stupak retired rather than face voters). The day the bill passed, I wrote a public memo to the members of Congress who voted for it:

> All 219 of you put blind adherence to a radical gov-
> ernment-first ideology ahead of the wishes of the
> American people. We are less free today than we
> were yesterday. Our health care will now likely be
> permanently politicized, subject to the whim of our
> often out-of-touch political class.
>
> Last night was your turn to vote. Your con-
> stituents made clear what they wanted, but you
> weren't listening. But you can't ignore voters for-
> ever. November is coming.[2]

Indeed the political energy and anger that built through the ObamaCare fight led to the landslide election of 2010 and a new Congress that may be able to do something about it. But until they succeed at repealing the law, we are living with its implications.

Up to now we've focused on failed elements of Obama's legislative agenda that have shifted inside the regulatory realm to bypass Congress and the American people. But it's also worth noting that Obama's two signature legislative achievements—ObamaCare and the Dodd-Frank financial regulation bill—both amount to the creation of vast new regulatory powers. Moreover, those vast new powers are vaguely defined, and much of the real decision-making was delegated by Congress to, in the case of ObamaCare, the Department of Health and Human Services (HHS) and the Centers for Medicare and Medicaid Services (CMS).

Although it was legislation passed by Congress, there is no greater example of the Obama administration's insistence on pushing the far-left envelope of public policy than the process by which the so-called Patient Protection and Affordable Care Act—better known as ObamaCare—was passed and by which it has so far been implemented.

There's no other way to say it: ObamaCare is an abomination. The bill that was passed into law was not even finished legislation— it was a jumbled mess of a draft bill that was passed into law as is because that was the only way to disregard Brown's election and the clear will of the American people. That jumbled mess is now being arbitrarily interpreted by unelected bureaucrats who are making a bad bill even worse.

ObamaCare is packed full of tax hikes that make a mockery of Obama's promise not to raise taxes on anyone but "the rich," as Obama adviser Austan Goolsbee made embarrassingly clear in testimony to the House Ways and Means Committee, claiming that tax increases are not tax increases. U.S. Rep. Pat Tiberi (R-Ohio) ran through a list of tax hikes, including the new excise tax on high-value health plans, the tax hike on over-the-counter medications, the limitation on tax deductibility for medical expenses, and the new cap on flexible spending account contributions. Goolsbee answered each question by saying he didn't consider the tax hikes to be tax hikes. Finally, Tiberi asked about the new 10 percent excise tax on indoor tanning services, and Goolsbee shrugged and laughed.[3] Of course, that tax is no laughing matter for thousands of small tanning businesses, and the other hefty tax hikes are no laughing matter for the rest of us.

ObamaCare gives politicians and bureaucrats control over private health decisions that should be left to patients and doctors. And, of course, it is unconstitutional—as two federal judges have now decisively concluded. (For the most up-to-date information on the legal challenges, see the Independent Women's Forum website: www.healthcarelawsuits.org.)

ObamaCare just keeps getting worse as waivers are granted to the administration's political allies while the rest of us are expected to comply with all of the new requirements of the law's vast new bureaucracies. Obama cheated the legitimate confirmation process, installing Don Berwick—who is romantic about the British system of health care rationing—as the new head of Medicare without so much as a single Senate hearing. Obama's Food and Drug Administration (FDA) is also cooperating in efforts to ration care by pulling approval for cancer drugs it deems too expensive.

As the various tentacles of this disastrous law reach into the lives of Americans, it's crucial that Congress uses all of its tools—Congressional Review Act resolutions of disapproval, oversight hearings, appropriations riders, and, ideally, the REINS Act—to slow, stall, stop, and restrict the abuse of regulatory powers as the law moves forward.

▶ ▶ ▶

*There is no alternative to repealing this disastrous law. Quite simply, the damage ObamaCare will do to the traditional relationship between government and the people is so serious that however long it takes, we cannot afford to stop pushing for repeal and using it as a yardstick for candidates.*

In the end, however, there is no alternative to repealing this disastrous law. Quite simply, the damage ObamaCare will do to the traditional relationship between government and the people is so serious that however long it takes, we cannot afford to stop pushing for repeal and using it as a yardstick for candidates.

# BAD PROCESS LEADS TO BAD POLICY

Barack Obama made a clear commitment on the campaign trail to reforming health care in an honest, above-board, and transparent fashion. Then he did precisely the opposite. His most infamous promise was to allow C-SPAN to film the negotiations. He said:

> I'm going to have all the negotiations around a big table. We'll have doctors and nurses and hospital administrators. Insurance companies, drug companies—they'll get a seat at the table, they just won't be able to buy every chair. But what we will do is, we'll have the negotiations televised on C-SPAN, so that people can see who is making arguments on behalf of their constituents, and who are making arguments on behalf of the drug companies or the insurance companies. And so, that approach, I think is what is going to allow people to stay involved in this process.[4]

Even PolitiFact, which has generally been very lenient on Obama, judged this as a "promise broken."[5] Instead of the promised open process, we saw a special-interest feeding frenzy in which the White House shopped special deals to buy the support of key players at the expense of patients.

The biggest special-interest beneficiaries were the union bosses, who were willing to put card check on the shelf temporarily to pursue ObamaCare. Consider the stakes for them—with private sector unions declining toward zero, they had the opportunity to create a vast new federal workforce of dues-paying union

▶ ▶ ▶

*Barack Obama made a clear commitment on the campaign trail to reforming health care in an honest, above-board, and transparent fashion. Then he did precisely the opposite.*

members: a unionized American National Health Service. By way of comparison, there are only three employers in the world larger than the unionized British National Health Service (NHS)—Walmart, the China National Petroleum Company, and Indian Railways. The NHS employs an astonishing 1.6 million people, one out of every 23 British citizens.[6] A similar ratio in the United States, a country of more than 310 million people, would be 13.5 million dues-paying, federalized health care workers. Clearly any step in that direction is a big win for union bosses.

> ▶ ▶ ▶
>
> *There are only three employers in the world larger than the unionized British National Health Service (NHS)—Walmart, the China National Petroleum Company, and Indian Railways.*

Democrats even tried at one point to exempt union workers from an excise tax that would apply to all other workers, although public pressure caused them to retreat from that provision.

The first special deal—ironic given Obama's statement about drug companies—was reached on July 7, 2009, with the pharmaceutical industry, represented by the Pharmaceutical Research and Manufacturers of America (PhRMA), which agreed to spend up to $150 million promoting the president's plan and to offer as much as $80 billion in Medicare discounts on drugs in exchange for four key White House promises to promote pharmaceutical interests: opposing prescription drug reimportation; opposing rebates in the Medicare prescription drug benefit; opposing the imposition of "negotiating" or price controls in the Medicare prescription drug benefit; and opposing "opening Medicare Part B," which meant protecting the higher reimbursement rates for infusion drugs currently covered by Medicare's physician program instead of its drug program.[7] Even with the discounts PhRMA offered, the companies stood to make significant profits from the president's plan, and they made good on their $150 million pledge, becoming the main financial backer of the ObamaCare effort.

That PhRMA money mostly ran through the union-backed front group Families USA, which along with Health Care for America Now (HCAN)—an umbrella organization of John Podesta's Center for American Progress Action Fund, the unions, MoveOn.org, and the usual left-wing protest crowd—copiloted the outside pressure for the legislation. Thus the key financial backers for ObamaCare were the pharmaceutical industry and the unions. The unions, in turn, organized the full array of left-wing pressure groups (including the union activists' radicalized wing, Association of Community Organizations for Reform Now, or ACORN). HCAN still lists 26 of ACORN's state affiliates as members as of this writing.[8]

Michelle Malkin revealed an internal ACORN memo, which explained the political rationale for their involvement:

> Why do they want Obamacare? An internal ACORN
> memo I obtained from August 2008 makes the mo-
> tives clear. "Over our 38 years, health care organiz-
> ing has never been a major focus either nationally
> or locally for ACORN," wrote ACORN Philadelphia
> region director Craig Robbins. "But increasingly,
> ACORN offices around the country are doing work
> on health care." The goal: "Building ACORN Power."
> The memo outlines the ACORN/HCAN partnership
> and strategy of opposing any programs that rely on
> "unregulated private insurance"—and then parlay-
> ing political victory on government-run health care
> "to move our ACORN agenda (or at least part of it)
> with key electeds that we might otherwise not be
> able to pull off."

The objective, in other words, is to piggyback and exploit Obamacare to improve and protect their political health.[9]

Although the union efforts were mostly funded by pharmaceutical companies, they continued to bash drug companies and accuse Republicans of being beholden to them.

The PhRMA deal was followed in short order by a White House deal with the hospitals, which supposedly had given back $155 billion in future Medicare reimbursements. Dennis Smith of The Heritage Foundation noted immediately, however: "These savings are really a mirage. Hospitals are likely to get more revenue than what they are pretending to give up."[10] He was right. As Medicare actuaries John Shatto and Kent Clemens concluded in an appendix to the Medicare Trustees Report, the purported cuts to Medicare payment rates would force large numbers of hospitals to stop taking Medicare patients—and therefore Congress will step in and prevent those cuts from happening.[11]

▶ ▶ ▶

*"Administration and congressional Democrats are literally bullying health care groups into cutting backroom deals to fund a government takeover of health care."*

—Speaker of the House JOHN BOEHNER

On the other hand, the so-called "Accountable Care Organization" concept embedded in ObamaCare is designed to reward hospitals.[12]

Speaker of the House John Boehner accurately described exactly what was going on: "Administration and congressional Democrats are literally bullying health care groups into cutting backroom deals to fund a government takeover of health care."[13]

# AARP SELLS OUT SENIORS

Perhaps the most politically significant special-interest deal of all was cut with the AARP, which Jim Martin of the 60 Plus Association, a fiscally conservative seniors group, has rightly called Americans *Against* Retired Persons.

Seniors hated the bill because they rightly feared steep cuts to Medicare with no meaningful cost containment mechanism other than rationing. The last Rasmussen poll before the final House passage vote showed opposition to the law among seniors running at 59 percent, versus just 37 percent support, with strong opponents outnumbering strong supporters more than two to one.[14]

Yet AARP ignored the overwhelming opposition among seniors, seen not just in polls but in emotional town hall confrontations all over the country. Why? Money. AARP is a major insurance company, whose offerings were uniquely well positioned to benefit from ObamaCare because the steep cuts to Medicare Advantage would force beneficiaries into traditional fee-for-service Medicare. Seniors in traditional Medicare typically buy so-called Medigap insurance policies to fill in what Medicare doesn't cover (but Medicare Advantage does). Sweetening the deal for AARP, the bill created a special, AARP-specific carve-out exempting its Medigap policies from the rate regulations applied to its competitors.[15]

An investigative report from the House Committee on Ways and Means found: "The Democrats' health care law, which AARP strongly endorsed, could result in a windfall for AARP that exceeds over $1 billion during the next 10 years."[16] The report also found that while AARP offers a Medicare Advantage plan through United Healthcare, it does so under a flat-fee licensing agreement that would give the company the same revenue even following savage cuts to Medicare Advantage enrollment. It was a win-win for AARP's bottom line, but at a devastating cost to the seniors it pretends to represent.

# INSURERS JOIN THE SPECIAL INTEREST FEEDING FRENZY

Even the health insurance companies, which Obama continued to vilify throughout the national debate, got in on the special-interest deal-making. While the White House staged a largely phony clash with insurance companies over a so-called public option—a path to a single-payer, Canadian-style system that the administration publicly supported to keep the left-wing base happy—the administration was quietly cooperating with insurers on the basic reform template that became ObamaCare: a mandate to buy insurance from the big insurance companies, combined with expensive regulations to put their smaller competitors out of business and hefty subsidies at taxpayer expense.

As I warned in August 2009, the public option debate was a distraction to pave the way for precisely the special-interest-driven bill that ultimately passed:

> The insurance companies will insist on, and probably receive, an individual health insurance mandate that will make it illegal not to buy their products. The penalty for violating the mandate will be a sizable new tax or garnishing your wages. President Obama beat Hillary Clinton in part by opposing such a mandate, but now he supports it. Call it a nod to political reality, or selling out to insurance companies if you're more harshly inclined.
>
> The big insurance companies will spend tens if not hundreds of millions of dollars supporting a mandates bill, because their smaller competitors will be regulated out of business while they can mint huge profits from all of the new customers now required by law to buy their products.

Why would big government central-planners support this type of legislation? Because even without a public option, the mandates are enough, over time, for Washington to exert total control over our health care. Under an individual mandate, politicians and bureaucrats would get to define what counts as "health insurance"...

Vast new subsidies will be required to ease passage of a bill that would otherwise slam lower income constituents—those subsidies mean businesses and the middle class will be slammed twice—once to pay higher premiums for the now-legally-mandated purchase of health insurance, and again with higher taxes to subsidize coverage for others.[17]

I wish I'd been wrong, but unfortunately things played out pretty closely to how I'd predicted. What I didn't anticipate, however, was how much worse the bill would get in its final back-room negotiations to buy the last few Democratic votes, including infamous payoffs like U.S. Sens. Ben Nelson's Cornhusker Kickback, Mary Landrieu's Louisiana Purchase, the U-Con for Chris Dodd (D-Conn.) that he intended to provide $100 million to the University of Connecticut hospital, and Bill Nelson's Gator Aid, which carved out 800,000 of his Florida constituents from the bill's Medicare Advantage cuts.[18]

Most of these deals were removed due to public outrage, but the Louisiana Purchase survived. Dodd's U-Con was drafted in such a way that a few other university hospitals were able to apply for it. The Obama administration chose Ohio State to receive the $100 million.[19]

None of these special-interest industry deals or single-senator sweetheart arrangements would have been possible if Obama had made good on his promise to have an open public debate. A disastrously bad process resulted in disastrously bad policy.

# HOW THE DEMOCRATS IGNORED MASSACHUSETTS VOTERS

The ObamaCare freight train looked, briefly, as if it had been stopped cold by the election of Scott Brown, who campaigned on being vote number 41 to sustain a filibuster to stop the bill. Brown arrived signing autographs with the number 41, and according to *The Christian Science Monitor*, "forced Democrats to review strategy for completing the health care reform bill that Brown campaigned to defeat."[20]

Indeed, even Democratic stalwart U.S. Rep. Barney Frank unambiguously ruled out efforts to pass ObamaCare in its current form after the election, saying:

> If Martha Coakley had won, I believe we could have worked out a reasonable compromise between the House and Senate health care bills. But since Scott Brown has won and the Republicans now have 41 votes in the Senate, that approach is no longer appropriate.
>
> I am hopeful that some Republican senators will be willing to discuss a revised version of health care reform because I do not think that the country would be well-served by the health care status quo. But our respect for democratic procedures must rule out any effort to pass a health care bill as if the Massachusetts election had not happened.[21]

That appeal to fairness and respect for the democratic process was short-lived. That same day a cleverly undemocratic proposal from Ron Pollack, the executive director of the PhRMA-funded union front Families USA suggested a way to do precisely what Frank had ruled out. As *Politico* reported:

Ron Pollack, a longtime health care insider and executive director of Families USA, has floated a variation on this theme with the administration and congressional aides: a two-step process that would reassure House members their wishes would be met in the bill.

Under Pollack's proposal, the House would take up the Senate bill only after the White House and congressional leaders struck a deal on key issues, such as taxes and the subsidies to purchase insurance. They would incorporate those changes into a separate budget reconciliation bill.

The House would pass both the Senate bill and the reconciliation bill, possibly on the same day. The Senate would then take up the reconciliation bill, which would require only 51 votes for passage.[22]

Pollack's strategy, and the payoff it brought for his union members and his PhRMA patrons, were eagerly embraced by congressional Democrats. It's worth nothing, however, that the seeds of Pollack's strategy were planted a month earlier, on the Senate floor, when Republican leadership made the fateful decision to enter into unanimous consent agreements with Democrats that paved the way for an initial draft bill to pass the Senate before they left for Christmas.

The first such agreement was blocked by stalwart conservative U.S. Sen. Jim DeMint, who forced a two-day delay before the Senate was able to vote on an amendment offered by U.S. Sen. Barbara Mikulski (D-Md.) that stripped the bill of embarrassing provisions, including one that would have excluded mammogram coverage for women younger than 50. There were substantive problems with the amendment—critics argued it would compel abortion coverage—but the more important tactical consideration was that withholding consent forced Harry Reid and the Democrats to burn two days per amendment under Senate rules. With all of the amendments they needed to have votes on, running out the clock would have gotten Republicans to the Massachusetts election and victory over ObamaCare.

Ultimately, DeMint could not do it alone. No other senators of either party joined his stalling effort, with Republican Whip Jon Kyl (R-Ariz.) explicitly opposing it, saying:

> Our strategy is not actually to delay. Our strategy is to have a lot of good amendments and highlight the problems in the bill. It is not our strategy to some-how slow things down.[23]

To be fair to Republican leadership, it was hard to believe that Brown—still far behind in the polls at that time—would pull off the Massachusetts miracle. Still, it would have been wonderful to stall Senate action and *guarantee* that stopping ObamaCare would be on the line with Brown.

Unfortunately, isolated and unable to be on the Senate floor all the time, DeMint backed down and allowed the bipartisan parade of amendments that led to Senate passage and laid the foundation for the Pollack maneuver that would circumvent the Massachusetts election. DeMint made a keen observation shortly thereafter:

▶ ▶ ▶

*"The problem in the Republican Party is that the leadership has gone to the left and the tea parties and the Republicans out across the country are right there where American principles have always been, and I'm trying to pull the party back to the mainstream of where America really is."*

—U.S. Sen. JIM DEMINT

The problem in the Republican Party is that the leadership has gone to the left and the tea parties and the Republicans out across the country are right there where American principles have always been, and I'm trying to pull the party back to the mainstream of where America really is.[24]

A new crop of conservative Republicans were indeed elected, and will now be challenged to slow down and stop the regulatory rollout of ObamaCare.

## REGULATORS TAKE CONTROL

Nancy Pelosi was right in more ways than she realized when she infamously said: "We have to pass the bill so that you can find out what is in it, away from the fog of the controversy."[25] Not only was the more than 2,000-page bill negotiated in secret and so densely complex that few humans could understand it, it also deferred most of the really difficult and important decisions to the regulators, including dozens of brand-new boards, committees, councils, and working groups. So even after ObamaCare had been passed there was no way to know what was really in it until the bureaucracy was assembled and began issuing regulations.

> ▶ ▶ ▶
>
> *One of the worst tragedies of the bill is that this new army of unionized federal bureaucrats will stand between patients and doctors.*

During the ObamaCare debate, opponents of the bill touted lengthy lists and convoluted charts to show the enormous bureaucratic overlay on top of the new taxes, mandates, and subsidies that captured most of the headlines. One of the worst tragedies of the bill is that this new army of unionized federal bureaucrats will stand between patients and doctors.

The Congressional Research Service was asked to produce the definitive number of new bureaucracies created by the bill, but was unable to even calculate it, saying:

> This report describes dozens of new governmental organizations or advisory bodies that are mentioned in PPACA, but does not include other types of entities that were created by the legislation (e.g., various demonstration projects, grants, trust funds, programs, systems, formulas, guidelines, risk pools, websites, ratings areas, model agreements, or protocols)...
>
> The precise number of new entities that will ultimately be created pursuant to PPACA is currently unknowable, for the number of entities created by some sections is contingent upon other factors, and some new entities may satisfy more than one requirement in the legislation.[26]

The most powerful person in this vast new regulatory apparatus is HHS Secretary Kathleen Sebelius, who was given frighteningly vast powers by the new law. Philip Klein of *The American Spectator* explained:

> There are more than 2,500 references to the secretary of HHS in the health care law (in most cases she's simply mentioned as "the Secretary"). A further breakdown finds that there are more than 700 instances in which the Secretary is instructed that she "shall" do something, and more than 200 cases in which she "may" take some form of regulatory action if she chooses. On 139 occasions, the law mentions decisions that the "Secretary determines."[27]

The Pollack plan also created a unique opportunity for regulatory excess—a bill that was intended as a discussion draft was, to circumvent Brown's historic win, passed into law as is. The result was a mass of conflicting provisions and ambiguities that created even more regulatory discretion.

The most obvious proof that the ObamaCare bill was never written to be passed into law is its Title X, which is a laundry list of amendments and changes to the bill itself. A leading employee-benefits attorney who was implementing the employment-related provisions for clients told me she has never seen such an inconsistent mess in a piece of final legislation.

Now Sebelius's office is issuing a whole string of official guidances and regulations that attempt to "correct" the draft law, often by asserting things that the law doesn't actually say.

> ▶ ▶ ▶
>
> *Sebelius's office is issuing a whole string of official guidances and regulations that attempt to "correct" the draft law, often by asserting things that the law doesn't actually say.*

Just days after the law passed, it became clear that, contrary to the promises of the White House and bill's authors, it was not actually written to require insurance companies to cover children with preexisting conditions. Sebelius sprang into action with regulations demanding what the legislation did not. She wrote to insurance executives:

> Health insurance reform is designed to prevent any child from being denied coverage because he or she has a pre-existing condition. Leaders in Congress have reaffirmed this in recent days in the attached statement. To ensure that there is no ambiguity on this point, I am preparing to issue regulations in the weeks ahead.[28]

That was one thing. It was "for the children." But the next major regulatory action under the new law was the so-called Grandfathered Health Plan rule. That rule was supposed to make good on the president's promise that "if you like your plan, you can keep it." Instead it did the opposite. U.S. Sen. Mike Enzi (R-Wyo.) forced a vote in September 2010 on overturning the rule, saying:

> An estimated 80 percent of small businesses are expected to lose their grandfathered status based upon the regulations the Administration wrote. That means the small firms that do offer health insurance won't be able to afford what they now provide.[29]

The one key exception, spared from the grandfather regulations, is for union plans. Those plans are protected for at least the life of the union contract, with a specific carve-out on page 81 of the regulations. According to *Investors Business Daily*:

> Unions that had a health plan under a collective bargaining agreement by March 23, 2010, can switch insurers as long as the collective bargaining deal is in effect and not forfeit the grandfathered exemptions from many ObamaCare provisions. But anyone else—large business, small business, [an] individual—who switches carriers loses their grandfathered status.[30]

It pays to be on Team Obama. Enzi's resolution failed on party lines.[31]

Some employers and their employees have been fortunate enough to keep their existing coverage by receiving waivers from HHS. The process appears to be somewhat arbitrary, with no clear standards specified by the statute. There is an interesting emerging pattern, however: the very unions who lobbied so hard for

ObamaCare to pass are now opting out in huge numbers, and HHS is happy to oblige. Of course, you and I are not offered the same opportunity to opt out.

An analysis by Michelle Malkin of the waivers granted through late January 2011 found that 182 of the 771 waivers granted were to unions, including 17 Teamster locals and seven SEIU affiliates.[32] On January 26, 2011, HHS granted blanket waivers to four states: Massachusetts, Ohio, New Jersey, and Tennessee.[33] All are considered politically important for Obama.

## OBAMA'S SCARY MEDICARE RATIONER

The means by which the Obama administration has pushed the ObamaCare law to the extreme and beyond gets even worse in the Medicare arena.

President Obama circumvented the Senate and the American public by using a recess appointment to install Dr. Donald Berwick at the helm of the CMS. It not only confirms the president's disregard for the legitimate legislative process, but also exposes the frightening big-government extremism of the president's health care agenda.

Berwick has said: "The decision is not whether we will ration care. The decision is whether we will ration with our eyes open."[34]

Obama's new Medicare boss goes even further, openly supporting giving the government centralized control over health care. Berwick specifically looks to the National Institute for Clinical Excellence in Britain as a model, with its measure of "quality adjusted life years." In Britain, they estimate that a year of your life—adjusted for "quality," (i.e., meaning how

▶ ▶ ▶

*In Britain, they estimate that a year of your life—adjusted for "quality," (i.e., meaning how sick you are)—is worth about $45,000. If you're too old or too sick to justify the cost, you're denied treatment.*

sick you are)—is worth about $45,000. If you're too old or too sick to justify the cost, you're denied treatment.[35]

Berwick said of the British National Health Service (NHS) rationing system:

> Cynics beware, I am romantic about the National Health Service; I love it. All I need to do to rediscover the romance is to look at health care in my own country. The NHS is one of the astounding human endeavors of modern times. Because you use a nation as the scale and taxation as the funding, the NHS is highly political.[36]

Not only does he love rationing, but he rhapsodizes about politicizing health care decisions. Now, thanks to Obama, he is in a position to impose his views on Medicare.

One of his first actions was to openly disregard the results of the contentious public debate over Medicare coverage for end-of-life counseling that were a major part of the 2009 summer of discontent that fueled the November 2010 electoral landslide.

As columnist Charles Krauthammer noted:

> Most people don't remember Obamacare's notorious Section 1233, mandating government payments for end-of-life counseling. It aroused so much anxiety as a possible first slippery step on the road to state-mandated late-life rationing that the Senate never included it in the final health-care law.
>
> Well, it's back—by administrative fiat. A month ago, Medicare issued a regulation providing for end-of-life counseling during annual "wellness" visits. It was all nicely buried amid the simultaneous release of hundreds of new Medicare rules.[37]

How could the president successfully install such an extreme advocate of rationing and government control of health care? By cheating the process. The Senate didn't hold a single hearing. Berwick wasn't filibustered, because Republicans didn't even have a chance—he was never put on the calendar.

This extremist—determined and, indeed, romantic about rationing health care while offering "end-of-life counseling"—was never even presented to the Senate or the American people. The ObamaCare law, already full of provisions seniors opposed, was, by the unilateral action of President Obama, handed over to a man clearly intent on pushing, and perhaps breaking, the limits in an effort to ration and restrict the availability of care.

> ▶ ▶ ▶
>
> *How could the president successfully install such an extreme advocate of rationing and government control of health care? By cheating the process.*

Berwick faced a perfunctory half hour of questions in the Senate Finance Committee on November 17, 2010, a full 213 days after he was nominated and 134 days after he was recess-appointed, but his first real congressional testimony was on February 20, 2011. In it, he touted ObamaCare as the solution to every health care problem. It was a stunning lack of intellectual honesty from the man who purports to be an expert in knowing what works and does not work in health care.

## THE RATIONING BEGINS

Shortly after Berwick was appointed, two cancer drugs were reviewed for exclusion from Medicare reimbursement: the prostate cancer vaccine Provenge and the breast cancer treatment Avastin. Both are expensive biotech drugs, and it was widely perceived that while cost was not supposed to be a factor, it was the overriding consideration. After a storm of criticism, Provenge survived, for now. Avastin did not.

Avastin has been shown to extend life for some late-stage breast cancer patients. For some patients, the treatment has been remarkably successful, as Sally Pipes noted:

> Avastin is a miracle drug. In the manufacturer's critical phase III study, tumors shrank in nearly 50% of patients receiving the medicine. Patients who received Avastin in conjunction with chemotherapy lived nearly twice as long as would otherwise be expected without their disease worsening.
>
> For some patients—known as "super-responders"—an Avastin regime translates into years of additional life.[38]

But in the Obama-Berwick era, Avastin's price tag of about $8,000 per month is a problem. Officially, the FDA is not permitted to consider cost, and claimed not to throughout its review process. However, Eric P. Winer, director of the Breast Oncology Center at the Dana-Farber Cancer Institute in Boston, was more honest, saying: "It's hard to talk about Avastin without talking about costs. For better or worse, Avastin has become in many ways the poster child of high-priced anti-cancer drugs."[39]

These advanced biotech drugs cost more than a billion dollars each to develop, but they hold the potential to be true miracle cures that will drive the next big jump in life expectancy. As Jim Pinkerton of Serious Medicine Strategy observed throughout the ObamaCare debate, we should be focused on getting the incentives right to develop cures and improve people's lives, not on the green-eyeshade questions of cost and insurance.[40] Unfortunately, cost-based rationing in the biotech realm has the potential to undercut research and development. We'll never know about the cures that will never exist as a result.

U.S. Sen. David Vitter (R-La.) underscored the stakes in a letter to the FDA, saying: "I fear this is the beginning of a slippery slope leading to more and more rationing under the government takeover of health care that is being forced on the American people."[41]

On December 16, 2010, the FDA made it official: it revoked the approval of Avastin for breast cancer treatment.[42] The drug's manufacturer, Genentech, appealed, and Medicare claimed the drug would remain covered pending the outcome of the appeal, but just three weeks later *The New York Times* reported that patients in South Carolina, Ohio, West Virginia, California, Nevada, and Hawaii lost Medicare coverage for Avastin.[43]

> ▶ ▶ ▶
>
> *"I fear this is the beginning of a slippery slope leading to more and more rationing under the government takeover of health care that is being forced on the American people."*
>
> —U.S. Sen. DAVID VITTER (R-La.)

The era of health care rationing had begun.

## OBAMACARE LAWSUITS AND THE REGULATORY POWER

The legal challenges to ObamaCare go to the heart of how expansive federal regulatory power is under the Constitution's interstate commerce clause. Randy Barnett, the Georgetown law professor who first made the constitutional case against ObamaCare, put it this way:

> The individual mandate extends the commerce clause's power beyond economic activity, to economic inactivity. That is unprecedented. While

Congress has used its taxing power to fund Social Security and Medicare, never before has it used its commerce power to mandate that an individual person engage in an economic transaction with a private company. Regulating the auto industry or paying "cash for clunkers" is one thing; making everyone buy a Chevy is quite another. Even during World War II, the federal government did not mandate that individual citizens purchase war bonds.[44]

The Congressional Research Service agreed that the individual mandate is the first time the federal government has tried to use its power to regulate commerce to compel the purchase of a product:

One could argue that while regulation of the health insurance industry or the health care system could be considered economic activity, regulating a choice to purchase health insurance is not...In general, Congress has used its authority under the Commerce Clause to regulate individuals, employers, and others who voluntarily take part in some type of economic activity...However, a requirement could be imposed on some individuals who engage in virtually no economic activity whatsoever. This is a novel issue: whether Congress can use its Commerce Clause authority to require a person to buy a good or a service and whether this type of required participation can be considered economic activity.[45]

> ▶ ▶ ▶
>
> *"Regulating the auto industry or paying 'cash for clunkers' is one thing; making everyone buy a Chevy is quite another."*
> —RANDY BARNETT, Georgetown law professor

Similarly, the Congressional Budget Office researched the mandate during the 1994 HillaryCare debate—when it was rejected—and noted: "The imposition of an individual mandate, or a combination of an individual and an employer mandate, would be an unprecedented form of federal action."[46]

South Dakota legislators introduced legislation requiring every citizen to buy a gun. They weren't seriously advocating passage of the bill but were rather demonstrating what would be legally permissible under the rationale offered for ObamaCare.[47] Proponents of ObamaCare might consider how the vast new power could be used to force them to buy things they don't want, need, or believe in.

Federal judges in Virginia and Florida have agreed that ObamaCare exceeds the legitimate regulatory power of the federal government, though they disagree on the crucial question of whether the rest of the law will stand if the individual mandate is struck down. As a practical matter, removing the mandate would undermine the White House's deal with the insurance companies and destroy the economics of that industry. That's because the law's other regulations would allow people to wait until they get sick to buy insurance—at the same rates as everyone else and without the possibility of being denied. So if the Supreme Court strikes down the individual mandate, all of ObamaCare will be imperiled, even if the court opts not to strike down the entire law.

Ultimately, nobody knows how the Supreme Court will decide until the decision is handed down. More than likely, it will depend on how Anthony Kennedy views the extent of the regulatory power under the Commerce Clause. We have already seen him join the court's big-government wing on critical cases like *Massachusetts v. EPA*, which set up all of the EPA mischief discussed in Chapter 2. So while we need to keep hoping for the best, we must focus on pressuring Congress to step in as well.

# FIGHTING BACK:
# BLOCK, STALL, REPEAL, AND REPLACE

Congress must bring all of its regulatory accountability tools to bear on ObamaCare. That means appropriate use of the Congressional Review Act to force politically challenging votes like the one Enzi forced on the grandfathering rule. It means conducting aggressive oversight hearings, hauling Sebelius and Berwick in front of committee after committee to answer questions about how they are exercising their broad discretion and for whose benefit. It means aggressively using the appropriations process to defund the law overall as well as its most objectionable provisions, including regulatory actions that stretch the law, as Berwick will certainly continue to do on his romantic mission to ration health care.

The funding fight will be the critical showdown, because it's where the House of Representatives has the most leverage. If Republicans are determined to deny funding for ObamaCare to move forward, the only recourse President Obama will have to stop them is to shut down the federal government. This was put to the test in April 2011, and the House Republicans backed down, removing language defunding ObamaCare in a compromise deal with the White House. If they are truly committed to stopping ObamaCare, they must hold their ground next time.

If there are not enough members of the House with the fortitude to outright deny funding—or if the political messaging battle is going Obama's way—there will be opportunities to, in a targeted way, repeal or deny funding for some of the most offensive provisions, like the grandfather rule that breaks the promise to let people keep their plans if they like them.

We have already seen Congress repeal one of the most outrageous elements of the law—the 1099 reporting requirement that would have imposed a ridiculous compliance burden on businesses to file a 1099 with their taxes for every vendor from whom they bought $600 or more of goods and services. Repeal was a top priority for the new Republican House, which passed its repeal bill, H.R. 4, by an overwhelming 314 to 112 margin.[48] After several failed Democratic attempts to attach tax hikes to the bill, it passed the Senate cleanly on a bipartisan 87 to 12 vote on April 5, 2011, and was signed into law by Obama on April 14.[49] While some on the right criticized that vote for improving a bad law, the provision actually had nothing to do with ObamaCare—it was just hitching a ride on the bill—but would have imposed enormous regulatory compliance costs on businesses. Therefore, 1099 repeal was a significant victory.

In one very important respect, congressional opponents of ObamaCare must be cautious not to undermine the legal challenges by helping Democrats "fix" the individual mandate. There is a real risk that if Republicans offer an amendment at some point to repeal the individual mandate, Democrats will counter with an amendment that allows people to opt out of the mandate but locks them out of health insurance markets completely if they do. Very few people would ever exercise that kind of opt-out, but it would correct the constitutional impropriety and disarm the legal challenges to the law. We must make sure free-market activists and the American people broadly understand that such an opt-out regime would be a ploy.

As I noted earlier, the only true solution to the ObamaCare nightmare is full repeal. It will be a long and challenging three-year fight—which has already begun—with a sustained effort to shine a light on how outrageous the law really is and how it continues to get worse in the implementation.

What's already been happening needs to be continued and followed by a genuine effort through 2012 and into the elections to describe what positive, patient-centered alternatives would look like:

- Medical liability reform to end the tort tax that drives up the cost of health care while enriching trial lawyers.
- Interstate competition to end the situation in which state legislators and insurance regulators are constantly

being lobbied by disease groups to add coverage mandates that drive up costs.[50]

- Expanded health savings accounts to let patients control their own health care dollars.

- Replacing the tax exclusion for employer-provided health insurance with an individual tax credit to put people who buy their own insurance on a level playing field with people who get insurance from their employers.

These types of big-picture changes would create a genuine free market for health care in which patients are empowered to control their own health care dollars and, with their doctors, their own health care choices.

To develop these basic ideas into a genuine reform bill, we need to have an honest, open, transparent process—the kind of process Obama promised but failed to deliver. Health care is too personal and too important to be left to Washington special interests—whether on the left or the right. We simply cannot have any confidence in health care policy unless we have confidence in the process that produces it.

Barring a total victory at the Supreme Court, the destiny of ObamaCare depends on the ability to drive a genuine health care reform effort through the 2012 election, and then sustain enough pressure to force full repeal in 2013, along with the adoption of genuine reforms that fix the real problems that already existed, but that ObamaCare made even worse.

In the meantime, one of the best ways to fight this disastrous law is to highlight the outrageous regulatory abuses that flow from it. Exposing those abuses will educate the American public, keep beating the drum for ultimate repeal and real reform, and advance the demand for an honest, above-board process. Congress needs to choose its battles wisely and force high-visibility votes on these regulatory issues, both to highlight the good that can be done in stopping some of the regulations and to move the ball forward with an eye toward 2013.

The efforts at the state level must also move forward. Arizona and Oklahoma have adopted state constitutional amendments to protect health care freedom. Georgia, Idaho, Louisiana, Missouri, Utah, and Virginia have adopted statutory versions. The Health Care Freedom Act concept was the brainchild of Dr. Eric Novack, a leading health care reform activist and orthopedic surgeon from Phoenix. The amendment protects two basic rights: the right to spend your own money to receive lawful health care services and the right to choose not to participate in any health care system without penalty or fine.

States are also taking the lead on what will replace ObamaCare by having more frank conversations than ever as to what role the federal government should be playing in regulation and decision-making for states where local control and understanding is more likely to yield better and more efficient results. Ultimately, strong voices for a decentralized, patient-centered approach from the states will make a big difference in whether Congress adopts real reform, just as the governors successfully led on welfare reform in the 1990s.

The bottom line is that ObamaCare is a bad law that is getting worse daily and clear proof both that we need much greater regulatory accountability and that we must eventually repeal the law and replace it with genuine patient-centered reform.

## CHAPTER 6

# The New Golden Rules: Regulations for Every Aspect of Your Financial Life

*"No one will know until this is actually in place how it works. But we believe we've done something that has been needed for a long time. It took a crisis to bring us to the point where we could actually get this job done."*[1]

—U.S. Sen. CHRIS DODD, chief Senate sponsor of the
Dodd-Frank financial regulation bill

*"It's a very creative way to put Elizabeth where she ought to be—running the agency."*

—U.S. Rep. BARNEY FRANK, chief House sponsor, on
Obama's decision to skip the Senate and install Elizabeth
Warren as a financial czar

The Dodd-Frank financial regulation bill is what happens when you let the most corrupt Washington special interests exploit a crisis to create vast new government powers. We are already seeing the end of free checking accounts, new fees on debit cards, and other assorted fees and lost services that have a real impact on consumers. The bailout process has now been institutionalized and guaranteed. And the big Wall Street firms are now more tightly integrated with Washington politics than ever before. Every left-wing special interest—from the trial lawyers, to the racial grievance groups, to the unions—got a special payoff in the bill. And like ObamaCare, Dodd-Frank was a massive piece of legislation that spawned a vast new regulatory apparatus with sweeping, unprecedented powers.

Even *The New York Times* acknowledged that the bill essentially punted all the real power and decision-making to regulators:

> The bill … is basically a 2,000-page missive to federal agencies, instructing regulators to address subjects ranging from derivatives trading to document retention. But it is notably short on specifics, giving regulators significant power to determine its impact—and giving partisans on both sides a second chance to influence the outcome.[2]

The most powerful of those regulators is a newly created Consumer Financial Protection Bureau (CFPB), which was initially opposed by Republicans on the grounds that a powerful new regulator with the power to interfere with every consumer financial transaction was unnecessary. In remarkable Washington fashion, however, an eventual "compromise" was reached in which the CFPB was housed in the Federal Reserve—and funded out of Fed operations, not congressional appropriations. The result is a brand-new agency with vast powers that is less subject to effective congressional oversight than any existing regulatory agency.

On top of that, President Obama appointed an extreme radical to the position of heading the new agency: Elizabeth Warren. When it became clear he could not appoint her the honest way because her radical views would be a problem for Senate confirmation, he bypassed the Senate by hiring her as his financial czar—a White House staffer charged with establishing the new agency. So we now have a new agency with frighteningly broad powers to interfere with our financial lives being assembled by a czar so radical the president chose not to even submit her name to the Senate.

For a law touted as a response to the financial crisis, what Dodd-Frank *didn't* do is also significant, because it failed to address any of the root causes of the financial crisis (the drafters of the bill did not even wait for the report of the commission they had created to determine what went wrong, the so-called Financial Crisis Inquiry Commission).

It did nothing to address Fannie Mae and Freddie Mac, the mortgage giants at ground zero of the housing bubble that spawned the economy's downward spiral via the financial markets.

It did not end "too big to fail," but instead institutionalized it by guaranteeing that banks and any other institutions judged by the Federal Reserve to pose a "systemic risk" would be subject to strict regulation and potential bailouts through a so-called "orderly liquidation fund." (If Congress had been serious about ending bailouts, it would have removed the emergency authority the Federal Reserve used under Section 13.3 of the Federal Reserve Act to conduct the vast majority of the bailout activities, which happened without the consent of Congress.)

> ▶ ▶ ▶
>
> *If Congress had been serious about ending bailouts, it would have removed the emergency authority the Federal Reserve used under Section 13.3 of the Federal Reserve Act to conduct the vast majority of the bailout activities, which happened without the consent of Congress.*

The funding for the "orderly liquidation fund" can be replenished by the Federal Deposit Insurance Corporation's (FDIC) new ability to levy fees—without congressional approval—on other banks to bail out the creditors of failing institutions.

The men to thank for this bailout-assuring regulatory assault on our financial lives are now-former U.S. Sen. Chris Dodd and U.S. Rep. Barney Frank.

## CHRIS DODD IS NO REFORMER

Chris Dodd, by any reasonable estimation, was a big part of the problem that created the housing bubble and the subsequent financial crisis. He was an inveterate opponent of reforming Fannie and Freddie. He was a cheerleader for subprime lending. He was even the recipient of a corrupt sweetheart deal from notorious subprime lender Countrywide Financial.

In 2004, Countrywide Financial refinanced two loans of Dodd's on homes he owned in Washington and Connecticut, at substantially below-market interest rates. He saved about $75,000.

Rick Green of *The Hartford Courant* summed it up:

> Because when you are U.S. Sen. Christopher Dodd, VIP, and you want a mortgage from Countrywide Financial, it appears to mean all kinds of fees are waived and the deal is sweeter than for anyone else who walks in the door.
>
> That is the difference between us poor suckers with millstone mortgages hanging around our necks and VIP Dodd.
>
> The chairman of the committee that oversees the banking industry offers a hilariously implausible explanation to those who dare ask what he was thinking, accepting loans starting in 2003 from Countrywide Financial after they told him he was in their "VIP" program.[3]

While Dodd denied knowing he received a special deal, Robert Feinberg, who was in charge of Countrywide's "VIP Program," told House and Senate ethics investigators that Dodd knew exactly why he was getting such a good deal—because he was a VIP friend of Countrywide CEO Angelo Mozilo.[4] Despite this revelation, Dodd continued to lie and claim he had no knowledge of special treatment.

Nonetheless, Dodd knew he could not face the voters of Connecticut again and decided to retire to avoid an embarrassing defeat. On January 6, 2010, Dodd announced he would not run for reelection. Democrats were relieved. This analysis from *Talking Points Memo* was typical of the reaction: "While usually a retirement by an incumbent is bad news for a party, in this case Dodd's retirement almost certainly improves Democratic chances for holding the seat with a stronger candidate."[5]

Indeed, the Democratic candidate, Richard Blumenthal, did go on to win the seat. Interestingly, Blumenthal, then the state attorney general, refused to investigate Dodd's Countrywide scandal, saying, "there's no evidence of wrongdoing on [Mr. Dodd's] part any more than victims who were misled or deceived by Countrywide."[6] Blumenthal reached this uninvestigated conclusion in the face of overwhelming evidence so clear that Dodd's political career was over. Of course, Blumenthal, who repeatedly lied about serving in Vietnam, has his own ethics challenges.

While still in the Senate, though, Dodd used his perch as the chairman of the Senate Banking Committee to repeatedly thwart efforts to reform the government-sponsored enterprises of Fannie Mae and Freddie Mac before they precipitated disaster. Naturally, in the Obama era, Dodd's ethical lapses and oversight failures prepared him to play the lead role in a sweeping regulatory attack on every aspect of our financial lives.

# BARNEY FRANK IS NO REFORMER

The other half of Dodd-Frank is Barney Frank, the irascible arch-liberal congressman from Massachusetts who openly supported a public option in ObamaCare as a step toward a Canadian-style, government-run system.[7]

Like Dodd, Frank was one of the leading opponents in Congress of taking any action to reduce the enormous risk to taxpayers from Fannie Mae and Freddie Mac. Frank's longtime lover Herb Moses was a top Fannie Mae executive from 1992 to 1998, while Frank was on the House Financial Services Committee pushing a series of measures that benefited Fannie Mae, while exposing taxpayers to what ultimately proved to be catastrophic risks.[8]

Dan Gainor of the Media Research Center pointed out the double standard that allowed the mainstream media to disregard this scandal:

> It's absolutely a conflict. He was voting on Fannie Mae at a time when he was involved with a Fannie Mae executive. How is that not germane? If this had been his ex-wife and he was Republican, I would bet every penny I have—or at least what's not in the stock market—that this would be considered germane. But everybody wants to avoid it because he's gay. It's the quintessential double standard.[9]

Judicial Watch named Frank to its list of "Ten Most Wanted Corrupt Politicians" in both 2009 and 2010 for his involvement in scandals involving the questionable steering of TARP bailout funds and his part in concealing the serious problems at Fannie Mae and Freddie Mac.[10]

Judicial Watch notes:

Congressman Barney Frank (D-MA) improperly intervened for Maxine Waters (D-CA) on behalf of his home-state OneUnited Bank to obtain Troubled Asset Relief Program (TARP) funds. When asked about the scandal, the Massachusetts Democrat admitted he spoke to a "federal regulator" but, according to the *Wall Street Journal* he didn't remember which federal regulator he spoke with. According to explosive Treasury Department emails uncovered by Judicial Watch in 2010, however, it appears this nameless bureaucrat was none other than then-Treasury Secretary Henry "Hank" Paulson![11]

Frank directly pressured the secretary of the Treasury for bailout funds for a bank in his district, and then claimed he couldn't remember with whom he spoke. Yet, he not only escaped an ethics investigation but managed to style himself a reformer.

Frank admitted that he missed repeated warning signs about Fannie Mae and Freddie Mac, telling *The Boston Globe* he was wearing "ideological blinders."[12] That's an interesting way to describe his decades of fierce opposition to the reforms that could have prevented or limited the impact of the housing bubble and collapse. Even worse, as the *Globe* revealed, Frank continued to mislead the public about Fannie and Freddie even when they were on the brink of collapse:

> In July 2008, then-Treasury Secretary Henry Paulson called Frank and told him the government would need to spend "billions of taxpayer dollars to backstop the institutions from catastrophic failure," according to Paulson's recent book. Frank, despite that conversation, appeared on national television two days later and said the companies were "fundamentally sound, not in danger of going under."[13]

Like Dodd, Frank was the opposite of a reformer. He was at the heart of all the corruption and scandals that allowed the housing bubble to inflate, violently collapse, and take down the financial system.

Once again, we turn to the wisdom of Judge Lloyd Rogers, who told me:

> We don't need any new agencies, and anything that comes from Chris Dodd and Barney Frank I don't want. These guys have showed me what kind of stuff they can come up with. I don't want anything they have their names tattooed on.[14]

They were a big part of the problem, and they should have been subject to ethics investigations—not empowered to write a massive so-called reform bill that would reward all the usual left-wing suspects. But that, unfortunately, is exactly what happened.

## THE LEFT-WING ACTIVIST COALITION

The biggest lobbying push for Dodd-Frank came, like ObamaCare, from an umbrella organization led primarily by the unions, self-styled consumer groups, racial grievance groups, and, of course, the Association of Community Organizations for Reform Now (ACORN). It called itself Americans for Financial Reform (AFR). Unlike Health Care for America Now, AFR went through the trouble of scrubbing ACORN from its official coalition list, although it remains listed on a February 1, 2010,

▶ ▶ ▶

*Like Dodd, Frank was the opposite of a reformer. He was at the heart of all the corruption and scandals that allowed the housing bubble to inflate, violently collapse, and take down the financial system.*

letter to Dodd urging the bill to include a new Consumer Financial Protection Agency.[15]

One of the members of AFR, its leader from a policy-development perspective, was a little-known group from Durham, North Carolina, called the Center for Responsible Lending (CRL). It was founded by Martin Eakes, who *Politico* called "the main intellectual engine driving Democratic responses to the housing crisis."[16]

Eakes played a major role in the creation of the subprime bubble and its disorderly collapse. He described his so-called Self-Help Credit Union as "one of the earliest subprime lenders in the nation."[17]

Eakes didn't just start subprime; he expanded it nationally. In 1994, his Self-Help Credit Union established the Home Loan Secondary Market Program, which profited by buying risky loans from banks and then reselling them to Fannie Mae. As Peter Roff noted, "This gave the original lenders a way to sell and offload the risk for non-conforming loans and other products they could not sell to Fannie directly. And then it was off to the races."[18]

The major financial backers of CRL were among the biggest financial beneficiaries of the financial crisis.

Hedge fund billionaire John Paulson, along with other notorious subprime kingpins Herb and Marion Sandler, funded the CRL to the tune of $15 million to shake down and harass banks into making bad loans to unqualified borrowers. CRL then turned around and lobbied for legislation to undermine the burgeoning subprime market it had helped create. CRL's efforts to push "cram-down" legislation that would have allowed judges to rewrite mortgage contracts—such as the Foreclosure Prevention Act of 2008 and the Emergency Home Ownership and Mortgage Equity Protection Act of 2007—never made it into law, but the uncertainty it created helped pop the subprime bubble.

Meanwhile, Paulson paid Goldman Sachs another $15 million to design collateralized-debt obligations composed of specific subprime mortgages that he selected. This bucket of investments may have included loans that he knew were unsound and were made only because banks were strong-armed by the CRL. It also may have included loans that he knew would be undermined by the CRL's extensive lobbying activities.[19]

Yet somehow CRL and Eakes had positioned themselves as the leading proponents of "reform," and not only in the left-wing advocacy community. They also had an inside man in the administration.

Treasury official Eric Stein, who helped design the Dodd bill, had been the longtime chief operating officer of the CRL. He was also reportedly one of the loudest voices inside the administration pressing for the inclusion of a vast new federal agency to regulate consumer financial transactions, what would become the Consumer Financial Protection Bureau. The CFPB and other new regulatory agencies in the bill would allow ever-greater interference and distortion in the housing markets and broader financial markets to advance the left-wing social policy goals of groups like CRL and their partners in Americans for Financial Reform, including the unions and ACORN.

▶ ▶ ▶

*This bucket of investments may have included loans that [Paulson] knew were unsound and were made only because banks were strong-armed by the CRL.*

## OBAMA'S RELATIONSHIP WITH WALL STREET

According to Obama, the banks were fighting against reform. But it wasn't really that simple. In fact, the biggest banks were much more interested in working with the administration and shaping the bill to their liking than with stopping it—and why not? Obama had consistently bailed them out with taxpayer dollars, and the biggest banks would be in the best position to cope with an onslaught of expensive, tedious new regulations. As usual, the little guys would be the losers.

In fact the Center for Responsive Politics reports Wall Street tilted more Democratic in 2008—the year of Obama—than it had it any year since 1990, giving 57 percent of its contributions to Democrats.[20] In 2008, scandal-plagued Goldman Sachs gave 75 percent of its contributions to Democrats, including nearly a million dollars to candidate Obama and $112,400 to Dodd, the Senate Banking Committee chairman.

Big-bank stocks reacted favorably to Obama's April 22, 2010, speech at Cooper Union in New York City calling for financial reform. That's because the basic framework of the bill institutionalized "too big to fail." It assured the banks access to Federal Reserve loans as needed. It made bailouts permanent.

> ► ► ►
>
> *In 2008, scandal-plagued Goldman Sachs gave 75 percent of its contributions to Democrats, including nearly a million dollars to candidate Barack Obama and $112,400 to Dodd, the Senate Banking Committee chairman.*

In a report on the repeated bailouts of Citigroup, the special inspector general for TARP reported that Secretary Timothy Geithner admitted: "In the future we may have to do exceptional things again if the shock to the financial system is sufficiently large."[21] This admission that "too big to fail" is still part of the government's strategy shows that Dodd-Frank did not end bailouts but rather normalized them as a likelihood in future financial crises.

While granting regulators the power to step in and claim province over firms they deem to be failing, it also gave regulators the power to seize firms they judge to pose a systemic risk, creating not just a bailout authority but a mechanism for government takeovers as well.[22]

The Dodd-Frank legislation was not so much an attack on the big banks as it was a symbiotic strategy—in coordination with Wall Street's biggest players—to assure them a protected status at taxpayer expense, in exchange for a vast new regulatory apparatus that will grow the power of Washington to interfere in the lives of regular Americans. In the end, however, the banks that went along for the ride will regret it, because they are being reduced to little more than regulated financial utilities with federal regulatory tentacles reaching into every aspect of their operations.

> ▶ ▶ ▶
>
> *This admission that "too big to fail" is still part of the government's strategy shows that Dodd-Frank did not end bailouts but rather normalized them as a likelihood in future financial crises.*

## SCOTT BROWN GOT DUPED

On the Dodd-Frank bill, Democrats didn't have to contrive to circumvent U.S. Sen. Scott Brown's election. Instead they deceived him into voting for the bill.

On July 12, 2010, Brown announced he would support what ended up being the final version of the bill. He said: "I appreciate the efforts to improve the bill, especially the removal of the $19 billion bank tax. As a result, it is a better bill than it was when this whole process started. While it isn't perfect, I expect to support the bill when it comes up for a vote."[23]

It was an unusual statement because the addition and subsequent removal of that particular bank tax was dwarfed by an *unlimited* tax on banks already built into the bill. It was right there, starting on page 356, where the FDIC is empowered to levy "risk-based assessments" on banks and nonbank financial institutions, which could potentially include nearly any large company in the country, to cover the costs of bailout operations.[24]

U.S. Sen. Kent Conrad made it clear in the floor debate that a bank tax was still very much in the final bill that Brown agreed to support. The issue being debated was that the removal of the $19 billion tax created a budget point of order because the overall bill now added to the deficit. Conrad, who styles himself a "deficit hawk," was explaining that the bank tax that was removed was unnecessary because of the bill's unlimited hidden tax. He said:

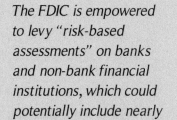

*The FDIC is empowered to levy "risk-based assessments" on banks and non-bank financial institutions, which could potentially include nearly any large company in the country, to cover the costs of bailout operations.*

The government will temporarily borrow funds from the Treasury. The financial industry will then reimburse the government and the taxpayers for 100 percent of the cost. Again, 100 percent of the money will be paid back by the banks. So the net impact on the deficit is zero.[25]

Translated from Senate-speak, "reimburse" means "tax." The bank tax was still in the bill. Brown got duped.

(Incidentally, Conrad, like Dodd, was also a beneficiary of Countrywide's "VIP Program." After the 2010 election, he chose to retire rather than face voters in 2012.)

# A DIZZYINGLY COMPLEX NEW REGULATORY MAZE

Echoing both Nancy Pelosi's infamous "pass the bill so you can find out what is in it" quote about ObamaCare and Rahm Emanuel's "you never want a serious crisis to go to waste," Dodd admitted:

> No one will know until this is actually in place how it works. But we believe we've done something that has been needed for a long time. It took a crisis to bring us to the point where we could actually get this job done.[26]

*The Wall Street Journal* summarized the scope of the regulatory onslaught:

> Dodd-Frank, with its 2,300 pages, will unleash the biggest wave of new federal financial rule-making in three generations... The law firm of Davis Polk & Wardwell needed more than 150 pages merely to summarize the bureaucratic ecosystem created by Dodd-Frank... The law will require no fewer than 243 new formal rule-makings by 11 different federal agencies.
>
> The SEC alone, whose regulatory failures did so much to contribute to the panic, will write 95 new rules. The new Bureau of Consumer Financial Protection will write 24, and the new Financial Stability Oversight Council will issue 56. These won't be one-page orders. The new rules will run into the hundreds if not thousands of pages in the Federal Register, laying out in detail what your neighborhood banker, hedge fund manager or derivatives trader can and cannot do.[27]

There is no aspect of finance in America that won't be touched by the regulatory emanations of Dodd-Frank. In fact, the estimate of 243 rulemakings may be an understatement. An analysis by the U.S. Chamber of Commerce found:

- The 2,300-page financial regulatory reform law will require thousands of pages of implementing regulations.
- A Chamber review of the law discovered that it calls for nearly 500 regulatory rulemakings, 60 studies, and 93 reports. By contrast, the Sarbanes-Oxley corporate governance legislation passed in 2002 required only 16 rulemakings and 6 studies.
- There are $20 billion of costs associated with the financial reform bill.[28]

The comparison with Sarbanes-Oxley is particularly notable because that law was also created as a crisis response. In the hothouse atmosphere after the fraud committed by Enron and WorldCom, Sarbanes-Oxley was rushed into effect as a poorly thought-out "do something," and has had an enormous negative impact on U.S. capital markets.

In 2001, the year before Sarbanes-Oxley took effect, nine out of the 10 companies that conducted initial public offerings (IPOs) in excess of $1 billion did so by listing on U.S. exchanges. By 2005, only one of the 24 largest IPOs in the world was listed on a U.S. exchange.[29] In 2000,

▶ ▶ ▶

*"A Chamber review of the law discovered that it calls for nearly 500 regulatory rulemakings, 60 studies, and 93 reports. By contrast, the Sarbanes-Oxley corporate governance legislation passed in 2002 required only 16 rulemakings and 6 studies."*

—U.S. Chamber of Commerce

50 percent of all the funds raised in IPOs were raised in the United States. By 2005, that number declined to only 5 percent.[30]

The great Nobel Prize–winning economist Milton Friedman, in one of his last interviews, identified Sarbanes-Oxley as the biggest problem facing the U.S. economy at that time, saying: "Sarbanes-Oxley is terrible. It ought to be eliminated. It's costing the country a great deal. Sarbanes-Oxley says to every entrepreneur, 'For God's sake, don't innovate. Don't take chances because down will come the hatchet. We're going to knock your head off.'"[31]

The one new agency created by Sarbanes-Oxley—the Public Company Accounting Oversight Board—has been a disaster and has already been found to be unconstitutionally constituted by the U.S. Supreme Court. That is just one agency. With Dodd-Frank, which is orders of magnitude more complex, cumbersome, and expensive than Sarbanes-Oxley, there will be hundreds of new rulemakings coming from dozens of bureaucracies, many of them newly created.

Given the extremism of the Obama administration's abuse of regulatory power in existing bureaucracies, we can safely assume that his new army of financial regulators will stretch and even break the limits of their legal authority in the pursuit of their big-government objectives. The onslaught will go on for years—perhaps indefinitely. The era of publicly traded companies and one of the most efficient capital markets in the world may be ending in America.

# ELIZABETH WARREN, FINANCIAL CZAR

On the day he signed Dodd-Frank into law, Obama said: "This is the central lesson not only of this crisis but of our history. Ultimately, there's no dividing line between Main Street and Wall Street."[32] He meant it. And he intends to regulate both.

Main Street America will pay big-time, and not only because we taxpayers will be on the hook for future bailouts. The vast agency created by the bill, the so-called Consumer Financial Protection

Bureau (CFPB), will have sweeping powers to disrupt and interfere with commerce down to even small businesses. The CFPB can regulate every consumer financial transaction and exists largely outside of congressional oversight, because it's funded directly by the Federal Reserve.

A Harvard professor, Elizabeth Warren led the TARP oversight panel away from its intended purpose of exercising oversight toward radical policy changes, including nationalization of the banks. As Thomas Cooley explained:

> Elizabeth Warren is the Gottlieb professor of law at Harvard University and chair of the Congressional Oversight Panel (COP) charged by Congress with evaluating how effectively the TARP money is being used... The COP, however, apparently decided that its mission was too narrowly defined. It didn't need to do more evaluation of what the Treasury was doing with the TARP funds. Instead, it should hold forth on how financial crises at large should be addressed...
>
> The report essentially argues for nationalization... Clearly, this is Elizabeth Warren's particular crusade against the banks, since a majority of panel members dissented from the direction the report took and two refused to sign off on it at all.[33]

So we had an ideologically motivated, left-wing crusader who had already hijacked one entity away from its intended purpose to advance her political agenda. Naturally, she was the dream pick of the left to head the new CFPB, with its vast, vaguely defined powers to regulate every consumer transaction in the economy—and almost no congressional oversight.

MoveOn.org kicked into gear, launching a national petition saying: "We need Elizabeth Warren at the CFPB!"[34]

*Huffington Post* columnist Jerome Karabel even argued that Warren was Obama's political salvation, saying, improbably:

> This is a toxic political environment for the Obama administration…But there is something that President Obama can do that would simultaneously help mend his strained relations with progressives and counter the popular perception that he is too cozy with Wall Street. He could immediately appoint Elizabeth Warren.[35]

While the hard left was enamored with Warren, her extremism gave her little chance of being confirmed by the Senate. Dodd himself said she was too radical. No Republicans offered support for her nomination. In fact, Obama never even nominated her.

Instead, Obama skipped the Senate by appointing her not to head the new agency, but as a special White House staffer—a czar—charged with creating the new agency. A distinction without a difference, except that it allowed Obama to sidestep the constitutional requirement of Senate confirmation. To be clear, she is unconstitutionally running the new agency, as Barney Frank, who hailed the Obama appointment, agreed when he said: "It's a very creative way to put Elizabeth where she ought to be—running the agency."[36]

Dodd himself criticized the move for making the new agency politically vulnerable, while U.S. Sen. Bob Corker (R-Tenn.) noted: "This is, in fact, the czar of all czars."[37]

U.S. Sen. Susan Collins, a Republican who voted for Dodd-Frank, said: "This is clearly a disingenuous effort to circumvent the Senate confirmation process. The last thing we need is another 'czar' that is unaccountable to Congress and the American people."[38]

To lead her communications effort, Warren turned to an experienced hand at spinning outrageous big-government regulatory power grabs: Jen Howard. Howard, a disciple of socialist Robert McChesney who served as McChesney's communications director at Free Press, came to the CFPB from the Federal Communications Commission (FCC) just days after its infamous three-to-two party-line vote to regulate the Internet. In her e-mail to reporters announcing the move to the CFPB, Howard wrote: "I am so proud of everything the agency has accomplished and I couldn't be more grateful to Chairman Genachowski for the opportunity to be a part of his team at such an exciting time."[39]

Having helped set the FCC on a path toward a regulatory stranglehold on a huge sector of the U.S. economy, Howard is moving on to be the PR flack for an even broader attack on our free-market economy at the CFPB.

Just how powerful could the new CFPB be? According to the Congressional Research Service's analysis, the scope is nearly unlimited:

> Section 1022 alone gives the CFPB broad rulemaking powers, authorizing it to prescribe such rules "as may be necessary or appropriate" to enable the Bureau to administer federal consumer financial protection laws. The act contains many other provisions that require or permit the Bureau to issue rules, most of which give the Bureau substantial discretion regarding whether rules need to be issued, the contents of those rules, and when they must be issued. The Bureau also assumes responsibility for certain transferor agencies' existing rules, proposed rules that have not been made final, and final rules that have not taken effect. Therefore, other than for about 20 rules that are specifically required in the statute, it is not currently possible to determine how many rules the Bureau will issue, or the contents of those rules.[40]

All that power is now being wielded by an unconfirmed, un-accountable czar overseeing and running a new agency with vast regulatory power that is not even subject to congressional oversight through appropriations, because it is funded by the Federal Reserve. The U.S. Constitution may not be perfect, but it's better than this.

## FINANCIAL REGULATION HITS YOUR WALLET

While Warren is busily setting up her new regulatory empire, the Federal Reserve is already moving forward with one of the biggest and most obvious regulatory changes to hit consumers. New regulations on debit cards are coming pursuant to an amendment that was slipped into the bill with little debate or understanding by U.S. Sen. Dick Durbin (D-Ill.) at the behest of big-box retailers. The amendment shredded the contracts between merchants and the payment card companies that required merchants to give customers the familiar choice of "credit or debit" when we use our bank cards.

Many of us, even though we are using bank debit cards, choose the "credit" option, which is actually a debit transaction that runs over the same Visa or MasterCard network that processes credit card transactions. There are lots of valid reasons for choosing "credit," from fraud detection, to bonus points, to network security, but many big merchants want to take the "credit or debit" choice away from customers.

The checkout process generally goes so smoothly that we don't even think about it, but these new regulations could create upheaval that undermines both the economics of the payment card industry and the practical experience of completing a retail purchase.

The provision that would take away the choice of credit or debit is labeled "transaction routing" and shreds the legitimate private contracts that Visa and MasterCard have with merchants that assure customers the ability to choose how their transactions are processed.

In Federal Reserve language:

The Board proposes to prohibit issuers and payment card networks from restricting the ability of a merchant to direct the routing of electronic debit transactions over any of the networks that an issuer has enabled to process the electronic debit transactions.[41]

That means merchants will be allowed to take the "credit or debit" choice away from customers, even though the contracts they agreed to with card networks guaranteed consumers that choice. They can force your transaction onto a network that may not offer fraud protection services or any of the other extras that come with using a brand-name network like Visa or MasterCard.

In effect, the federal government is tearing up legitimate contracts that have served consumers very well in order to allow merchants to choose. It is bad news for consumers who rely on the value-added features of their cards that are only available when transactions are routed over credit networks, including fraud protection, a better audit-trail including a signature, and other features like integrated lines of credit and transaction-timing flexibility offered by some banks and credit unions.

> ▶ ▶ ▶
>
> *Government cannot make things less expensive by imposing price controls without serious consequences.*

The new regulations also impose explicit price controls on all debit transactions, limiting the fee charged for each transaction to 12 cents, based on the Fed's calculation of what Dodd-Frank calls the "incremental cost incurred" by the bank or credit union that issued your card. It's a huge, approximately 85 percent cut from the existing, market-based transaction fees. But government cannot make things less expensive by imposing price controls without serious consequences.

As John Berlau argued in a piece calling for Dodd-Frank repeal legislation to be called the Free Checking Restoration Act:

> Yet over the past few months, the middle class has seen a beneficial feature of modern banking—free checking—begin to vanish due to these "reforms" and the substantial loss of bank revenues that they've caused.
>
> There are two main culprits in free checking's demise: the Federal Reserve's new rules, in effect since July, that restrict banks from charging overdraft fees when customers overdraw their checking accounts; and the amendment from Sen. Dick Durbin (D., Ill.) in Dodd-Frank that puts price controls on the interchange fees that merchants pay to banks and credit unions to process debit cards.[42]

Fed Chairman Ben Bernanke, who is reluctantly moving to implement the price controls, said: "It's going to affect revenue of small issuers. And it could result in some smaller banks being less profitable or even failing."[43]

Defying that warning, on June 8, 2011, 12 Senate Republicans who should have known better joined 33 Senate Democrats to *block* an amendment that would have delayed the price-control rule long enough to study what its effects would be.[44]

The resulting disappearance of free checking and the imposition of new consumer fees are among the first unintended consequences of the 500 or so new regulations to come.

# THE RACIAL GRIEVANCE GROUPS GET THEIR PAYOFF

Among the many new regulatory agencies and offices under Dodd-Frank is the creation of new Offices of Minority and Women Inclusion. The offices are grafted on to many existing federal agencies and departments, as well as the newly created ones under the bill. These new offices explain the presence of identity politics groups on the long list of members of Americans for Financial Reform. They do not have anything to do with regulating the financial system.

As Horace Cooper of the Heartland Institute explained:

> Based on the faulty premise that somehow having more women and minority bankers will result in banks issuing more loans to women and minorities, the racial quotas provision doesn't in any way address risk or efficacy of loans being issued. Yet risk is the number one issue that any reform should be assessing. And even with the dubious association between workforce representation and lending, it is especially troublesome that Congress may be using an unconstitutional means—race-based preferences—to achieve its objectives.
>
> The so-called affirmative action provision is found in Section 342 of the bill. It creates the Offices of Minority and Women Inclusion in at least 20 federal financial services agencies. These offices will be tasked with implementing "standards and procedures to ensure, to the maximum extent possible, the fair inclusion and utilization of minorities, women, and minority-owned "financial institutions, investment banking firms, mortgage banking firms, asset management firms, brokers, dealers, financial

services entities, underwriters, accountants, investment consultants, and providers of legal services."[45]

These provisions will force financial institutions to make race-
based decisions instead of accurately assessing financial risk. This
will lead to more shakedowns and scandals. And they will not improve either the stability or efficiency of our financial system.

## THE TRIAL LAWYERS GET THEIR PAYOFF

The trial lawyers did not allow a 2,300-page grab bag of left-wing
ideas to pass through Congress without getting a nice piece of the
pie for themselves. What they got were Dodd-Frank's whistle-blower
provisions, which apply not just to financial companies, but to every publicly traded company.

These provisions incentivize employees to file reports of securities
law violations with the Securities and Exchange Commission (SEC)
and Commodity Futures Trading Commission (CFTC) by promising
them bounties of between 10 and 30 percent of settlements.

There is no requirement to first report violations internally
at a company—ironic given the enormous resources companies
were forced to dedicate to internal controls under Sarbanes-Oxley.
Tipsters can remain anonymous, and to do so they are required to
hire an attorney. There are new protections against retaliation, and
there is no meaningful penalty for filing false claims.

It is simply a wet kiss to plaintiff lawyers that undermines
internal-compliance programs and turns workers against their
employers on any perceived opportunity to hit a whistle-blower
jackpot.

According to Susan Hackett, senior vice president of the
Association of Corporate Counsel, which represents the general
counsels of more than 270 companies that filed comments with the
SEC opposing the new rules, this issue has raised more alarms than

any other in the 22 years she has worked there. That it was slipped into Dodd-Frank with little debate or public awareness shows the downside to the Pelosi/Dodd pass-the-bill-first style of legislating.

Hackett said:

> The proposals cut to the very core of what it is that every responsible U.S. company has been trying to do for the last couple of decades, which is to create effective, robust compliance reporting systems. This just pulls the legs off the stool.[46]

In America, the first impulse of an employee who discovers something wrong at his or her own company shouldn't be to run to a lawyer or the SEC.

## THE UNIONS GET THEIR PAYOFF

With the unions providing most of the manpower and funding for the Dodd-Frank push, they, of course, had a lot to gain from its passage. Beyond their obvious interests in a bigger, more powerful unionized federal bureaucracy and the politicization of financial decisions over which they could exert influence, the longtime union priority of proxy access was included in the bill.

Proxy access has been a longtime dream of the political left because it would give the unions, through their pension funds, incredible leverage to accomplish the political objectives they have been unable to accomplish in Congress instead through corporate boardrooms.

Several years ago, when the SEC was considering a proxy-access proposal that was ultimately defeated, I wrote:

> The SEC purportedly is considering a rule that would allow shareholders with as little as a 3 percent

stake in a company to nominate directors to that company, with the requirement that those directors be included on the company's proxy statement. The result would be special interests—primarily labor unions through their pension funds—gaining seats on corporate boards, or using the threat of director nomination to leverage their anti-market agendas.

By way of their pension funds, unions have big stakes in virtually every significant corporation today. A shareholder-access rule would allow them to achieve through the back door what they have been unable to accomplish through honest collective bargaining. Card-check agreements would be just the beginning since the unions will insist not only on leveraging the companies they have stakes in to unionize, but will place the same demands on corporate partners and suppliers. The unions could undermine free trade by requiring companies to shift away from foreign suppliers, or by pushing an anti-market dream list of measures—ranging from Kyoto-like carbon restrictions to interference in foreign policy through the manipulation of defense contractors. Empowering unions and other pressure groups to influence corporate-governance decisions on this basis will substitute coerced political judgment for business judgment.

That's called socialism.[47]

Now a version of proxy access is the law, smuggled in as part of Dodd-Frank. The SEC adopted a proxy access rule the month after the bill passed. This rule is the first time the SEC has ever trumped state law by creating substantive shareholder rights.

As former SEC Commissioner Paul Atkins explained, the rule is calibrated to specifically benefit special interests at the cost of all other shareholders:

> A fundamental principle of state corporation laws is that all shareholders holding the same class of securities have the same rights. The new rule will discriminate among shareholders, since the SEC would increase the clout of special-interest groups at the expense of the vast majority of shareholders...
>
> In a cynical game of picking numbers, the SEC considered 5%, 3%, 2% and 1% of outstanding shares and various holding periods as thresholds before which shareholders can use the new rule. The winner, after much behind-the-scenes maneuvering with favored parties: 3% and three years. The idea was to find the magic number where "good" shareholder groups (like state pension funds) are in, but "bad" groups (politically incorrect shareholders, like hedge funds) are out.
>
> It's no coincidence that only unions and cause-driven, minority shareholders want this coveted access. They would use it to advance their own labor, social and environmental agendas instead of the corporation's goal of maximizing long-term shareholder wealth. The rule will give them pressure points with which to hold companies hostage until their pet issues are addressed. Many corporate managements and boards will acquiesce to avoid a contested director election.[48]

The strategy builds on an idea in the Saul Alinsky playbook. In *Rules for Radicals* he wrote:

> Remember that the objective of the proxies approach is not simply a power instrument with reference to our corporate economy, but a mechanism providing for a blast-off for middle-class organization—beginning with the proxy, it will then begin to ignite other rockets on the whole political scene from local elections to the Congress. Once a people are organized they will keep moving from issue to issue. *People power is the real objective; the proxies are simply a means to that end.*[49]

The SEC's new proxy access rules under Dodd-Frank are presently stayed, pending a legal challenge by the U.S. Chamber of Commerce and the Business Roundtable. If the rules stand up in court, Congress must step in and overturn them.

## FIGHTING BACK: BLOCK, STALL, REPEAL, AND REPLACE

Dodd-Frank massively expands bureaucratic control over not only the financial sector but every public company and every aspect of our financial lives. Its unintended consequences will hamper the economic recovery, limit the availability of credit, and harm those the bill was intended to protect—and guarantee future bailouts at taxpayer expense. Ultimately, our goal must be to repeal it in its entirety.

In the meantime, however, we need to use the available tools to exercise oversight and limit the most outrageous aspects of the regulatory onslaught as it moves forward. The simplest and most effective is to limit funding. Indeed, by using continuing resolutions instead of appropriations bills, Congress has already greatly limited the ability of federal regulators to move forward in implementing Dodd-Frank.

One of the most significant but underappreciated implications of Senate Republicans blocking an omnibus spending bill in the 2010 lame-duck session was that a continuing resolution passed without funding for Dodd-Frank implementation. As Pat Garafalo of the Center for American Progress lamented:

> However, the resolution does not include funding for the implementation of the Dodd-Frank financial reform law. Under the omnibus, the Securities and Exchange Commission would have seen its budget increase to $1.3 billion from $1.1 billion, and the CFTC would have gone from $169 million to $286 million.
>
> Already, the SEC has halted implementation of a variety of measures under the law as it waits for funding. Included in this halt are new regulations for credit rating agencies and an office for financial markets whistleblowers. The Commodity Futures and Trading Commission (which is charged with implementing the derivatives title of the bill) has said that its current funding level "is far less than what is required to properly fulfill our significantly expanded role." "The implementation of that good and historic law is in jeopardy if the CFTC doesn't have increased resources," Bart Chilton, a CFTC commissioner, has said.[50]

▶ ▶ ▶

*Dodd-Frank massively expands bureaucratic control over not only the financial sector but every public company and every aspect of our financial lives. Its unintended consequences will hamper the economic recovery, limit the availability of credit, and harm those the bill was intended to protect—and guarantee future bailouts at taxpayer expense.*

David Dayen, a left-wing blogger, noted that the way Dodd-Frank punted nearly all real decision-making to regulators leaves it particularly vulnerable to funding restriction:

> Dodd-Frank was more a promise to write a bill than a bill itself. Congress seems determined to deny the resources to the bill writers to get that done. This is part of the danger of a purely regulatory and not a statutory approach.[51]

Republicans can and must limit funding going forward to slow and stall the creation of the bill's regulatory machinery. Unfortunately and outrageously, the CFPB is insulated from oversight via the appropriations process because it is funded directly out of Federal Reserve operations and required no congressionally appropriated funds. Congress can and should, however, prohibit any federal funds from being spent to carry out the directives of Elizabeth Warren, an unconfirmed White House staffer who has no legitimate authority to direct the CFPB.

Other strategies will also be needed. The financial regulatory issues are some of the most complex and challenging in the whole Obama regulatory agenda, and at stake is whether Obama's strategy of ruling by nearly unchecked regulatory power will be allowed to stand. Congressional Republicans must therefore wisely choose at least one or two major high-profile issues emanating from Dodd-Frank to elevate as gut-check level, politically charged votes. The issue could be either a rulemaking by the CFPB that Congress can overturn via the Congressional Review Act or a key nomination they can contest. They must also continue to press for broad regulatory reform, including the REINS Act.

For far too long we have allowed public policy fights to end when legislative action ends, which is why Congress is increasingly writing bills that leave all the real policymaking to unelected, unaccountable regulators. It has to stop. That means this bill, the most egregious example of this phenomenon yet, cannot be allowed to stand.

The more this regulatory nightmare unfolds, the more citizens—as consumers, shareholders, and taxpayers—must demand Congress step in and repeal this law. If we don't keep the pressure dialed up, it will be all too easy to accept the vast new financial bureaucracy as a way of life, and a future Republican president will consider appointing Republicans to run all these new agencies a viable solution. We have to stay angry and stay focused on repealing Dodd-Frank and replacing it with financial reform that eliminates the wasteful, overlapping, confusing regulatory agencies that already exist and instead establishes simple rules of the road that will let markets work.

*For far too long we have allowed public policy fights to end when legislative action ends, which is why Congress is increasingly writing bills that leave all the real policymaking to unelected, unaccountable regulators. It has to stop.*

CHAPTER 7

# Drilling Down: Assault on Offshore Energy

*"A massive campaign must be launched to restore a high-quality environment in North America and to de-develop the United States... Resources and energy must be diverted from frivolous and wasteful uses in overdeveloped countries to filling the genuine needs of underdeveloped countries. This effort must be largely political."*[1]
—JOHN P. HOLDREN, Assistant to the President for Science and Technology

*"Barack Obama and Senator Biden, you've said no to everything in trying to find a domestic solution to the energy crisis that we're in. You even called drilling—safe, environmentally friendly drilling offshore—as raping the outer continental shelf."*[2]
—SARAH PALIN, on the campaign trail in 2008

When President Obama took office, the average price of a gallon of gasoline in the United States was $1.83. What has happened since was not an accident, but the result of a consistent set of anti-energy policies designed to make prices skyrocket so that we can't afford to use as much gasoline and electricity. I explained the EPA's backdoor global warming taxes in Chapter 2, but they are only the tip of the iceberg. Add unlawful moratoria in the Gulf of Mexico and Alaska, and a vicious assault on access to onshore resources (discussed in Chapter 8), and you have a recipe for doubling or tripling prices at the pump—which Obama has done.

Recall that the famous 2009 "summer of discontent" over health care was preceded by an equally intense, and perhaps even broader-based, summer of anger on the issue of American energy production the previous year. As prices at the pump went to three and then four dollars, people began to ask why vast American energy resources were being held off-limits by the federal government.

In July 2008 President George W. Bush lifted the moratorium on exploration and production in the Outer Continental Shelf that his father had established. By September, even Nancy Pelosi was forced to relent and allow the congressional offshore ban to expire.

But then came November, and the election of a new president profoundly hostile to developing American energy resources. Quite simply, the Obama administration has refused to offer any leases in the former moratorium waters that should have been opened when the ban was lifted in 2008. Obama promised a very small lease sale off the coast of Virginia, in an area unlikely to have much oil or gas, then seized on the BP oil spill to reverse course and reinstitute the old George H. W. Bush and Bill Clinton moratorium—and worse.

Never willing to let a good crisis go to waste, the Obama administration manipulated the data to unlawfully impose a moratorium in the Gulf of Mexico and to cancel leases in Alaskan waters. With the Gulf's number-two industry—tourism—already suffering a severe decline as a consequence of the spill, Obama imposed an even worse disaster by walloping the Gulf's number-one industry: oil and gas. That moratorium, though officially lifted, lives on in an outrageous "permitorium," an unofficial *de facto* moratorium in which the Department of the Interior refuses to issue permits. Rigs are being towed to other countries and will likely never come back. Companies are filing for bankruptcy. And prices at the pump are going back up as we shut off more and more of the American energy supply.

Three years after Congress was forced to lift the offshore drilling ban, thanks to an administration that doesn't care what Congress or the American people want, we have less access to American energy than ever before.

## DRILL, BABY, DRILL: HOW ACTIVISTS LIFTED THE OFFSHORE BAN IN 2008

Before it became the year of the financial crisis and the year of Obama, 2008 was the year of soaring oil and gasoline prices. As prices climbed higher, Americans were increasingly outraged that American energy resources were being held almost completely off-limits by the federal government. The shortage that was driving prices higher was entirely artificial, a product of bad policy decisions rather than the physical scarcity of supply.

Throughout the summer, grassroots activists grew increasingly agitated, demanding that Congress allow exploration and production in the Outer Continental Shelf. Newt Gingrich launched the brilliantly succinct "Drill Here, Drill Now, Pay Less" campaign that collected more than 1.5 million signatures.[3]

At the 2008 Republican National Convention an even simpler slogan became a rallying cry: "Drill, baby, drill." Michael Steele, the former lieutenant governor of Maryland who would later become RNC chairman, explained: "It's a call to action. It's about making our country less dependent on foreign oil."[4]

Sarah Palin scored big points when she used the slogan in the vice presidential debate, answering Biden's claim that her energy policy is "drill, drill, drill":

The chant is "drill, baby, drill." And that's what we hear all across this country in our rallies because people are so hungry for those domestic sources of energy to be tapped into. They know that even in my own energy-producing state we have billions of barrels of oil and hundreds of trillions of cubic feet of clean, green natural gas...

Barack Obama and Senator Biden, you've said "No" to everything in trying to find a domestic solution to the energy crisis that we're in. You even called drilling—safe, environmentally friendly drilling offshore—as raping the outer continental shelf.[5]

It was, until the financial crisis hit, the key issue that drove the McCain-Palin ticket higher in the polls and put the candidates in a surprising position to potentially pull off an unlikely upset. The pressure on Obama was so intense that he even reversed his opposition, claiming on August 1, 2008, that he would support offshore drilling under some circumstances:

My interest is in making sure we've got the kind of comprehensive energy policy that can bring down gas prices. If, in order to get that passed, we have to compromise in terms of a careful, well thought-out drilling strategy that was carefully circumscribed to avoid significant environmental damage I don't want to be so rigid that we can't get something done.[6]

The offshore drilling issue that summer, in an important sense, laid the foundation for the online activism that would grow into the tea party movement the following winter. Throughout the summer of 2008, online and grassroots activists came together around the issue. The "#dontgo movement" sprang up on Twitter to protest Congress leaving for August recess while the country suffered from high prices at the pump. (Many of its organizers would go on to become key organizers of the 2009 tax day tea parties.) Large numbers of activists began showing up all over the country, and chanting—as Palin observed—"drill, baby, drill," because they were tired of political elites in both parties holding our energy supplies off-limits.

It worked, but it took sustained pressure by grassroots activists on Congress and the Bush White House to adopt the strategy that ultimately proved successful. The key was recognition—once Bush lifted the executive branch moratorium in July 2008—that the legislative ban was not a permanent policy but rather an annually renewed appropriations rider. (A lesson we should remember when we consider defunding strategies for some of the other threats noted in this book is that funding limitations can be renewed annually for decades.)

Because the ban was part of the annual appropriations process, it ended each year at the end of September. While Congress usually enacted a new ban as a matter of course, there was no way it could justify enacting a new ban for the upcoming fiscal year, given public opinion about high energy prices.

I explained how the grassroots victory occurred in 2008 on *National Review Online*:

> The normal process of funding the U.S. government through appropriations bills broke down this year, forcing Congress to prepare a continuing resolution to keep the government funded at last year's levels. Proponents of American oil and gas production have long suspected that the Democrats would use the resolution to hide an extension of the wildly unpopular bans on offshore drilling and oil-shale development. The theory was that by simply extending last year's Interior Appropriations act, which included the bans, they could hide an extension without even mentioning it in the text of the bill.

To pre-empt this strategy, Jim DeMint in the Senate and Jeb Hensarling and John Shadegg in the House collected signatures from enough members of Congress to make it clear that an expected presidential veto of any such extension of the drilling ban would be sustained. Meanwhile, free-market and conservative groups presented a united front to Congress and the White House, urging lawmakers to let the ban expire. Facing organized opposition in Congress and overwhelming public opinion in favor of drilling, Democrats signaled late last week [mid-September 2008] that a continuing resolution would not include an extension of the drilling bans.

But that's when the financial crisis struck and everything on Capitol Hill was thrown into the air.

With the Treasury's proposed financial-market intervention drawing attention away from the energy debate, anti-drilling House Democrats were temporarily emboldened. On Monday they inserted language into their continuing-resolution draft that would permanently ban oil drilling within 50 miles of the U.S. coast, where the vast majority of offshore oil and gas is believed to be.

Their political calculation was that the White House would be willing to sign this into law and go along with the charade that it represented a real increase in offshore drilling. That calculation was wrong. News broke last night that President Bush threatened to veto the continuing resolution unless it allowed the bans to cleanly expire. As a result, Democrats backed down—no doubt aware of the strength of public opinion on the underlying policy issue.[7]

Bush's veto threat held and the Democrats backed down. Nancy Pelosi raised the white flag. U.S. Sen. Jim DeMint, U.S. Rep. Jeb Hensarling (R-Texas), then-U.S. Rep. John Shadegg, (R-Ariz.), and millions of Americans demanding offshore drilling had won. The offshore drilling ban that had been in place for the Outer Continental Shelf since 1982 ended on October 1, 2008.

Ben Lieberman, then an energy policy analyst with The Heritage Foundation and now a key staffer on the House Energy and Commerce Committee, summarized what that meant for domestic energy supply:

> Recent DOI estimates are that these off-limits offshore areas contain 19.1 billion barrels of oil, the equivalent of 30 years of current imports from Saudi Arabia. It should also be noted that these initial energy estimates often prove to be low. For example, in the central and western Gulf of Mexico—the only offshore area not severely restricted—production has already exceeded original expectations by several billion barrels, and it is ongoing.[8]

It was a remarkable turn of events, and if we had actually begun leasing and allowing exploration and production in those areas, we would be well on the way to more secure and affordable oil and gas. Unfortunately, the month after the offshore ban was lifted, Barack Obama was elected president, and—notwithstanding his campaign trail promise—he had no intention of allowing offshore drilling to move forward, ban or no ban.

## OBAMA'S FOOT DRAGGING

The first order of business for Ken Salazar, Obama's new secretary of the Interior, was to stop the pending opening of the former moratorium waters that had been put in motion by the outgoing Bush administration. Salazar's first public policy statement, just weeks after being confirmed as the new head of the Department of the Interior (DOI), focused on stopping the opening of the Outer Continental Shelf:

> the Bush Administration's midnight action acceler-
> ated by two years the regular process for creating a
> new plan for the outer continental shelf. It opened
> up the possibility for oil and gas leasing along
> the entire eastern seaboard, portions of offshore
> California, and the far eastern Gulf of Mexico…
>       It was a headlong rush of the worst kind. It was
> a process rigged to force hurried decisions based on
> bad information. It was a process tilted toward the
> usual energy players, while renewable energy com-
> panies and the interests of American consumers and
> taxpayers were overlooked. But the time for reform
> has arrived.[9]

He started by reopening the docket for public comments on the offshore drilling plan and beginning a rigged process in which there would be only one public hearing on the East Coast in Atlantic City, New Jersey, and one public hearing on the West Coast in San Francisco—cities that are especially hostile to sensible offshore production. It meant stalling and disregarding the American people and the clear intent of Congress manifest in the lifting of the moratorium.

During the reopened public comment period, the American public continued to heavily favor expanded offshore drilling. In fact, the 530,000 comments that were filed with the DOI ran two to one in favor of expanded drilling. To avoid embarrassment, the administration tried to cover up the results of the prolonged comment period, but American Solutions filed a series of Freedom of

Information Act requests that confirmed the two-to-one ratio in favor of expanding drilling.[10] It also uncovered this e-mail in which Interior Department official Liz Birnbaum explained how Salazar could "honestly" dodge the questions about it:

> Although we do have a preliminary tabulation of the comments, it has not yet gone to the Secretary because Steve [Black] wanted to suggest some revisions in the presentation and analysis. (Steve, if you could get those comments to me, we'll get it completed.) So the Secretary can honestly say in response to any questions that he's [sic] has not yet seen the analysis of the comments—staff is still working on it. I did, however, confirm to him the 2-1 split that these guys are emphasizing.[11]

The policy stance of the Obama administration throughout 2009—a year of severe economic weakness—was to ignore the overwhelming desires of the American people and do nothing to move forward on the no-cost, genuine stimulus policy of allowing access to offshore oil and gas.

# OFFSHORE DRILLING ... IN BRAZIL

Obama was doing nothing to advance drilling, of course, unless the oil and gas in question was off the coast not of the United States but of Brazil, where the Obama administration appeared keenly interested in moving forward as quickly as possible—with the backing of U.S. taxpayers—to assist the Brazilian national oil company, Petrobras, in its offshore plans.

On April 14, 2009, the Obama administration's Export-Import Bank granted preliminary approval for $2 billion of loan guarantees to Petrobras.[12] *The Wall Street Journal* editorialized under the headline "Obama Underwrites Offshore Drilling":

> The U.S. is going to lend billions of dollars to Brazil's state-owned oil company, Petrobras, to finance exploration of the huge offshore discovery in Brazil's Tupi oil field in the Santos Basin near Rio de Janeiro. Brazil's planning minister confirmed that White House National Security Adviser James Jones met this month with Brazilian officials to talk about the loan.
>
> The U.S. Export-Import Bank tells us it has issued a "preliminary commitment" letter to Petrobras in the amount of $2 billion and has discussed with Brazil the possibility of increasing that amount. Ex-Im Bank says it has not decided whether the money will come in the form of a direct loan or loan guarantees. Either way, this corporate foreign aid may strike some readers as odd, given that the U.S. Treasury seems desperate for cash and Petrobras is one of the largest corporations in the Americas.
>
> But look on the bright side. If President Obama has embraced offshore drilling in Brazil, why not in the old U.S.A.?[13]

▶ ▶ ▶

*The United States economy was reeling, and Obama's stimulus policies were failing. Giving the green light to offshore drilling here would have created more than 160,000 well-paying American jobs.*

Good question.

The United States economy was reeling, and Obama's stimulus policies were failing. Giving the green light to offshore drilling here would have created more than 160,000 well-paying American jobs.[14] Yet we had government policy preventing the creation of these jobs by stalling and denying access to offshore resources when unemployment was around 10 percent.

When the American people learned that the administration was approving offshore projects not here, but in Brazil, they were, not surprisingly, outraged. Public comments flooded the Department of the Interior, demanding they stop stalling and take action. Eventually they did. Sort of.

## OBAMA'S PHONY DRILLING PLAN

More than a year later, on March 31, 2010, Obama finally announced his official policy on offshore drilling. *The New York Times* headline made it look like he was delivering on his campaign promise. It read: "Obama to Open Offshore Areas to Oil Drilling for First Time."[15]

The article went on to explain the Obama plan:

> The proposal—a compromise that will please oil companies and domestic drilling advocates but anger some residents of affected states and many environmental organizations—would end a long-standing moratorium on oil exploration along the East Coast from the northern tip of Delaware to the central coast of Florida, covering 167 million acres of ocean.
>
> Under the plan, the coastline from New Jersey northward would remain closed to all oil and gas activity. So would the Pacific Coast, from Mexico to the Canadian border...The first lease sale off the coast of Virginia could occur as early as next year in a triangular tract 50 miles off the coast.[16]

This was typical of the coverage of the Obama announcement throughout the mainstream media. Even the governor of Virginia, Republican Bob McDonnell, who had campaigned on developing offshore resources, praised the Obama announcement, saying:

> I thank the President and Secretary of the Interior Ken Salazar for ensuring Virginia will be the first state on the East Coast to explore for and produce energy offshore. The President's decision to allow energy exploration off Virginia's coast will mean thousands of new jobs, hundreds of millions in new state revenue and tens of billions of dollars in economic impact for the Commonwealth...
>
> With today's announcement, oil and gas can be produced in an environmentally-safe manner 50 miles off Virginia's coast. Virginians will benefit from the thousands of jobs that will be created and the economic activity and development that will accompany this vital industry's arrival in the state.[17]

But what had Obama really done for Virginia? He was promising to allow a limited lease sale for waters beyond 50 miles—past where geologists think most of the oil and gas is. And contrary to the spin from the administration picked up by *The New York Times* and others, he had dragged his feet for more than a year after Congress had voted to end the offshore ban, and was now canceling five lease sales in Alaska while imposing new restrictions in the Atlantic and Pacific.

This was my public statement on the day of Obama's supposed drilling plan:

> Obama is talking about lifting a nonexistent ban! Bush lifted the executive ban in July 2008, and Congress lifted the legislative ban in October 2008. There is no legal impediment to drilling now, except

that the Obama administration refuses to offer leases. So the idea that this is a big concession in exchange for which Congress should jumpstart climate legislation is ridiculous. I'll believe they are really allowing drilling when they actually offer leases. Also, the 50-mile restriction means he is actually *adding* a *new* moratorium on waters inside of 50 miles.[18]

Obama's left-wing allies in Congress knew what was going on, but they feigned outrage at his "shift to the center" to make the president appear moderate. Obama's supposed "pro-drilling" policy didn't last long, however.

# THE BP SPILL: A CRISIS NOT TO WASTE

Less than a month after Obama's drilling announcement, tragedy struck in the Gulf of Mexico on BP's Deepwater Horizon drilling platform. On April 20, 2010, an explosion on that platform killed 11 men and injured 17 others.[19] The ensuing oil spill was the largest accidental marine spill of all time.[20] While the administration's legitimate crisis response was lackluster (James Carville memorably said its "political stupidity is unbelievable, to say the least"[21]), its political crisis exploitation—an Obama administration specialty—shifted into high gear.

This was an opportunity, it seemed, not only to shut down any possibility of access to offshore resources in the former moratorium waters, but to shut down production where it already existed, in the Gulf of Mexico, and possibly even to jump-start efforts to pass the flagging cap-and-trade bill. There were a couple of problems with these ambitions, however.

First, the cap-and-trade bill that was being developed by U.S. Sens. John Kerry (D-Mass.), Joe Lieberman (ID-Conn.), and Lindsey Graham (R-S.C.) relied on compromise language to encourage offshore drilling to attract support from Republicans. That language was now a nonstarter for left-wing Democrats, so there was no real impetus to restart the failed push for global warming legislation because of the BP spill.

Second, the public still strongly believed that America needed to develop its offshore energy resources. One of the key elements of political crisis exploitation is that the crisis precipitate a shift in public opinion that makes it politically possible to push the envelope further than would otherwise be the case. That simply didn't happen. The majority of Americans continued to support offshore drilling throughout the crisis. A Rasmussen Reports poll conducted two weeks after the incident found support for offshore drilling at 58 percent, and it rose from there, reaching 64 percent by August and hovering around that level.[22] Opposition to offshore drilling was in the low-20s, so proponents of offshore oil drilling still outnumbered their opponents by a politically potent three-to-one ratio.

Unfortunately, while the political reality limited the ability of the Obama administration to exploit the BP crisis to pass legislation, the administration had a free hand to exploit the crisis through its own unilateral executive actions. And it did.

Obama imposed an emergency moratorium shutting down all deepwater production while a task force was commissioned to make recommendations on how to proceed. When the task force reported, its major recommendation was a six-month moratorium on all deepwater drilling activities. It was a sweeping recommendation with a dramatic negative impact on a regional economy already suffering from lost tourism and idled fishing boats as a consequence of the spill. As James Carville put it: "You take fishing and you take petroleum away down here and you don't have a whole lot left."[23] But the recommendation for a moratorium was not supported by the authors of the task force report. They wrote this letter to Louisiana Gov. Bobby Jindal and U.S. Sens. David Vitter and Mary Landrieu:

A group of those named in the Secretary of Interior's Report, "Increased Safety Measures for Energy Development on the Outer Continental Shelf" dated May 27, 2010 are concerned that our names are connected with the moratorium as proposed in the executive summary of that report. There is an implication that we have somehow agreed to or "peer reviewed" the main recommendation of that report. This is not the case.

As outlined in the attached document, we believe the report itself is very well done and includes some important recommendations which we support. However, the scope of the moratorium on drilling which is in the executive summary differs in important ways from the recommendation in the draft which we reviewed. We believe the report does not justify the moratorium as written and that the moratorium as changed will not contribute measurably to increased safety and will have immediate and long term economic effects. Indeed an argument can be made that the changes made in the wording are counterproductive to long term safety.

The Secretary should be free to recommend whatever he thinks is correct, but he should not be free to use our names to justify his political decisions.[24]

They went further in their public statement, opposing the moratorium that their findings had been manipulated to support:

A blanket moratorium does not address the specific causes of this tragedy. We do not believe punishing the innocent is the right thing to do. We encourage the Secretary of the Interior to overcome emotion with logic and to define what he means by a "blanket moratorium" in such a way as to be consistent with the body of the report and the interests of the nation.[25]

An investigation by the DOI inspector general, requested by Vitter and U.S. Rep. Steve Scalise (R-La.), revealed that it was White House staff who rewrote the report's executive summary to give the false impression that the expert panel had recommended the moratorium. The key White House player? None other than Carol Browner, motivated by the same ideas she endorsed as a member of the Socialist International Commission for a Sustainable World Society, discussed in Chapter 2. The investigation found:

> At 2:13 a.m. on May 27, 2010, Browner's staff member sent an e-mail back to [Steve] Black that contained two edited versions of the Executive Summary. Both versions sent by the staff member contained significant edits to DOI's draft Executive Summary but were very similar to each other. Both versions, however, revised and re-ordered the Executive Summary, placing the peer review language immediately following the moratorium recommendation causing the distinction between the Secretary's moratorium recommendation—which had not been peer-reviewed—and the recommendations contained in the 30-Day Report—which had been peer-reviewed—to become effectively lost.[26]

The political manipulation of the report by Browner and Steve Black (the same Interior Department official who tried to cover up the public comments supporting offshore drilling) paved the way for the imposition of a sweeping new moratorium. The Obama administration did this with full knowledge that it would put more than 23,000 Americans out of work at a time of record-high unemployment. As *The Wall Street Journal* reported:

> ▶ ▶ ▶
>
> *An investigation by the DOI inspector general, requested by Vitter and U.S. Rep. Steve Scalise (R-La.), revealed that it was White House staff who rewrote the report's executive summary to give the false impression that the expert panel had recommended the moratorium.*

Senior Obama administration officials concluded the federal moratorium on deepwater oil drilling would cost roughly 23,000 jobs, but went ahead with the ban... The new top regulator on offshore oil exploration, Michael Bromwich, told Interior Secretary Ken Salazar that a six-month deepwater-drilling halt would result in "lost direct employment" affecting approximately 9,450 workers and "lost jobs from indirect and induced effects" affecting about 13,797 more.[27]

The blanket moratorium shut down operations not just in the Gulf and Alaska, but in California as well. The *Ventura County Reporter* noted:

Three offshore drilling platforms in the Santa Barbara Channel, which extends into Ventura County waters, have been ordered by the U.S. Department of the Interior to cease drilling operations. Platforms Heritage, Gail and Houchin have had to respond to the issued moratoria by capping their wells and suspending operations...

The platforms in the Santa Barbara Channel, which make up about 80 percent of the drilling platforms in the Pacific, have been producing from the same oil fields for close to 40 years, said Hull, and these fields are not under the kinds of pressure encountered by Deepwater Horizon. If the moratorium, which is supposed to be lifted in November, is overly prolonged, Hull suggested that it would impact more than 100,000 barrels of oil a day from these local platforms, resulting in more lost jobs, more dependence on foreign oil and less energy security.[28]

Shutting operations in Santa Barbara had broad historic significance because it was ground zero for the antidrilling environmental movement, dating back to a 1969 spill. But by the summer of 2008, the Santa Barbara County Board of Supervisors had voted to urge the state to *expand* offshore drilling.[29] Now even the limited production they already had was being shut down by Salazar and Obama.

The politically motivated moratorium was unlawful and economically devastating. On June 23, 2010, U.S. District Court Judge Martin Feldman issued a stinging 22-page decision, issuing an injunction to overturn the moratorium based on the political manipulation and the Interior Department's utter failure to justify the breadth of the moratorium. Feldman wrote:

> How these studies support a finding that shear equipment does not work consistently at 500 feet is incomprehensible. If some drilling equipment parts are flawed, is it rational to say all are? Are all airplanes a danger because one was? All oil tankers like Exxon Valdez? All trains? All mines? That sort of thinking seems heavy-handed, and rather overbearing...

An invalid agency decision to suspend drilling of wells in depths of over 500 feet simply cannot justify the immeasurable effect on the plaintiffs, the local economy, the Gulf region, and the critical present-day aspect of the availability of domestic energy in this country. Accordingly, the plaintiffs' motion for preliminary injunction is GRANTED. An Order consistent with this opinion will be entered.[30]

The Obama administration turned to the Fifth Circuit Court of Appeals for an injunction to stay Feldman's ruling, and it was rejected.[31] Nonetheless, Salazar reimposed a very similar moratorium, disregarding the rulings of the two courts. He explained: "We will only lift the moratorium when I as secretary of Interior am comfortable that we have significantly reduced those risks."[32] Feldman held Salazar and the Interior Department in contempt of court, but the unlawful moratorium continued.

▶ ▶ ▶

*Secretary Salazar reimposed a very similar moratorium, disregarding the rulings of the two courts. He explained: "We will only lift the moratorium when I as secretary of Interior am comfortable that we have significantly reduced those risks."*

## MORATORIUM ENDS, PERMITORIUM CONTINUES

On October 12, 2010, Obama and Salazar were finally comfortable enough to end their illegal moratorium on deepwater drilling. Some of the key pressure that got them to finally relent came from Landrieu, who was holding up Obama's nominee for budget director to oppose the ongoing moratorium. But the end of the formal

moratorium didn't put anyone back to work, because the administration continued to drag its feet on permitting.

Kerry Chauvin, chief executive of Gulf Island Fabrications Inc.
of Houma, Louisiana, a builder of steel platforms used in develop-
mental oil and gas wells, pointed out:

> It doesn't matter if they lift the ban if the wells
> can't get permitted—and right now the guidelines
> are still vague, and the Bureau of Ocean Energy
> Management is too understaffed to process permits
> in a timely manner.[33]

It was a fact of life long clear to the shallow-water operators
who had been sidelined by an informal moratorium via permitting
delays—a "permitorium"—that had already shut them down, even
though they were not subject to the official deepwater ban.[34]

By February 2011, there were more than 100 Gulf of Mexico
permits pending at the Interior Department's newly created regulator, Bureau of Ocean Energy Management, Regulation and
Enforcement, which had not approved a single permit since the
moratorium was supposedly lifted.[35] According to the Greater New
Orleans Regional Economic Alliance's Gulf Permit Index:

> No deep-water permits were issued during January
> 2011. The current three-month trailing average is
> 0.67 permits, representing a 5.13—or an 88%—
> monthly reduction from the historical monthly av-
> erage of 5.8 permits per month.
>
> Shallow-water permit issuance also lags behind
> the historical average of 7.1 permits per month. In
> the past three months, 5 shallow-water permits, on
> average, were issued. The deficit of 2.1 represents
> a 30% decrease in permit issuance. Only two new
> shallow-water permits were issued in January 2011.[36]

On February 12, 2011, Seahawk Drilling Inc. filed for bankruptcy and liquidated its assets.[37] It was a casualty of the continuing unlawful moratorium.

The state of Alaska sued the Interior Department in September 2010, alleging that the cancellation of lease sales, suspension of Shell's approval to drill exploratory wells, and refusal to grant permits there amounted to an illegal stealth moratorium. In February 2011, Shell gave up and pulled the plug on its Alaskan offshore operations, saying it couldn't justify investing more than $100 million with the continued regulatory uncertainty. CEO Peter Voser said:

> Despite our investment in acreage and technology and our work with the stakeholders, we haven't been able to drill a single exploration well. Critical permits continue to be delayed and the timeline for getting these permits is still uncertain.[38]

In March 2011, a small number of deepwater permits in the Gulf were finally approved, after Exxon and other major oil and gas companies developed a Marine Well Containment Company to contain future blowouts that took away one of Salazar's last excuses.[39] But it's clear the administration remains committed to blocking as much offshore oil and gas production as possible. It did not let the BP crisis go to waste.

# JOHN HOLDREN, OBAMA'S ANTIENERGY ADVISER

Remarkably, Carol Browner is not Obama's most extreme adviser with respect to energy policy. That honor is reserved for John P. Holdren, a longtime collaborator of neo-Malthusian blowhard Paul Ehrlich, and one of the leading opponents of economic growth, prosperity, development, and modern technology. Barack Obama made Holdren the director of the White House Office of Science and Technology Policy (OSTP), which describes itself this way:

> Congress established the Office of Science and Technology Policy in 1976 with a broad mandate to advise the President and others within the Executive Office of the President on the effects of science and technology on domestic and international affairs.[40]

OSTP should have provided the president with an understanding of the technology of offshore drilling, the specific problems with the BP Deepwater Horizon rig, and the same sensible recommendation not to adopt a moratorium that other qualified scientists and engineers had recommended. But under Holdren, it was always a given that the only advice the president would get would be to stop fossil fuel use at all costs.

Holdren is such an extremist and so out of touch with reality that as recently as 2009 he claimed that more than a billion people would die from global warming by 2020.[41] That's one person in six dead less than a decade from now. Anyone who believed such a thing would be desperate to stop oil and gas production at all costs.

Holdren has gone much further, however, calling for the outright rationing of energy as a way to deliberately shift wealth out of the United States. Consider this quote from one of the books he coauthored with Ehrlich:

> A massive campaign must be launched to restore a high-quality environment in North America and to de-develop the United States...Resources and energy must be diverted from frivolous and wasteful uses in overdeveloped countries to filling the genuine needs of underdeveloped countries. This effort must be largely political.[42]

Or this one, another of many Holdren statements catalogued by Robert Bradley of the Institute for Energy Research:

> Only one rational path is open to us—simultaneous de-development of the [overdeveloped countries] and semi-development of the underdeveloped countries (UDCs), in order to approach a decent and ecologically sustainable standard of living for all in between. By de-development we mean lower per-capita energy consumption, fewer gadgets, and the abolition of planned obsolescence.[43]

To the truly radical greens, restricting access to energy is an imperative because energy drives all human activities—and they want to stop nearly all human activities. As Holdren observed in a moment of clarity:

> A reliable and affordable supply of energy is absolutely critical to maintaining and expanding economic prosperity where such prosperity already exists and to creating it where it does not.[44]

Yet his policy proposals—which are also Obama's—are designed to restrict energy and therefore to restrict prosperity. When Obama was constantly attacking my group, Americans for Prosperity, on the campaign trail as a vacuous name akin to "Moms for Motherhood," I pointed to the administration's anti-energy policies, including the Gulf moratorium, as clear proof that it placed other values above prosperity.

▶ ▶ ▶

*To the truly radical greens, restricting access to energy is an imperative because energy drives all human activities—and they want to stop nearly all human activities.*

# OCS IS OFFICIALLY CLOSED

On November 2, 2010, voters overwhelmingly elected a new Congress that was pro-offshore oil drilling. And, as with so many issues, the Obama administration acted swiftly to disregard the election and accomplish the opposite of what Americans wanted through unilateral executive action.

On December 1, 2010, Salazar officially announced the reimposition of the old moratorium that Congress had lifted on October 1, 2008. What the American people wanted didn't matter. What Obama himself had promised the previous year didn't matter. Instead, the attention was focused on the ongoing efforts of the Interior Department to cripple production where it had previously existed. So opening up the former moratorium waters fell by the wayside.

A poll by Rasmussen Reports on December 3 and 4, 2010, found that 60 percent of Americans still supported offshore drilling, 54 percent of Americans believed the new ban would increase gas prices, and 54 percent believed it would hurt the U.S. economy—versus only 11 percent who thought it would help.[45]

The majority of Americans, including the hundreds of thousands of people who filed comments supporting increased offshore drilling, were ignored. The deal with Virginia Gov. McDonnell was shelved, spurring him to correctly say:

> I am extremely disappointed that the Obama Administration has unilaterally blocked environmentally responsible, and economically crucial, offshore energy exploration and development in Virginia, along the Atlantic Coast and throughout other broad swaths of offshore territory nationwide. This is an irresponsible and short-sighted decision. It demonstrates a complete lack of confidence in the entrepreneurial spirit of American industry and its ability to fix the problems experienced in the Gulf

spill, and no confidence in the ability of the U.S. government to better plan for and react to offshore emergencies.[46]

We ended up with the inverse of what happened in so many other policy areas, where Congress rejected legislation and Obama acted as if it had passed anyway. Here, the Congress had passed something with overwhelming public support—the end of the moratorium in the Outer Continental Shelf—and Obama insisted on disregarding it to keep the old moratorium firmly in place.

And he pushed way beyond that, seizing on a crisis to impose an unlawful moratorium on nearly all offshore production in the United States. Not surprisingly, with the oil and gas industry firmly under the thumb of the administration, prices at the pump began steadily creeping back up in 2010 and 2011, just as they had steadily declined when it looked like America was finally going to tap its vast offshore energy resources. This is not just an issue for Alaska, Louisiana, and Texas. It is an issue for every American who fills a gas tank or pays a home heating bill.

It will be a big challenge to get this administration to finally approve permits even in nonmoratorium waters. With a combination of court orders, public anger, and an aggressive Congress using all of its oversight tools, however, it is possible. In March, Salazar softened his stance, by beginning—albeit slowly—to again issue permits in the Gulf of Mexico. It will take an even stronger push to get back to normal,

> ▶ ▶ ▶
>
> *It will be a big challenge to get this administration to finally approve permits even in nonmoratorium waters. With a combination of court orders, public anger, and an aggressive Congress using all its oversight tools, however, it is possible.*

and it will depend on bringing pressure to bear on senators who are not from energy states. The energy industry, contrary to the complaints from the left, simply does not have enough lobbying clout to take on this administration in Congress without a sustained, direct effort from consumers standing up for their own interests.

But we also need to aim our sights higher. We need to access oil and gas in the Outer Continental Shelf and should demand Congress develop a way to bypass the intransigent regime at the DOI. One approach would be to give the states discretion to approve energy exploration and production off their shores, while also assuring them a share of the revenues.

We need to directly pressure Obama on this issue, given his repeated broken promises to allow drilling and his present complete disregard for the will of the people and of Congress. If "drill, baby, drill" can be as potent a political movement in the run-up to 2012 as it was in 2008, he will have no choice but to relent and allow us to finally begin to access American offshore energy resources.

## CHAPTER 8

# Property in Peril: Obama's Shocking Land Grabs

*"America has undergone a massive period of galloping government land acquisition with essentially no oversight or accounting whatsoever. Every time any level of government takes more land, there is less for the use of a free and productive society, less for use in producing the food, fiber, minerals, and energy, less for private ownership, private conservation, and pursuing the American dream."*[1]

—R. J. SMITH, the father of free-market environmentalism

P resident Obama aims high: he wants to control all the land and all the water in the United States. Toward that end, there were several significant failed legislative efforts to steamroll property rights in the last Congress that were emphatically rejected in the 2010 election, but have continued to move forward by other means. Perhaps the biggest upset of the 2010 cycle was the defeat of U.S. Rep. Jim Oberstar (D-Minn.), the powerful chairman of the House Transportation and Infrastructure Committee and an appropriator who consistently brought large sums of federal tax dollars home to Minnesota. By any conventional political analysis, Oberstar should have been unbeatable. But a combination of an extremely anti-incumbent, antispending mood and Oberstar's obsession with a land and water grab that was directly contrary to the interests of his constituents ended his career. The bill, called the Clean Water Restoration Act, would have expanded the jurisdiction of the Environmental Protection Agency (EPA) and the U.S. Army Corps of Engineers to all the land and all the water in the United States. Obama is now attempting to accomplish elements of the bill through the improper use of guidance documents—and he must be stopped, or not only will access to energy resources be shut off but private property rights will be trampled throughout the country.

Another assault on private property that follows the familiar pattern of the administration disregarding the voters and Congress is the massive omnibus public lands bill that Senate Majority Leader Harry Reid pushed throughout 2010 before the election, and then again in the lame-duck session, that was stymied by public outrage. It would have created many new wilderness areas that would have shut off access and added to the inventory of tragically mismanaged federal lands. Unfortunately, one of the first actions taken by Interior Secretary Ken Salazar after the failure of the omnibus lands bill was Secretarial Order 3310, which created "Wild Lands"—wilderness areas without the consent of Congress. This policy has already been put on ice—at least temporarily—by Republicans in the House who blocked its funding. A key success, and an indication that Obama's power grabs can, in fact, be stopped.

In yet another attack on property, leases have been canceled to stop onshore energy production, and a vast expanse of Alaska has been designated critical habitat for polar bears—another attempt to impose global warming regulations without the consent of Congress. It is just the latest example of how the Endangered Species Act is out of control and trampling property rights.

Finally, and perhaps most frightening, internal Interior Department memos reveal a plot for the largest land grab in history using the trick of designating as many as 13 million acres as "national monuments" under the Antiquities Act, one of the largest federal land grabs in history—without any meaningful input from Congress or local communities.

Taken together, these land grabs (and others too numerous to mention) amount to the stealth destruction of private property rights in America and all-out war on the West. They also lock up our onshore energy resources just as surely as the administration's outrageous policies to block offshore energy.

> ▶ ▶ ▶
>
> *Taken together, these land grabs … amount to the stealth destruction of private property rights in America and all-out war on the West. They also lock up our onshore energy resources just as surely as the administration's outrageous policies to block offshore energy.*

## HOW OBERSTAR'S LAND AND WATER GRAB ENDED HIS CAREER

Jim Oberstar, until his stunning defeat in the 2010 election, was the chairman of the House Transportation and Infrastructure Committee. He was elected to Congress in 1975, after serving 12 years as a congressional staffer. In other words, he spent his entire life in Washington, D.C. He lost touch with his rural Minnesota district so much that he became singularly obsessed with an extreme piece of legislation supported by radical green groups, but with nearly zero support from his own constituents. It was a bill to dramatically expand the Clean Water Act to give the EPA and the Army Corps of Engineers control over all the water—and all the land—in the United States.

The Oberstar bill, variously known as the "Clean Water Restoration Act," the "America's Commitment to Clean Water Act," or simply the "Oberstar Wetlands Bill," was the most extreme assault on property rights in the history of the United States. It was also an affront to the Constitution, which established a federal government of limited, enumerated powers.

When the Clean Water Act was originally debated in Congress in 1972, the idea of federal water regulation was novel. Regulating and protecting the water supply had always been a local responsibility, and there was no clear federal authority in the Constitution to encroach on this area. So Congress turned to the same overworked clause recently employed to try to justify a national health care mandate—the Commerce Clause. To make that work, the Clean Water Act was written to apply its regulatory requirements to "navigable waters" of the United States.

That's why the Clean Water Act falls under the jurisdiction of the House Transportation and Infrastructure Committee—it's supposed to regulate the waterways of interstate commerce.[2] Unfortunately, in short order the EPA and the Army Corps of Engineers went far beyond a reasonable interpretation of navigable waters, going so far as to base regulation of isolated intrastate waters on the "migratory bird theory" that birds are engaged in interstate commerce.

This would logically subject a bird feeder in your backyard to federal regulatory jurisdiction. This outlandish legal theory was rejected by the Supreme Court in 2001, when it ruled in *SWANCC* (Solid Waste Agency of Northern Cook County) that the Clean Water Act does not apply to isolated wetlands, rejecting the Army Corps of Engineers' argument that migratory birds using the isolated waters were engaged in interstate commerce. The court further limited Clean Water Act jurisdiction in 2006, when it ruled in *Rapanos* that the word "navigable" in the Clean Water Act actually has limits.

John Rapanos is a hero. His 175-acre Michigan property is 20 miles from the nearest navigable waterway, but the state issued a cease-and-desist order against development based on the Clean Water Act. Rapanos proceeded anyway, saying: "When the government tells you to cease and desist when you're not breaking the law, what do you do, if you're an American?"[3] Rapanos was arrested on criminal charges—simply for pouring sand on land he owned that was nowhere near a navigable waterway. Rapanos was convicted in 1995, but granted a new trial by Federal District Court Judge Lawrence P. Zatkoff, who said of Rapanos, shortly after sentencing an illegal immigrant on drug charges:

> So here we have a person who comes to the United States and commits crimes of selling dope, and the government asks me to put him in prison for 10 months. And then we have an American citizen who buys land, pays for it with his own money, and he moves some sand from one end to the other and government wants me to give him 63 months in prison. Now, if that isn't our system gone crazy, I don't know what is. And I am not going to do it.[4]

Unfortunately Zatkoff was reversed on appeal and ordered to sentence Rapanos, and eventually did sentence him to probation.[5] The civil case went to the Supreme Court, which split four to four along ideological lines, with Justice Anthony Kennedy partially concurring with conservative justices and limiting the scope of Clean Water Act jurisdiction to wetlands with a "significant nexus" to navigable waters.

The Oberstar Wetlands Bill was an attempt to strike back at the court and expand the Clean Water Act further than ever previously contemplated by deleting the word "navigable" from the law and expanding the Clean Water Act to all the waters in the United

States, whether or not there is any connection to interstate commerce. This, of course, ignores the fact that navigability was the basis for the Clean Water Act's original claim to federal constitutional authority.

Moreover, the bill would have expanded regulatory authority to "activities affecting these waters," an extremely broad provision to regulate *land* hidden inside a *water* bill. With an expansive ability to regulate any land that can affect any water—however small and isolated—the bill creates federal jurisdiction over all the land and all the water in the United States.

In testimony to Congress in 2007, Reed Hopper of the Pacific Legal Foundation, the lead counsel in the successful *Rapanos* Supreme Court case, said this about the Oberstar bill:

> This definition of federal authority is not a "restoration" of congressional intent. It far exceeds the jurisdictional scope of the current Clean Water Act as it appears in the text of the statute. It even exceeds the extravagant scope of the existing federal regulations on which this definition is, in part, based. Indeed, with its claim of authority over "all interstate and intrastate waters" this bill pushes the limits of federal power to an extreme not matched by any other law, probably in the history of this country. Neither an ornamental pond nor the proverbial kitchen sink are excluded.[6]

Not surprisingly, such an astonishing land and water grab had very little support in northeastern Minnesota. In fact, Don Parmeter of the National Water and Conservation Alliance observed: "This affects northern Minnesota and Minnesota in general, probably more than any other state in the country."[7]

Oberstar's opponent, Chip Cravaack, campaigned aggressively against the bill. This newspaper account made clear how strongly he opposed the bill:

"This flies directly in the face of the 10th Amendment on state's rights," said Cravaack. "If we allow this to go through, what's next? What other bill are they going to impose upon us that takes away our property rights and our personal freedoms?"

Cravaack said the bill would put 98 percent of Koochiching County under federal control because Koochiching County is 98 percent wetlands.

"If you're a farmer or a rancher, this bill opens up a litigation toolbox for every environmental lawyer, every environmental group who will challenge you with everything they've got," he said.

"If you read the bill, it says nothing about clean water," Cravaack said. "It has everything to do with jurisdiction and who's going to own your property."[8]

On Election Day, Oberstar suffered the biggest surprise defeat in the country. National Water and Conservation Alliance's Parmeter observed that the defeat was a direct consequence of his wetlands bill:

The citizens of Minnesota's 8th Congressional District have historically and aggressively opposed this kind of expansive federal legislation. Mr. Oberstar had won reelection since 1974 by such wide margins that he failed to see how people in water-rich northern Minnesota would be economically devastated by his legislation.[9]

"If you read the bill, it says nothing about clean water. It has everything to do with jurisdiction and who's going to own your property."
—Chip Cravaack

## OBERSTAR BY OTHER MEANS: EPA'S CLEAN WATER ACT GUIDANCE

Oberstar's wetlands bill was so controversial it never even received a vote in Congress, but rather than dying with his congressional career, the bill, like so many threats to our rights in this administration, shifted inside the agencies. In this case, the EPA and the Army Corps are acting to dramatically expand Clean Water Act jurisdiction in open defiance of the Supreme Court and without congressional authorization.

There is legitimate confusion stemming from Kennedy's decision in *Rapanos*, which Congress should step in and clarify by limiting jurisdiction to legitimately navigable waters legislatively. In the absence of congressional action, there have been calls for certainty from developers and property owners that arguably lend support for the EPA's guidance approach.

For instance, Don Parrish, the American Farm Bureau Federation's senior director of regulatory relations, has argued for a rulemaking to clearly define Clean Water Act jurisdiction because, he says: "It's unfair to landowners in a way that disadvantages them and gives the agency power and authority over economic decisions."[10]

Unfortunately, the EPA chose a path forward that actually exacerbates this problem, expanding both its own power and its discretion through the use of guidance. As *Western Farm Press* put it: "The legislation died and EPA now is seeking to address the issue in guidance documents."[11]

The EPA leaked draft guidance in December 2010 that stated explicitly that the goal was to dramatically expand federal jurisdiction:

> This guidance clarifies and refines the agencies' interpretation of the "significant nexus" standard many waterbodies must meet to be jurisdictional under the CWA that is more consistent with Justice Kennedy's

opinion and the science of aquatic ecosystems. The guidance also addresses how to determine the jurisdictional status of waters not addressed by the previous guidance (for example, interstate waters). Therefore, the agencies expect that the number of waters found to be subject to CWA jurisdiction will increase significantly compared to practices under the 2003 *SWANCC* guidance and the 2008 *Rapanos* guidance.[12]

The EPA and the Army Corps were asserting the power to judge—on a case-by-case basis—whether just about any drop of moisture on your property combines with any other waters in any way that affects waters under its jurisdiction. In other words, *almost* anything goes. I say *almost* because there is at least acquiescence to the Supreme Court on the issue of migratory birds, about which EPA's draft guidance said: "Consideration of use by migratory species is not relevant to the significant nexus determination."

Relying on guidance documents is even worse than regulators pushing the envelope of their powers with rulemakings. As Jonathan Adler observed:

> If the Obama administration is going to assert excessive authority, the industry would rather have that embodied in a clear, final action under a rule, because if the industry wanted to challenge the administration, they would have this final act to challenge.[13]

Fortunately, Congress pushed back. A bipartisan group of 170 House members, led by U.S. Rep. Bob Gibbs (R-Ohio), who defeated Zach Space (one of the many 2010 cap-and-trade casualties), wrote a stinging April 14, 2011, letter to EPA Administrator Lisa

Jackson and Assistant Secretary for the Army (Civil Works) Jo-Ellen Darcy. The letter said:

> This "Guidance" would substantively change the Agencies' policy on waters subject to jurisdiction under the Clean Water Act; undermine the regulated community's rights and obligations under the Clean Water Act; and erode the Federal-State partnership that has long existed between the States and the Federal Government in implementing the Clean Water Act. By developing this "Guidance," the Agencies have ignored calls from state agencies and environmental groups, among others, to proceed through the normal rulemaking procedures, and have avoided consulting with the States, which are the Agencies' partners in implementing the Clean Water Act.
>
> The Agencies cannot, through guidance, change the scope and meaning of the Clean Water Act or the statute's implementing regulations. If the Administration seeks statutory changes to the Clean Water Act, a proposal must be submitted to Congress for legislative action. If the Administration seeks to make regulatory changes, a notice and comment rulemaking is required.[14]

Among the letter's signatories were Oberstar's two successors: the man who took his seat in Congress, Cravaack, and the man who took his gavel as the chairman of the Transportation and Infrastructure Committee, John Mica (R-Fla.). Mica said:

> This massive federal jurisdiction grab has failed to pass in previous Congresses, and now the EPA and the Administration are attempting to achieve the

same economically stifling results by ignoring the proper rulemaking process.[15]

The letter from 170 members of Congress had an impact. When the EPA and the Army Corps published their draft wetlands guidance in the *Federal Register* on May 2, 2011, the language about "jurisdiction will increase significantly" was removed and the document was generally toned down. They also promised to follow the guidance with rulemaking.[16]

Nonetheless, the basic threat remains. The EPA and the Army Corps want to do through guidance or rulemaking what Oberstar ended his career trying and failing to get through Congress. The initial push back from the new Congress bought some time and forced the EPA and the Army Corps to at least use regulations, rather than guidance documents, for some of their power grab. Congress must now go further and pass legislation to strictly limit federal authority to legitimate interstate commerce, as the Constitution requires.

## 'WILD LANDS'—WILDERNESS AREAS WITHOUT CONGRESS

After the 2010 election the Democrats launched a last-ditch attempt to pass a massive omnibus public lands bill, dubbed "a Frankenstein" by House Natural Resources Committee Chairman Doc Hastings.[17] The bill, among other outrages, would have locked up more than 2 million acres in new wilderness area—on top of the biggest federal land grab in history, enacted in 2009 via the omnibus lands bill. These massive expansions of federal control are, as R.J. Smith of the Competitive Enterprise Institute has eloquently argued, undermining the American dream:

America has undergone a massive period of galloping government land acquisition with essentially no oversight or accounting whatsoever. Every time any level of government takes more land, there is less for the use of a free and productive society, less for use in producing the food, fiber, minerals, and energy, less for private ownership, private conservation, and pursuing the American dream.

American taxpayers have a right to know how much land that the government owns—and we should demand a clear accounting. The most careful accounting by various organizations suggests that governments now own approximately 50% of all the land in the nation.[18]

Smith went on to discuss the severe restriction placed on land given a wilderness designation:

Another area of concern is the ever-growing amount of American land being locked up in wilderness areas in the National Wilderness System. While these lands are predominantly government lands, they are incorporated into a federal regulatory system which prohibits all exploration for and development of natural resources, minerals, or energy resources. There is no oil and gas exploration or development, no access to minerals, no timber harvest.

All mechanized and motorized equipment is prohibited from use in Wilderness, including bicycles, chainsaws to clear trails after storms or fires and helicopter landings to rescue injured hikers.

Currently, the total acreage in federally designated wilderness areas is 107,514,938 acres. That is larger than the entire state of California plus the states of New Jersey, Delaware, and Rhode Island, and the District of Columbia.[19]

Fortunately, the 2010 omnibus lands bill was stopped cold by the same grassroots mobilization that stopped most of the rest of the Democrats' lame-duck agenda. So the good guys won, right? Wrong.

On December 23, 2010, just days after the omnibus lands bill collapsed, Salazar announced Secretarial Order 3310, which "directs the Bureau of Land Management (BLM), based on the input of the public and local communities through its existing land management planning process, to designate appropriate areas with wilderness characteristics under its jurisdiction as 'Wild Lands' and to manage them to protect their wilderness values."[20]

The new category of "Wild Lands" has no statutory basis and seems to be a new term that could accurately be described as "Wilderness Areas without Congressional Approval," an unprecedented power grab in which the secretary of the Interior intends to arbitrarily assert that federal lands beyond the already astonishing 109 million acres designated as wilderness should—on his sole authority—be closed to energy and mineral development, vehicles, and any other human activity that he deems a threat to the "wilderness characteristics" of the "Wild Lands."

Moreover, the term "wilderness characteristics" is frightening and indeterminately broad. "Wilderness" is defined by the Wilderness Act of 1964 as an "area of undeveloped Federal land retaining its primeval character and influence," but wilderness *characteristics*? It would seem the whole world has some of the *characteristics* of wilderness. The potential for abuse under this new concept is nearly unlimited. Almost all federal lands could potentially be locked up as "Wild Lands."

The environmental left's obsession with locking up ever larger expanses of land under government ownership and strict "wilderness" controls stems from a false religion that worships the creation, rather than the Creator. It is a view at odds with the way most Americans view the stewardship relationship between human beings and the natural world.

As Alston Chase observed, the philosophy of radical environmentalism rejects the conventional stewardship view. He wrote:

> In the environmentalists' scheme of things, however, man can stand apart from nature, and when he does he often commits the worst sin of all, the sin the ancient Greeks called *hubris*—usurping the role of God. By playing God he stands apart and thereby does evil. Yet they also seemed to suggest that human beings *should* stand apart from nature as well. For the ethic of protectionism was nothing more than *protecting nature from man.*
>
> Human beings, according to this growing idea, could do nothing right. They were damned if they did stand apart, and damned if they didn't. On the one hand we were all part of an indivisible, sacred reality. On the other hand, we must be kept away from nature. Rather than pantheism, therefore, the new environmental perspective was something else; in fact, it was hopelessly confused.[21]

Chase got it exactly right. The environmental extremists are conflicted in their core beliefs, and seem to agree only that human beings are a malevolent force that must be constrained and from which nature—the wilderness—must be protected.

Unfortunately, the tragic consequences of those views are on full display and should be deeply disturbing to Americans who still believe we have a duty to exercise good stewardship. The nine-to-five government workers who manage vast expanses of federal land will simply never take care of them as effectively as the 24-hours-a-day owners who have a property interest in managing their lands. Experience has borne this out, according to researchers at the Property & Environment Research Center:

Federal land management has largely resulted in poor stewardship of America's most treasured natural areas. Maintenance, in particular, has been dismal. The Forest Service estimates a backlog of $5 billion in deferred maintenance projects and the National Park Service has a backlog of more than $10 billion. The outcome is overflowing sewer systems, failing roads and ruined cultural resources... Consider the millions of acres of wildfire-prone forests that span the West. Decades of fire suppression and restrictions on logging have created unnaturally dense forests prone to catastrophic wildfires.[22]

Federal land management agencies have too much land already and are incompetent to manage it. But whenever they get more money they use it to acquire more land, not to deal with their disastrous failure to protect the lands they have. We should be selling federal lands, not subjecting them to greater restrictions.

Fortunately, Congress has successfully pressed pause, if not stop, on the Wild Lands secretarial order. It was included on page 304 of the budget compromise House Republicans negotiated with the White House to avoid a government shutdown in April 2011. That compromise was disputed among conservatives who disagreed on whether it cut spending enough, but everyone who believes in economic freedom should credit the Republican leadership for a hugely significant victory on Wild Lands.

The language was included at the behest of U.S. Rep. Mike Simpson (R-Idaho), who chairs the House Appropriations Subcommittee on Interior, Environment, and Related Agencies, which oversees funding for the Department of the Interior. During the tense negotiations over the bill, Simpson said: "The Department has overstepped its authority. Only Congress has the authority to create new land designations, and I intend to restore that authority by including this provision."[23]

He succeeded, which is powerful evidence that an engaged Congress and public pressure can successfully stop an Obama administration regulatory power grab. The compromise spending bill, however, will expire at the end of the fiscal year, September 30, 2011. That means starting in October, the Wild Lands policy can move forward unless Congress extends the prohibition. We must build on this success by demanding Congress permanently block Salazar's Wild Lands land grab.

# THE LEFT'S DESIRE TO STOP ALL ENERGY ACCESS

The religious antihuman environmental fervor reaches its peak intensity in opposition to energy development—regardless of the type of energy source. The U.S. Chamber of Commerce, for instance, has catalogued hundreds of environmental lawsuits not only against fossil fuel development but also against wind and solar power.[24] In the environmentalist classic *The Arrogance of Humanism*, David Ehrenfeld explained the extreme antipathy toward energy from the antidevelopment perspective:

> If a source of power is to be called "clean," that judgment can only be made if all the consequences and effects of the power have been traced—from the time of its generation to the time the last kilowatt has been dissipated as irrecoverable heat...
>
> It will be used to manufacture more snowmobiles, which will destroy more of the winter vegetation of the north...It will be used to make more laser bombs and surface-to-surface missiles and Rome plows and anti-crop defoliants. It will be used to provide more electric outdoor billboards, which will help accelerate the destruction of the meaning

of language. It will power the pumps of tube wells in the world's dry grasslands, thus permitting more cattle to be grazed, and more deserts to be formed... It will be used to produce more synthetic nitrogen fertilizer... The adjective "clean" cannot be applied to such a train of consequences.[25]

And indeed the impulse to shut down all of the supposedly harmful activities of modern civilization by shutting off access to energy has been one of the driving forces of this administration, as we discussed in the global warming context and the offshore drilling context. It has been very much the same story onshore.

Shortly after taking office, Salazar canceled land leases for energy development on 77 parcels of land in Utah.[26] Then he canceled a pending oil-shale lease sale based on his expert judgment that it "didn't meet the smell test."[27]

Overall there has been a steep drop-off in leasing on federal lands. According to an analysis by the Western Energy Alliance, 2010 saw a 79 percent drop in leasing in Colorado, Montana, New Mexico, North Dakota, Utah, and Wyoming from 2005 levels. Total onshore royalties dropped 33 percent in just two years.[28]

The Interior Department's Office of Surface Mining Reclamation and Enforcement is pursuing tight restrictions on coal mining under a so-called "Stream Protection Rule" that the agency admits would destroy 7,000 of the country's 81,000 coal-mining jobs.[29]

The EPA has virtually shut down mountaintop removal mining in Appalachia using guidance documents. "It could mean the end of an era," said Luke Popovich of the National Mining Association. "That is tantamount to saying the intent is to strictly limit coal mining in Appalachia."[30]

One of the first tests of the Wild Lands policy (if the appropriations rider freezing it is not made permanent) will be on the North Slope of Alaska, where environmental groups are already agitating for a Wild Lands designation to block oil and gas development in, of all places, the National Petroleum Reserve Alaska. U.S. Rep. Don Young (R-Alaska) observed: "The extreme environmentalist groups couldn't get their wilderness bill past Congress and so now they are circumventing this country's legislative body and having the agencies do their dirty work."[31]

Federal agencies are using every lever at their disposal to stall, revoke, and deny permits and leases and to block access to energy resources.

## POLAR BEARS AND SPOTTED OWLS

Another land grab and energy lockup comes from abuse of the Endangered Species Act (ESA) (another assault on property rights, generally) that has been contorted into a global warming law without Congress's consent through the listing of the polar bear as threatened—despite the fact that polar bear populations are at an all-time high and rising.[32]

As a consequence, the Department of Interior officially designated 187,157 square miles (an area larger than California!) along Alaska's North Slope as critical habitat for polar bears on November 24, 2010.[33] That designation places an enormous burden on oil and gas, adding litigation and uncertainty that will stall development, imposing costs that even the U.S. Fish and Wildlife Service concedes is "too speculative to quantify."[34]

It's a tragic story we've seen before—the misuse of the ESA, using species protection as a pretext for an assault on resource use and economic development. It was the spotted owl, which in the 1980s and early 1990s was a singular obsession for green groups and the mechanism with which they stopped logging on millions of acres of old-growth forest. As a result, 30,000 Americans lost their jobs.[35]

It caused a regional economic disaster in the Pacific Northwest, where the timber industry was crippled, as the acreage under federal protection went from 690,000 in 1986 to 11.6 million in 1991.

Oregon's timber output collapsed, going from 4.9 billion board feet in 1988 to just 240 million in 2009.[36]

And the spotted owl is still disappearing, because as it turns out the threat wasn't from loggers—it was from another species of owl, the native barred owl, which is outcompeting the spotted owl.

According to *The Oregonian*, the bureaucrats at the U.S. Fish and Wildlife Service, having already put 30,000 people out of work, have a new plan to save the spotted owl: "taking to the woods with shotguns."[37] They actually plan to kill 1,200 to 1,500 barred owls in three study areas, to lessen the competition on the spotted owl. They are desperate to save the spotted owl at this point not so much because they cherish it as a species (the barred owl is a closely related species with a recent common ancestor that fills the same ecological niche) but because their real goal—shutting down the timber industry—would be imperiled if they no longer had the spotted owl as an excuse for locking up forestland.

The ESA—as we've seen in these examples and other recent high-profile disasters, like the ongoing battle between farmers and the delta smelt in California's Central Valley—is an affront to basic property rights and is readily abused as a pretext for sweeping anti-industrial, antidevelopment activism. The latest antienergy ESA abuse is an attempt to list the abundant three-inch dunes sagebrush lizard to shut down oil production in West Texas.[38]

As recently as 2005, a strong ESA reform bill that would have, among other reforms, protected property owners by giving them certainty about their land-use decisions and assuring them of just compensation for the lost value imposed by land-use restrictions, passed the House and should have passed the Senate, but was scuttled by then-Republican Sen. Lincoln Chafee of Rhode Island (now the independent governor of that state). It's an idea whose time has come again.

# THE ABUSE OF THE ANTIQUITIES ACT

Perhaps the biggest threat to energy access, and to property rights, comes from the Antiquities Act of 1906.

The law was originally signed by President Theodore Roosevelt to give the president broad authority to designate "historic landmarks, historic and prehistoric structures, and other objects of historic or scientific interest" as national monuments without going back to Congress for approval.[39] While there may be some circumstances in which that still makes sense, the power has been so badly abused that Congress needs to take some responsibility and put itself back in the decision loop regarding the creation of monuments.

The most notorious Antiquities Act abuse was on September 18, 1996, when President Bill Clinton locked up an astonishing 1.7 million acres of southern Utah as the Grand Staircase-Escalante National Monument. That unilateral action of the president locked up an estimated 62 billion tons of coal under the Kaiparowits Plateau.[40]

Former U.S. Rep. Bill Orton (D-Utah) correctly criticized the move, saying:

> The reality is, the world is going to be using coal for the next 50 or 100 years. Are we going to use the dirtiest coal in the world, creating acid rain and air pollution? Or are we going to use the cleanest-burning coal that could have been developed with the least environmental impact? That's what we're leaving in the ground on the Kaiparowits.[41]

But the bipartisan outrage was not sufficient to spur Congress to step in and undo what Clinton had done. And now Obama is poised to up the ante. U.S. Rep. Rob Bishop (R-Utah) unearthed Obama's plan to create 14 massive national monuments under the Antiquities Act, and Fox News's William La Jeunesse broke the story in February 2010.[42]

The new monuments would lock up more than 13 million acres. U.S. Rep. Denny Rehberg (R-Mont.) has uncovered the full plan and posted the Department of the Interior memo, emblazoned "Internal Draft—NOT FOR RELEASE" on his website.[43]

La Jeunesse summarized some of the most significant of Obama's rumored land grabs:

- Otero Mesa, New Mexico: The area stretches over 1.2 million acres and is home to 1,000 native species. Gov. Bill Richardson has sought protection for Otero Mesa for years, but the Bush administration targeted it for oil and gas development.

- Heart of the Great Basin, Nevada: Researchers call it a "globally unique assemblage of cultural, wildlife and historic values" that includes thousands of petroglyphs and stone artifacts dating back 12,000 years.

- Owyhee Desert, Oregon: Called one of the most remote areas of the United States, the Owyhee is home to the largest herd of California bighorn sheep.

- Bodie Hills, California: Located in the fast growing eastern Sierra Nevada mountains, Bodie contains the Golden State's best preserved ghost town. But the area is also loaded with gold, and several mining permits are pending.

- The Modoc Plateau, California: Spanning close to 3 million acres in the northwest corner of California, the Modoc Plateau is "laden with biological and archeological treasures." Interior officials call it the second largest unprotected landscape in the state.[44]

These sites and the others rumored also have tremendous oil, gas, coal, and mineral resources. As Bishop said, "Outrage. In a country as dependent on foreign oil as this one, this kind of action on public lands is simply unacceptable."[45]

Clearly, Clinton raised the expectations of the environmental groups with Grand Staircase-Escalante and there is nothing in the extreme record of Obama and Salazar to suggest they won't push even more. Bruce Babbitt, who was Clinton's Interior secretary, explained that he convinced Clinton to pursue his final frantic land lockups to surpass Teddy Roosevelt's total acreage. "It all came down to one word," Babbitt wrote: "legacy."[46]

The Antiquities Act is—in the hands of a man like Barack Obama who is intent on accomplishing his goals by any available means—a frightening public policy weapon. We have to take very seriously the possibility that he may create all 14 of the rumored monuments. He may, like Clinton, see it as his legacy.

Unfortunately, even the Republican-controlled House has already failed one test of stopping the Antiquities Act. On February 19, 2011, an amendment offered by then-U.S. Rep. Dean Heller (R-Nev.)[47] that would have barred funding for the creation of any new monuments under the act failed on a vote of 209 to 213.[48] There were 34 Republicans who joined 179 Democrats in voting "no." Only five Democrats voted "yes." That 34 Republicans in the House believe Obama should have the unilateral power to create vast monuments that lock up land and block energy development means we have a huge amount of work to do in this area.

> ▶ ▶ ▶
>
> *The Antiquities Act is—in the hands of a man like Barack Obama who is intent on accomplishing his goals by any available means—a frightening public policy weapon.*

One potentially promising approach is a compromise bill offered by U.S. Rep. Devin Nunes (R-Calif.) and U.S. Sen. Mike Crapo (R-Idaho) that would require Congress to approve any new monuments within two years of their designation. If Congress does not approve the monuments, the lands would revert to their previous status. It's a step in the right direction, but the Antiquities Act is an antiquity itself, and it should be repealed. Federal land grabs should at least require a vote of Congress.

# FIGHTING BACK:
# THE PROPERTY RIGHTS MOVEMENT
# AND THE TEA PARTIES MUST UNITE

The issues in this chapter are challenging ones for me as a lifelong East Coaster because I don't live them daily the way people do in the West and in rural America. (I hope rural readers will give me some leeway for any errors or omissions for that reason.) But federal land and water policies are the bluntest and cruelest instruments of big government exercising control over people's lives and property, not in a theoretical or abstract sense but in the most practical way possible—they physically prevent people from enjoying the fruits of their labor.

The property rights movement has long been one of the major social movements in this country, and has often flexed its political muscles. Where it has successfully fused with the tea party movement—Oberstar's defeat being the most prominent example—the results have been explosive. We must foster more of that collaboration. We must join forces between the tea party activists who entered the fray over the past few years and the longtime warriors for private property rights who have long been fighting a federal government that is, for landowners, outrageously intrusive.

As the Cato Institute's great constitutional scholar Roger Pilon wrote:

> The Founders would be appalled to see what we did to property rights over the course of the 20th century. One would never know that their status, in the Bill of Rights, was equal to that of any other right.

The time has come to restore respect for these most basic of rights, the foundation of all of our rights. Indeed, despotic governments have long understood that if you control property, you control the media, the churches, the political process itself. We are not at that point yet. But if regulations that provide the public with benefits continue to grow, unchecked by the need to compensate those from whom they take, we will gradually slide to that point—and in the process will pay an increasingly heavy price for the uncertainty and inefficiency we create.[49]

We must be unified in pressing for action on these issues because fundamental American principles are at stake. But our prosperity is also at stake. When the federal government locks up vast expanses of land, it locks up resources, including energy. That forces prices higher and hits every consumer. That's another angle from which we can create political pressure on urban members of Congress who think federal land grabs are a free vote they can give to the environmental left. We must create political downsides based on the principles involved, as well as the enormous economic consequences.

The American people voted for smaller, less expensive, less intrusive federal government in the 2010 election. We cannot allow the bureaucratic machinery of the EPA, the Interior Department, and other federal land-management agencies to expand government's reach. We cannot allow the secretary of the Interior to create wilderness areas by dictate.

The failed vote to stop abuse of the Antiquities Act is an opportunity to flex the muscles of a property rights-tea party alliance. We should try to convince the 34 Republicans—and a fair number of Democrats—that they made a mistake voting against stopping Obama's land grabs. We need to go further and demand Congress

permanently stop the Wild Lands secretarial order, the EPA's wetlands guidance, and all the rest of the Obama administration's outrageous land lockups. And we need to persuade them to act as soon
as possible—before more of our land, and freedom, is gone.

## CHAPTER 9

# The Back Door to the Back Door: Phony Regulatory Reform

*"In what sense is the money in our pockets and bank accounts fully 'ours'? Did we earn it by our own autonomous efforts? Could we have inherited it without the assistance of probate courts? Do we save it without support from bank regulators? Could we spend it (say, on the installment plan) if there were no public officials to coordinate the efforts and pool the resources of the community in which we live?"[1]*

—CASS R. SUNSTEIN, Administrator of the White House Office of Information and Regulatory Affairs

P resident Obama knows he's politically vulnerable on regulation. He knows that if the public understands that his extreme left-wing agenda has not slowed down at all but merely shifted inside the agencies and departments that he will be unable to reinvent himself as a centrist for the 2012 campaign. So in January 2011 he took to the pages of *The Wall Street Journal* to announce a new executive order calling for a comprehensive review of federal regulations. He wrote:

> We're looking at the system as a whole to make sure we avoid excessive, inconsistent and redundant regulation. And finally, today I am directing federal agencies to do more to account for—and reduce— the burdens regulations may place on small businesses. Small firms drive growth and create most new jobs in this country. We need to make sure nothing stands in their way.[2]

It would be wonderful news if it could be believed, but it can't. U.S. Sen. Rand Paul accurately described what Obama was doing: "He senses what the public wants. And it's a little bit *Nineteen Eighty-Four*-ish. He'll tell you he agrees with you, while at the same time doing the exact opposite. So, a lot of big words and high-flowing rhetoric, but not a lot of substance."[3]

In light of the astonishing regulatory agenda described in the preceding chapters, the idea of Obama being a regulatory reformer is, depending on your disposition, somewhere between farce and tragedy. Remarkably, Obama pointed to perhaps the single most corrupt regulatory power grab of his administration to date—the "put nothing in writing ever" secret car-rule shakedown discussed in Chapter 2—as his model of good regulation that should be followed throughout the government.

▶ ▶ ▶

*"[Obama] senses what the public wants. And it's a little bit* Nineteen Eighty-Four-*ish. He'll tell you he agrees with you, while at the same time doing the exact opposite. So, a lot of big words and high-flowing rhetoric, but not a lot of substance."*

—U.S. Sen. RAND PAUL

Not only is the regulatory review's objective undermined by the administration's extreme regulatory agenda moving full-steam ahead, but it is, on its own terms, a recipe not for less expensive and more accountable regulation but for more *effective* regulation. Given that the objectives of this administration are redistribution of wealth and centralized economic control, moving more effectively in that direction would simply speed up our trip down the road to ruin.

Moreover, the review will be conducted through the White House's Office of Information and Regulatory Affairs (OIRA), whose administrator is Cass Sunstein—a prolific writer and thinker who has a distinctly paternalistic view of the relationship between government and the people.

From his perch at OIRA, Sunstein is already able to review and shape many federal regulations before they become final. Obama's regulatory review empowers Sunstein further, which means his extremism must be subject to even greater scrutiny. Glenn Beck has dubbed him "the most dangerous man in America."

Finally, Obama's review—which he has initiated by executive order, rather than by calling on Congress to pass legislation—is limited to executive branch agencies. So-called independent agencies, which would require congressional action to review, are completely exempt. Those independent agencies, among others, include the National Labor Relations Board (NLRB), the Federal Communications Commission (FCC), the Federal Trade Commission (FTC), the Federal Reserve Bank—including its new Consumer Financial Protection Bureau (CFPB)—the Securities and Exchange Commission (SEC), the Commodity Futures Trading Corporation (CFTC), and the Federal Deposit Insurance Corporation (FDIC).

Most of the very agencies most aggressively implementing Obama's regulatory power grabs get a pass.

In short, Obama has found a way to craft a "regulatory review" that allows him to politically posture as a moderate on regulation, while greasing the path for his extreme regulatory agenda to move even more swiftly and effectively toward control of our economic lives.

# OBAMA'S BIG FAKE MOVE TO THE CENTER

As noted earlier, in January 2011, Obama wrote an op-ed for *The Wall Street Journal* that launched a new charm offensive with the business community. It was titled: "Toward a 21st-Century Regulatory System," with the subtitle: "If the FDA deems saccharin safe enough for coffee, then the EPA should not treat it as hazardous waste." A reasonable point, but one that begged the question of why that same logic didn't apply to carbon dioxide—safe enough to carbonate soft drinks—but now subject to the sweeping EPA global warming regulations the administration is zealously pursuing.

The first paragraph was a paean to free-market capitalism:

> For two centuries, America's free market has not only been the source of dazzling ideas and path-breaking products, it has also been the greatest force for prosperity the world has ever known. That vibrant entrepreneurialism is the key to our continued global leadership and the success of our people.[4]

He got that exactly right, but as the agenda detailed in this book shows, his actions have undermined basic American free-market principles. Speaking directly to America's business leaders, Obama was telling them what they wanted to hear. But a deeper reading showed that Obama was not really promising a change of direction but rather offering a defense of his existing regulatory approach—including all of the ongoing power grabs and regulatory back doors to his failed legislative objectives. He wrote:

> Over the past two years, the goal of my administration has been to strike the right balance. And today, I am signing an executive order that makes clear that this is the operating principle of our government.[5]

In other words, he was merely codifying existing policy. Everything would continue. Consider the example he used of a balanced, pro-business regulatory approach:

> One important example of this overall approach is the fuel-economy standards for cars and trucks. When I took office, the country faced years of litigation and confusion because of conflicting rules set by Congress, federal regulators and states. The EPA and the Department of Transportation worked with auto makers, labor unions, states like California, and environmental advocates this past spring to turn a tangle of rules into one aggressive new standard.[6]

Those fuel-economy standards were the first time the 1970 Clean Air Act was twisted into becoming a global warming law, opening the door to the full regulatory cascade discussed in Chapter 2. It was also accomplished by the infamous, backroom, "put nothing in writing" shakedown described in that chapter. The litigation and confusion Obama referred to was created by his own administration's policy choice to provide California with a waiver to adopt its own emissions standards, in turn creating a very real fear that other states would follow suit and that the auto industry would be crippled by overlapping and conflicting state and federal standards. Having engineered the threat, the Obama administration then—in secret—coerced the industry into accepting an expensive new regulation that will make cars less affordable and less safe by reducing vehicle weight. And regulators were emboldened to begin ratcheting up regulatory requirements to 62 mpg, starting another shakedown, with the same risk of California and other states adopting their own standards still hanging over the heads of the auto industry.

Not only was the car rule corrupt, it was also probably illegal. As U.S. Reps. Darrell Issa (R-Calif.) and James Sensenbrenner (R-Wis.) noted:

> This coordinated effort, led by Carol Browner, to leave no paper trail of the deliberations within the White House appears to be a deliberate and willful violation of the Presidential Records Act. This Act requires the President to take, "all such steps as may be necessary to assure that the activities, deliberations, decisions, and policies that reflect the performance of his constitutional, statutory, or other official or ceremonial duties are adequately documented and that such records are maintained as Presidential records." Clearly, Browner's actions were intended to leave little to no documentation of the deliberations that lead to the development of stringent new CAFE standards.[7]

Now Obama's regulatory review proposal—positioned as a pro-business move to the center—was touting as a model the single worst abuse of the regulatory process that had occurred in his administration. While the president was rhetorically shifting to the center, the clear signal to his key left-wing constituencies—the greens, the unions, and the hard-left community organizers—was that nothing had changed.

The EPA didn't even play along with the charade, saying on the day of Obama's *Wall Street Journal* piece: "EPA is confident that our recent and upcoming steps to address greenhouse gas emissions under the Clean Air Act comfortably pass muster under the sensible standards the president has laid out."[8]

The FCC and FTC were, as independent agencies, exempt. So their net neutrality efforts could proceed without review. The NLRB, also an independent agency, is exempt and free to continue pursuing its backdoor card-check agenda without additional scrutiny. The various entities at the heart of Dodd-Frank—the Fed, the SEC, CFTC, CFPB, and FDIC—are also independent agencies exempt from the review.

The regulatory power grabs were full-steam ahead. Perhaps they would be dressed up in business-friendly language, paying lip service to the benefits of free-market capitalism, but the bareknuckled, backroom, extralegal shakedown was ratified as the model moving forward.

Obama is also, of course, rolling out the two biggest expansions in federal regulatory power in a generation—both encompassing hundreds of rulemakings and vast arrays of brand-new bureaucracies. In a speech to the U.S. Chamber of Commerce that was meant to be part of his new centrist charm offensive, Obama underscored that the extremely costly regulatory burdens emanating from ObamaCare and Dodd-Frank are his new, "good" kind of regulation, saying:

> I also have to point out the perils of too much regulation are also matched by the dangers of too little. And we saw that in the financial crisis, where the absence of sound rules of the road, that wasn't good for business. Even if you weren't in the financial sector it wasn't good for business. And that's why, with the help of Paul Volcker, who is here today, we passed a set of common-sense reforms.
>
> The same can be said of health insurance reform. We simply could not continue to accept a status quo that's made our entire economy less competitive, as we've paid more per person for health care than any other nation on Earth. Nobody is even close. And we couldn't accept a broken system where insurance companies could drop people because they got

sick, or families went into bankruptcy because of medical bills.[9]

The clear takeaway was that the 2010 election would force Obama to moderate his rhetoric only somewhat—and his actions not at all.

# A MEANINGLESS EXECUTIVE ORDER— OR WORSE

The regulatory review Obama promised in *The Wall Street Journal* was embodied in Executive Order 13563, "Improving Regulation and Regulatory Review,"[10] posted the same day as the op-ed piece.

As Andrew Langer of the Institute for Liberty has pointed out to me, the executive order actually has no more teeth than *The Wall Street Journal* op-ed, which is to say, none. As Wayne Crews of the Competitive Enterprise Institute observed:

> This executive order is hardly a war on red tape, and no affected businesses or consumers are going to be able to sue anybody to force compliance—it's just an "order" to agencies to behave. And, as my colleague Gregory Conko points out, it should be noted that there is already an Executive Order in effect that does what President Obama says this one will do. Both balancing safety against economic growth and requiring a review of existing rules are features of President Clinton's EO 12866, which Obama reaffirmed when repealing Bush's EOs 13258 and 13422.[11]

Indeed the text of the new Obama executive order reaffirms the previous executive order. If the administration were genuinely concerned with reducing the federal regulatory burden, the tools already existed for it to do so. Instead, it is overseeing an unprecedented onslaught of new red tape.

The new executive order is the regulatory parallel to the Obama administration's strategy on federal spending, which is to spend at astonishing, record rates and rack up trillions of dollars in deficits while paying lip service to fiscal responsibility by establishing a fiscal commission. (In an all-too-familiar pattern, by the way, that fiscal commission was established by executive order after the Senate rejected creating it legislatively, for fear that it would propose massive tax hikes, which it did.) The commission report was dead on arrival, but Obama was able to use it as a political tool to create the appearance that he was doing something about spending.

Similarly, his regulatory review will make recommendations that will be largely dead on arrival, while he continues to pursue an agenda that makes the problem of excessive regulation much worse. To the extent the regulatory review results in anything, it may actually *exacerbate* the country's regulatory problems by helping the administration find ways to accomplish its radical objectives of central economic control more effectively.

There are two individuals who loom large in the regulatory review process and suggest it may, despite its stated intentions, well be used as a cover for larger and more intrusive government: John Holdren and Cass Sunstein. Holdren—the extreme antienergy zealot discussed in Chapter 7—is in charge of making sure that executive agency heads "ensure the objectivity of any scientific and technological information and processes used to support the agency's regulatory actions."[12]

Sunstein plays an even larger role as the White House's top regulatory staffer. The regulatory review executive order explains OIRA's role this way:

> Within 120 days of the date of this order, each
> agency shall develop and submit to the Office of

Information and Regulatory Affairs a preliminary plan, consistent with law and its resources and regulatory priorities, under which the agency will periodically review its existing significant regulations to determine whether any such regulations should be modified, streamlined, expanded, or repealed so as to make the agency's regulatory program more effective or less burdensome in achieving the regulatory objectives.[13]

Think about that. OIRA is reviewing a plan from each executive agency not just to reduce regulatory burdens, but to make the thousands of regulations that already overburden American businesses, consumers, and families "more effective." That could prove a very dangerous mandate if the person put in charge of implementing it wants regulations to be "more effective" at achieving very destructive ends. Unfortunately, in Sunstein, we have such a person.

## CASS SUNSTEIN, OBAMA'S REGULATOR IN CHIEF

Cass Sunstein has a formidable pedigree. After receiving his law degree from Harvard, he clerked for Supreme Court Justice Thurgood Marshall and then served in the Justice Department in the Carter administration before moving to the University of Chicago Law School, where he remained for decades as a leading legal theorist and scholar. He moved to Harvard Law School in 2008 but took a leave of absence shortly thereafter to serve as Obama's OIRA administrator.

OIRA has a central role in the regulatory process, serving as the administration's official eyes and ears on all regulatory proposals moving through the agencies and executive departments. That role is now, under Obama's regulatory review plan, expanded to overseeing new review processes for all existing executive branch regulations to make them "more effective."

So it's crucial to understand how Sunstein views the purposes of federal regulation toward which he is tasked with increasing effectiveness. And there are many insights into how he thinks in his wide-ranging, freewheeling body of academic and popular writing. Let's start with his view of private property, which comes close to rejecting its very existence. In a celebration of April 15 and the joy of paying taxes, Sunstein wrote:

> In what sense is the money in our pockets and bank accounts fully "ours"? Did we earn it by our own autonomous efforts? Could we have inherited it without the assistance of probate courts? Do we save it without support from bank regulators? Could we spend it (say, on the installment plan) if there were no public officials to coordinate the efforts and pool the resources of the community in which we live?[14]

So what's ours is not ours. What's ours is everyone's—or the government's—to redirect consistent with the social purposes of the regulations he is now overseeing. Without those wonderful bank regulators, we would all have nothing. Right.

More recently, Sunstein has developed a theory of the role of government regulation that he calls "libertarian paternalism," an obvious contradiction in terms that he tried to defend in a May 2003 paper. The abstract summarized the view as follows:

> Equipped with an understanding of behavioral findings of bounded rationality and bounded self-control, libertarian paternalists should attempt to steer people's choices in welfare-promoting directions without eliminating freedom of choice. It is also possible to show how a libertarian paternalist

might select among the possible options and to as-
sess how much choice to offer. Examples are given
from many areas, including savings behavior, labor
law, and consumer protection.[15]

Sunstein and his coauthor, Richard Thaler, further developed
this concept in the book *Nudge*. The radical environmentalist website *Grist* prefaced an interview with Sunstein about "green nudges"
this way: "With Sunstein in the role of President Obama's 'regulation
czar,' Americans should prepare to get nudged."[16] In the interview,
Sunstein said:

> I think on a lot of problems, including environmen-
> tal problems, we can make progress without getting
> stuck on issues that divide people. The price system
> can be used in a way that fits with people's moral
> obligations. If you're inflicting harms on other peo-
> ple but the costs of your actions (become) higher,
> then you're probably going to inflict lower harms on
> other people. One of the great tasks of the next de-
> cade is to ensure that when people are creating risks
> through their daily activities, that they bear the cost.
>
> I believe also that one big motivator of behav-
> ior is economic and another big motivator is moral,
> and for certain environmental activities we should
> appeal to people's conscience. A lot of people are
> buying hybrids not because they save money, which
> they might, but because it's the right thing to do. I
> just bought a hybrid myself. The reason I bought it
> was moral.[17]

This man is now charged with reviewing the EPA's regulations
to make them "more effective." But more effective to him may well
mean an embrace of the 62 mpg mandate the administration is pro-

posing as a way to "nudge" us into hybrids. It may mean more creative ways to force the cap-and-trade concept through regulatory back doors. It almost certainly will not mean an overall reduction in regulatory burden, as Obama's rhetoric promised. Sunstein, after all, sees this as a moral obligation.

It's the same story in the other high-stakes regulatory areas he is likely to review. Consider his proposed government response to "conspiracy theories," which amounts to something like a propaganda ministry:

> What can government do about conspiracy theories? Among the things it can do, what should it do? We can readily imagine a series of possible responses. (1) Government might ban conspiracy theorizing. (2) Government might impose some kind of tax, financial or otherwise, on those who disseminate such theories. (3) Government might itself engage in counterspeech, marshaling arguments to discredit conspiracy theories. (4) Government might formally hire credible private parties to engage in counterspeech. (5) Government might engage in informal communication with such parties, encouraging them to help. Each instrument has a distinctive set of potential effects, or costs and benefits, and each will have a place under imaginable conditions. However, our main policy idea is that government should engage in *cognitive infiltration of the groups that produce conspiracy theories*, which involves a mix of (3), (4) and (5).[18]

A form of this tactic was actually used during the ObamaCare debate, when MIT economist Jonathan Gruber was hired as a consultant for the administration, a fact that was not disclosed to the public when he was deployed to discredit "conspiracy theories" about the costs of the bill.[19] That tactic will likely continue to be employed as Sunstein reviews the wide array of new regulations that will come down under ObamaCare.

In a 2001 interview, Sunstein called for something very close to a Fairness Doctrine for the Internet, saying:

> The sites of one point of view agree to provide links to other sites, so that if you're reading a conservative magazine, they would provide a link to a liberal site. And vice versa, just to make it easy for people to access to competing views. Or maybe a popup on your screen that would show an advertisement or maybe even a quick argument for a competing view. If we could get voluntary arrangements in that direction, it would be great and if we can't get voluntary arrangements, maybe Congress should hold hearings about mandates.[20]

▶ ▶ ▶

*A form of this tactic was actually used during the ObamaCare debate, when MIT economist Jonathan Gruber was hired as a consultant for the administration, a fact that was not disclosed to the public when he was deployed to discredit "conspiracy theories" about the costs of the bill.*

While the FCC is exempt from Sunstein's review—it is still legally an independent agency, notwithstanding the close relationship between Chairman Julius Genachowski and the president—Sunstein is a close adviser to the president and his views likely hold sway beyond his formal responsibilities.

Consider Sunstein's more recent proposal for Internet censorship, from a book he wrote that was released after he joined the Obama administration:

On the Internet, in particular, people might have a right to "notice and take down." Under this approach, modeled on the copyright provisions of the Digital Millennium Copyright Act, those who run websites would be obliged to take down falsehood upon notice.[21]

And Sunstein's support for restricting speech goes beyond "falsehoods" (to be judged by whom?) to the more radical agenda of the Free Press crowd discussed in Chapter 3. Sunstein embraces the idea that government should step in and regulate the media to "free us" from corporate control. Accordingly, he wrote:

A legislative effort to regulate broadcasting in the interest of democratic principles should not be seen as an abridgement of the free speech guarantee. On the contrary, such an effort would respond to the powerful threats to democratic principles that come from the current marketplace for speech.[22]

Fortunately, his proposal to regulate political speech is a legislative one (although Obama has reportedly considered implementing a version of it by executive order[23]) that would, I hope, be dead on arrival in the Republican-controlled House. But it certainly suggests he will take a questionable view of any free-speech issues that might be implicated by the regulations he reviews.

The idea of Sunstein's "nudge" philosophy is that the fatal conceit of central economic planning can somehow succeed if it is subtly hidden from view. Sunstein thinks that if he imposes regulations that steer our choices instead of outright forcing them, he can achieve desirable social objectives. But this suffers from the same knowledge problem that makes socialism untenable, albeit on a smaller scale— the central planner cannot have all of the knowledge necessary to know in what direction individual choices should be steered.

Sunstein's view of the Constitution will not be a meaning-ful constraint on regulation. During the confirmation debate over Samuel Alito to the Supreme Court, he took this derisive view of the idea that the Constitution means what it says:

> Some conservative legal thinkers like Justice Scalia and Justice Thomas think that the Constitution means what it originally meant. That means we should understand the document by going into a kind of "Time Machine" and capturing the public understanding of the public that ratified the document a century, or more than a century, ago.[24]

Given Sunstein's views and the central role he will have in re-shaping federal regulation to be "more effective," we need to be deeply concerned that any changes that come out of the process may make regulation less apparent but no less costly—and more ef-fective at crushing genuine individual choice and responsibility and substituting the judgment (even if by a nudge instead of a shove) of a central planner.

## CALLING OBAMA'S BLUFF

While Obama's regulatory review effort, as such, is likely to be ei-ther ineffective or, under Sunstein's guidance, highly destructive, it does create a genuine opportunity to focus attention on regulatory compliance costs and the need for real reform. While Obama was trying to inoculate himself against the political consequences of his astonishing regulatory agenda, he conceded that we have far too much regulation already, and that it is far too costly.

That means we now have a broad consensus that federal regula-tions need to be reviewed and reduced. As I wrote in *The Washington Times* in immediate reaction to the Obama proposal:

If President Obama is serious about regulatory reform, he should immediately end all efforts to use regulatory back doors to achieve failed elements of his legislative agenda. He should go further and issue an executive order calling for a moratorium on all new federal regulations until his review of existing regulations is complete and the compliance burden has been cut at least in half from its present level of $1.75 trillion.[25]

Of course, he wasn't serious about regulatory reform, and no such regulatory time-out or commitment to reducing the compliance burden was forthcoming from the White House.

By simply agreeing that overregulation is a serious problem, the White House provided an opportunity for Republicans to trumpet the severe costs of the administration's regulatory policies and get out in front demanding real reforms. Leading the effort has been U.S. Rep. Darrell Issa (R-Calif.), chairman of the House Committee on Oversight and Government Reform. Issa credited the president for recognizing the problem, saying: "The president has recognized the value in examining the regulatory barriers impeding private sector job creation," and got out in front on the push for identifying particular problematic regulations.[26]

Issa requested feedback from 171 businesses and trade associations on their regulatory challenges and launched a website at www.AmericanJobCreators.com to make it easy for businesses to engage the regulatory review process.[27] Issa had more than 200 detailed responses ready for the White House when it began its own regulatory review process. The comments specified roughly 100 regulations that businesses are hamstrung by and would like to see altered or eliminated. About half of those were environmental regulations.

Issa explained that his "effort is meant to complement what the president has ordered and should be a starting point for the broader discussion that will unfold about the regulatory barriers to job creation."[28]

House Republicans are shrewdly taking seriously a process that was intended to be political and forcing a discussion of real actions to reduce out-of-control regulations. The White House is therefore potentially in a position of defending its indefensible regulatory agenda, rather than being able to use the sham review process to inoculate itself to the political charge of overregulation while proceeding anyway.

We need to drive that conversation forward and demand that Obama follow through on his promise to reduce regulatory burdens, or face political consequences for a failure to do so. He has put himself to the test. We also need to demand that Congress move forward with its own regulatory process reforms.

# FIGHTING BACK: REAL REGULATORY REFORM

Real reform to the regulatory process will require legislation. The most significant regulatory reform proposal before Congress is the REINS Act, which must be our top priority. But both before and after the REINS Act passes, there are many other aspects of the regulatory process that need to be reformed to get the $1.75 trillion and growing federal regulatory burden under control.

So we must seize on the opportunity presented by Obama's gambit to push for genuine reforms in Congress. We may never again have a time where the leadership of both parties so clearly agree regulatory burdens must be reduced. This creates a real opportunity.

How about that regulatory time-out? If we all, supposedly including the president, agree that federal regulations are already too numerous and too expensive, why don't we take a time-out from all new regulations until after we can significantly reduce the burdens of existing regulations? Obama cannot have this both ways. If it's crucial that the agency agendas outlined in this book move forward, and it's also true that we have too much regulation already, then he should propose massive deregulation of many other sectors. Clearly he has not done so. A time-out would demand that real regulatory review and reform take place before the massive new pending regulations could take effect.

▶ ▶ ▶

*Codifying Obama's regulatory review in legislation would be difficult for congressional Democrats and the White House to oppose, because it could be positioned as agreeing with the administration.*

Or less ambitiously, Congress should codify the president's regulatory review process in legislation—extending it to the so-called independent agencies, creating a credible mechanism for feedback from businesses and consumers, and giving the results real teeth— rather than simply being advisory for Obama and Sunstein to twist toward their own ideological purposes. Codifying Obama's regulatory review in legislation would be difficult for congressional Democrats and the White House to oppose, because it could be positioned as agreeing with the administration.

Another idea with considerable merit is a regulatory "pay-as-you-go," or pay-go, system, championed by U.S. Sen. Mark Warner (D-Va.). Susan Dudley, who was Cass Sunstein's predecessor at OIRA, explained why she supports Warner's concept:

> His legislation "would require federal agencies to identify and eliminate one existing regulation for each new regulation they want to add." Under his "regulatory pay-go system," regulatory agencies, with oversight from the Office of Management and

Budget (OMB) and either the Congressional Budget Office (CBO) or the Government Accountability Office (GAO), would catalogue existing regulations and develop estimates of their economic impacts. Then, before issuing a new regulation, agencies would be required to eliminate one outdated or duplicative regulation of the same approximate economic impact...

By focusing on the costs of regulations and allowing agencies to set priorities and make tradeoffs among regulatory programs, it might remove some of the contentiousness surrounding benefit-cost analysis. How it would affect agencies' incentives for estimating costs is uncertain. In developing a baseline estimate of the costs of existing regulations, they may have incentives to overstate costs, particularly for regulations they may want to trade in exchange for new initiatives. Providing an entity outside of the executive branch (CBO or GAO) the resources and mandate to evaluate and critique agency estimates of regulatory costs could be critical to a regulatory pay-go's success. While it will never be possible to estimate the real social costs of regulations with any precision, a regulatory pay-go should provide incentives for agencies, affected parties, academics, Congressional entities and non-governmental organizations to improve upon the rigor of regulatory impact estimates.[29]

While this proposal wouldn't reduce the regulatory burden, it would, if the practical challenges could be overcome, stop it from expanding. Given the difficulty of actually passing reform legislation in this environment, it also raises an important question for supporters of the approach, foremost among them Warner himself: will he support Republican efforts to block the major regulatory power grabs outlined in this book, on the basis that they will not be paired with the elimination of any previous regulations?

If Warner allows these regulatory power grabs to move forward by refusing to vote to stop them, it will suggest that he, like Obama, is advancing a regulatory reform proposal more as an exercise in political outreach than for substantive reasons. Warner has expressed concerns about the REINS Act, saying that having Congress so closely involved in the regulatory process would not be good.[30] That suggests he may be unwilling to accept political responsibility for regulatory actions. That said, Warner deserves credit for advancing a proposal to limit the regulatory burden, and his bill would be a step in the right direction.

One solution to the need for credible independent cost estimates might be the creation of a new Joint Committee on Regulation (JCR) in Congress. The JCR would be modeled on the Joint Committee on Taxation (JCT), which is Congress's official scorekeeper for the impact of tax changes.

The JCT, of course, is far from perfect. In fact, its flawed "static scoring" methodology consistently overstates the revenue losses from tax cuts and understates the revenues raised by tax hikes, creating a persistent pro-tax bias. That element, failure to model macroeconomic impacts, is not something that should be modeled in a JCR, but rather something that must be fixed at JCT.

The upside to creating a Joint Committee on Regulation is that it would be composed of members of Congress, who could be held responsible for its functioning. It would be less likely than an outside scoring agency to become captive to big-government special interests. And the members who were on the committee would have an automatic platform to keep regulatory cost issues front and center with the public and in the news cycle.

Having accurate, credible cost estimates for federal regulations is an essential reform in itself because it would make it much easier to generate public awareness and political opposition needed to prevent or overturn costly regulations. It is also a crucial prerequisite to structural reforms that rely on credible official cost estimates, including the REINS Act, which requires congressional approval only for regulations with an economic impact greater than $100 million—to prevent opponents of the bill arguing it would consume too much of Congress's time to vote on every federal rule. If agencies are permitted to do their own scoring only under the supervision of a pro-regulation OIRA, we could see a lot of rulemakings that happen to score at $99 million to sidestep the congressional approval requirement.

Another worthy reform idea is a Federal Sunset Act, long championed by U.S. Rep. Kevin Brady (R-Texas) and based on the sunset process used in Texas. The bill would create a 12-member Sunset Commission, which would include eight members of Congress. Half would be appointed by the speaker of the House and half by the Senate majority leader, and the members of Congress on the commission would be equally divided by party. The commission would set an expiration date for every federal agency not specifically required by the Constitution. The expiration time would be no longer than 12 years. When an agency reaches its sunset date, it would automatically cease to exist unless Congress acted to reauthorize it.

The Sunset Commission would conduct hearings for input from taxpayers, regulated businesses, and state and local governments regarding how the agency is performing and whether it is necessary. They will then make recommendations as to whether each agency should be abolished, streamlined, reorganized, or reestablished. If the agency survives, a new sunset date would be set for its next review.

Tom Schatz of the limited-government group Citizens Against Government Waste explained the power of requiring federal regulatory authority to automatically sunset:

> For those in Congress who are committed to cutting wasteful spending, a federal Sunset Law is a powerful tool. No longer will federal agencies, once created, assume immortality. Sunsetting shifts the burden of proof, forcing agencies to regularly justify their existence to American taxpayers who will have a real say in whether they deserve our precious tax dollars. We support the Federal Sunset Act and encourage members of Congress to join Representative Brady in bringing accountability to our massive federal bureaucracy.[31]

While the budgetary savings would be significant, the savings in terms of regulatory compliance costs would be even greater. Not only because some unnecessary agencies would likely be shuttered but also because agencies that have to justify their very existence will spend much more time ensuring they are accomplishing their core mission and much less time looking for creative ways to expand their authority and accomplish major policy changes that Congress—which could allow them to sunset—never intended.

U.S. Rep. Geoff Davis sees the sunset approach as a complement to the REINS Act, saying:

> I think sunsetting all regulations is a very important thing to do...I think the imperative aspect. That would ultimately be a very heavy lift, but it would force accountability. I'm for anything that tightens the dialogue and reduces the ability for an imperial presidency.[32]

While the most immediate tasks for Congress are to step in and stop the specific power grabs like the EPA's global warming agenda, the FCC Internet takeover, the NLRB's backdoor card-check efforts (the latter two of which are beyond the reach of Obama's regulatory review), and the rest of the threats detailed in previous chapters, broader regulatory reform must also be on the agenda to create institutional constraints that prevent such acts of regulatory tyranny in the future.

Our challenge to Congress must be not only to stop the usurpations of its legislative power that are ongoing but to fix the process so that it won't have to fight these fights in the future.

It comes back to Lloyd Rogers and Article I, Section 1 of the U.S. Constitution: "All legislative Powers herein granted shall be vested in a Congress of the United States, which shall consist of a Senate and House of Representatives."

The goal of real regulatory reform must be to bring accountability to bear on the branch of government in which legislative power is supposed to rest. Therefore the REINS Act is the gold standard of regulatory reform.

# Restoring the Republic

I n 2010, voters who worked hard, played by the rules, paid their mortgages, paid their taxes, and took care of their own lives told arrogant, big-government politicians to stop telling them what to do. Obama's "fundamental transformation" agenda—an agenda to greatly centralize power, redistribute wealth, and tell people how to live their lives—was decisively rejected.

In a display of arrogance appropriate for a would-be central planner, Obama repeatedly attacked his political opponents and accused them of, essentially, using free-market ideology to fool the voters into opposing him. It's an idea right out of Friedrich Engels, who called it false consciousness.[1]

Obama thinks Americans who disagree with him must not understand what's best for them. Consider these remarks at a Democratic fund-raising dinner two weeks before Election Day, when it was increasingly clear his party would lose by a landslide:

> Part of the reason that our politics seem so tough right now, and facts and science and argument does

[sic] not seem to be winning the day all the time, is because we're hard-wired not to always think clearly when we're scared. And the country is scared, and they have good reason to be.[2]

To disagree with Obama, we're told, is to not think clearly. To believe in the dynamism of freedom and markets versus the scientific precision of the regulator's design is to be defective—or misled by fear.

To Obama, ignoring the elections and continuing to pursue his agenda by other means is doing us a favor. He thinks he is saving us from our own primitive inability to understand what's best for us.

In his press conference the day after the election, Obama answered a question about voters rejecting ObamaCare by saying: "we'd be misreading the election if we thought that the American people want to see us for the next two years relitigate arguments that we had over the last two years."[3] And he answered a question about the EPA by saying: "Cap-and-trade was just one way of skinning the cat; it was not the only way. It was a means, not an end."

Obama is simply unable to admit that he has fallen victim to the fatal conceit—the idea that he and his regulators can make better choices for us than we can make for ourselves. History proves otherwise.

As the great free-market philosopher and economist F. A. Hayek observed:

> At least before the obvious economic failure of Eastern European socialism, it was widely thought ... that a centrally planned economy would deliver not only "social justice," but also a more efficient use of economic resources. This notion appears eminently sensible at first glance. But it proves to overlook the facts just reviewed: that the totality of resources that one could employ in such a plan *is simply not know-*

*able to anybody*, and therefore can hardly be centrally controlled...

Yet after seventy years of experience with socialism, it is safe to say that most intellectuals outside
the areas—Eastern Europe and the Third World—
where socialism has been tried remain content to
brush aside what lessons might lie in economics,
unwilling to wonder whether there might not be
a *reason* why socialism, as often as it is attempted,
never seems to work out as its intellectual leaders
*intended.*[4]

We now have another 20 years of proof, and are even watching
the Western European "social democracy" model crack up before
our eyes. But the dream dies hard.

Obama will continue to *say* wonderful things about free markets,
entrepreneurship, business. Even regulatory review and reform.

As Lloyd Rogers put it:

I don't trust anything the man says. He talks out of
both sides of his mouth. It looks good to say you're
going to do a regulatory review, but he does this all
the time. He's on television every day with something, and he doesn't follow through.[5]

Obama may even pass some bipartisan legislation in Congress—
so long as it doesn't interfere with his regulatory agenda. But the real
action, his real ambitions, will proceed via regulation unless we can
succeed in getting Congress to stop them.

## THE CHALLENGE BEFORE US

Our challenge is to change the political calculus to elevate regulatory fights to the appropriate level in the public consciousness. We

must make sure the American people understand that a disastrously bad idea becomes even worse when it's implemented by backdoor, unaccountable, illegitimate means.

Obama's regulatory extremism is both a danger and an opportunity. We must repeatedly and unrelentingly, on the full array of regulatory issues, deliver these two key messages to Congress:

- You can delegate authority, but you can never delegate responsibility.
- If you fail to stop out-of-control regulators, voters will hold you accountable.

It's that simple, and the best way to put Congress to the test is to demand it pass the REINS Act and take responsibility, as the legislative branch, for writing the laws.

We cannot afford to spend $10,500 per worker every year on federal regulatory compliance.[6] We cannot let each and every federal regulator destroy 98 private sector jobs per year.[7] We cannot allow regulators to take away our freedom to make our own economic decisions, and substitute their own judgment—which can never allocate resources as effectively as a free market.

We cannot allow an administration that claims to support cutting federal regulation succeed in its pursuit of a dizzying array of unaccountable power grabs, doing violence to basic constitutional principles.

The conservative movement has done an excellent job of elevating the issue of judicial tyranny in the minds of voters and activists, and as a consequence judicial confirmation hearings have high stakes and are politically charged. Decisions that amount to legislating from the bench are roundly condemned.

Our challenge is to replicate that success with regulatory tyranny. To show how regulators are usurping the legitimate legislative function, elevate regulatory confirmation fights, and demand

Congress stand up for itself and exercise its powers as the legitimate legislative branch of government.

We must hold the president responsible, showing how his moderate rhetoric conceals extreme ambitions that continue to move forward by other means. Obama's mask must be torn off to reveal who he is—a true believer in big government. His science adviser, John Holdren, wants to "de-develop" the United States. His top regulatory adviser, Cass Sunstein, proudly describes himself as a paternalist, eager to nudge us in the direction of his choosing.

Given this extremism, the stakes are very high in the 2012 presidential election. Four more years of this regulatory assault on the American economy will do enormous damage to our freedom and our prosperity.

But we must also be wary of believing that electing a new president will, by itself, reverse the trend. We should learn from the cautionary tale of the civil libertarians who worked hard to elect Obama based on his promises to end Bush's abuses of presidential power, only to see them expand to nearly every area of domestic economic policy. Andrew Cohen put it well early in the Obama presidency: "If you were hoping that the Obama team would come into the White House and aggressively undercut its own power it's time to change dreams."[8]

Similarly, we cannot count on the next president to give up the expanded regulatory powers that Obama has seized without sustained political pressure and action by Congress.

The only answer, then, is to build that political reflex to hold Congress accountable and to restore the balance between the branches. We, as citizens and voters, must commit to holding Congress accountable not just for the legislation they pass but for the regulation they fail to stop.

Unfortunately, we have been through cycles of government expansion before, and each time government remained permanently larger, more expensive, and more intrusive than it was before the crisis.

Which brings us back to Robert Higgs, who closed his 1988 classic on a sobering note:

> We know that other great crises will come. Whether they will be occasioned by foreign wars, economic collapse, or rampant terrorism, no one can predict with assurance. Yet in one form or another, great crises will surely come again, as they have from time to time throughout human history. When they do, governments almost certainly will gain new powers over economic and social affairs...For those who cherish individual liberty and a free society, the prospect is deeply disheartening.
>
> Can such an outcome be avoided? I think not, but I hope I am wrong. Americans have been brought to their present inauspicious circumstances by, above all else, changes in the prevailing ideology. If ideologies are not mere superstructure, if ideas can gain sway through rational consideration in the light of historical evidence and moral persuasion, then there remains a hope, however slight, that the American people may rediscover the worth of individual rights, limited government, and a free society under a true rule of law.[9]

So far, in the Obama era, we have tragically failed to avoid another ratchet up in big government. But the biggest, most significant, longest-lasting fights are still in front us. Most of Obama's ambitions remain unfulfilled, and most of what he has done can still be undone.

The battle will take place in the hearts and minds of the American people, and unlike the previous ratchets up in the power of big government, we now have a remarkable mass movement dedicated not to their own personal interests as such but to the broad principles of limited government.

Obama is also our best ally, in a sense, because of his extremism. His utter refusal to accept the verdict of the American people and Congress will alienate and anger Americans who would otherwise accept the rationale of increased government power in response to crisis.

Turning Higgs's crisis theory on its head, we may have now reached a crisis point in the workings of our system of government, a crisis of unchecked regulatory power that threatens to render Congress irrelevant and trample our economic freedoms. This crisis, made clear by the ambitiousness of Obama's "fundamental transformation" agenda, can, if well communicated, arouse enough opposition to reverse a multi-decade trend toward ever-greater regulatory power.

This time, it can be different. This time we can win.

# NOTES

## Preface

1. Glenn Beck's official website, "Glenn Beck: Slaughtering the Constitution," March 16, 2010, www.glennbeck.com/content/articles/article/198/37989/ (accessed April 20, 2011).
2. Glenn Beck, "Is 'Slaughter Rule' the 'Courage' Obama Called For?" Wednesday, March 16, 2010, www.foxnews.com/story/0,2933,589583,00.html (accessed March 2, 2011). Video available at www.ObamaChart.com.

## Introduction—Crisis and Transformation

1. Hayley Tsukayama and Liz Lucas, "Thousands Cheer Obama at Rally for Change," *Columbia Missourian*, October 30, 2008, www.columbiamissourian.com/stories/2008/10/30/obama-speaks-crowd-40000/ (accessed March 1, 2011).
2. Barack Obama, interview, WBEZ-FM, 2001, *Naked Emperor News*, www.youtube.com/watch?v=iivL4c_3pck (accessed March 1, 2011).
3. Susan Jones, "'Spread the Wealth Around' Comment Comes Back to Haunt Obama," *CNS News*, October 15, 2008, www.cnsnews.com/node/37539 (accessed March 2, 2011).
4. F. A. Hayek, *The Fatal Conceit* (Chicago: University of Chicago Press, 1988), 77.
5. Robert Higgs, *Crisis and Leviathan* (New York: Oxford University Press, 1987), 67.
6. Higgs, *Crisis and Leviathan*, 261.
7. Rahm Emanuel, cited in "Bum Rap for Rahm," *FactCheck.org*, January 13, 2011, www.factcheck.org/2011/01/bum-rap-for-rahm/ (accessed March 1, 2011).

8. Higgs, *Crisis and Leviathan*, 73.

9. Quoted in Elizabeth Drew, "Power Grab," *New York Review of Books*, June 22, 2006, www.nybooks.com/articles/archives/2006/jun/22/power-grab (accessed March 1, 2011).

10. Drew, "Power Grab."

11. For a lengthy list of comparisons of Bush to Hitler claims from the left, see: http://semiskimmed.net/bushhitler.html (accessed March 1, 2011).

12. Text of speech by Al Gore, "A Constitutional Crisis," January 17, 2006, www.alternet.org/rights/30905/?page=entire (accessed March 1, 2011).

13. *The Wall Street Journal*, "Obama Channels Cheney," March 7, 2009, http://online.wsj.com/article/SB123638765474658467.html (accessed March 3, 2011).

14. Jonathan Weisman, "Signing Statements Reappear in Obama White House," *The Wall Street Journal*, March 12, 2009, http://online.wsj.com/article/SB123688875576610955.html (accessed March 1, 2011).

15. Cited in Dan Miller, "Constitutional Scholar Obama on Signing Statements," *PJ Tatler*, April 16, 2011, http://pajamasmedia.com/tatler/2011/04/16/constitutional-scholar-obama-on-signing-statements/. Video available at www.youtube.com/watch?v=seAR1S1Mjkc& (accessed April 20, 2011).

16. Barack Obama, "Statement on Signing the Department of Defense and Full-Year Continuing Appropriations Act, 2011," April 15, 2011, http://www.whitehouse.gov/the-press-office/2011/04/15/statement-president-hr-1473 (accessed April 20, 2011).

17. Bruce Ackerman, *The Decline and Fall of the American Republic* (Cambridge, Mass.: Belknap Press, 2010), 40.

18. Ibid., 41.

19. David M. Herszenhorn and David E. Sanger, "Senate Abandons Automaker Bailout Bid," *The New York Times*, December 11, 2008, www.nytimes.com/2008/12/12/business/12auto.html (accessed March 2, 2011).

20. Todd Zywicki, "Chrysler and the Rule of Law," *The Wall Street Journal*, May 13, 2009, http://online.wsj.com/article/SB124217356836613091.html (accessed March 2, 2011).

21. Phil Kerpen, "The Apollo Alliance: Unifying Activists on the Left," *Foundation Watch*, October 2009, Capital Research Center, www.capitalresearch.org/pubs/pubs.html?id=704 (accessed March 6, 2011).

22. Keith Schneider, "Recovery Bill Is Breakthrough on Clean Energy, Good Jobs," *Apollo News Service*, February 17, 2009, http://apolloalliance.org/feature-articles/at-last-federal-

government-signs-up-for-clean-energy-economy/ (accessed March 6, 2011).

23. Apollo Alliance website, www.apolloalliance.org/about/endorsers (accessed March 6, 2011).

24. Apollo Board of Directors, Apollo website, www.apolloalliance.org/about/board (accessed March 6, 2011).

25. Eliza Strickland, "The New Face of Environmentalism," *East Bay Express*, November 2, 2005, www.eastbayexpress.com/gyrobase/the-new-face-of-environmentalism/Content?oid=1079539 (accessed March 6, 2011).

26. Ibid.

27. "Van Jones, Senior Fellow," Center for American Progress, www.americanprogress.org/experts/JonesVan.html (accessed March 6, 2011).

28. "Van Jones, Distinguished Visitor," Princeton University, www.princeton.edu/africanamericanstudies/people/fellows (accessed March 6, 2011).

29. "Van Jones Among Honorees at NAACP Image Awards Show," *The Wall Street Journal*, February 23, 2010, http://blogs.wsj.com/speakeasy/2010/02/23/van-jones-among-honorees-at-naacp-image-awards-show/ (accessed March 6, 2011).

30. Video and transcript available at http://ironicsurrealism.blogivists.com/2009/02/19/trader-tea-party-rick-santelli-rant-video-full-transcript as of March 6, 2011.

31. Phil Kerpen, "Live From a Tea Party—The Atmosphere Is Electric!" *FoxNews.com*, April 15, 2009, http://replay.waybackmachine.org/20090417005924/http://foxforum.blogs.foxnews.com/2009/04/15/kerpen_tea_party (accessed March 6, 2011).

32. Nicole Crain and Mark Crain, "The Impact of Regulatory Costs on Small Firms," for U.S. Small Business Administration Office of Advocacy under contract number SBAHQ-08-M-0466, September 2010, http://archive.sba.gov/advo/research/rs371tot.pdf (accessed March 3, 2011).

33. James Gattuso, Diane Katz, and Stephen Keen, "Red Tape Rising: Obama's Torrent of New Regulation," *Heritage Foundation Backgrounder 2482*, October 26, 2010, www.heritage.org/Research/Reports/2010/10/Red-Tape-Rising-Obamas-Torrent-of-New-Regulation (accessed March 3, 2011).

34. Crain and Crain, "The Impact of Regulatory Costs on Small Firms."

35. Gattuso, Katz, and Keen, "Red Tape Rising: Obama's Torrent of New Regulation."

36. Clyde Wayne Crews, Jr., *Ten Thousand Commandments: An Annual Snapshot of the Federal Regulatory State* (Washington, DC: Competitive Enterprise Institute, 2011), http://cei. org/10kc (accessed April 20, 2011).

37. T. Randolph Beard, George S. Ford, Hyeongwoo Kim, and Lawrence J. Spiwak, *Regulatory Expenditures, Economic Growth and Jobs: An Empirical Study*, Phoenix Center Policy Bulletin 28 (April 2011), www.phoenix-center.org/PolicyBulletin/ PCPB28Final.pdf (accessed April 20, 2011).

## *Chapter 1—The REINS Act*

1. U.S. Const. art. I, sec.1.

2. John Locke, *Second Treatise on Government*, 1690, Section 141, http://constitution.org/jl/2ndtr11.htm (accessed March 1, 2011).

3. "John Adams and the Massachusetts Constitution," Massachusetts Supreme Judicial Court, www.mass.gov/courts/ sjc/john-adams-b.html (accessed March 2, 2011).

4. James Madison, The Federalist No. 47, "The Particular Structure of the New Government and the Distribution of Power Among Its Different Parts," *New York Packet*, January 30, 1788.

5. Lloyd Rogers, telephone interview by Phil Kerpen, February 8, 2011.

6. Patrick Crowley, "Rogers Joins GOP Hopefuls for Lucas' Seat," *The Cincinnati Enquirer*, April 27, 2003, 1C.

7. Rogers, interview.

8. Ibid.

9. Ibid.

10. Dennis Cauchon, "Cities Slap Fees on Storm Runoff," *USA Today*, March 29, 2010, www.usatoday.com/tech/news/2010-03-28-runoff-fees_N.htm (accessed March 2, 2011).

11. Rogers, interview.

12. Ibid.

13. Michael Barone and Richard E. Cohen, *Almanac of American Poltitics*, (Washington, D.C.: United Book Press, 2009), 636.

14. U.S. Rep. Geoff Davis, interview by Phil Kerpen, Washington, DC, February 28, 2011.

15. Davis, interview.

16. Text provided by Davis.

17. Davis, interview.

18. Ibid.

19. *Immigration and Naturalization Service v. Chadha*, 462 U.S. 919 (1983).
20. Jonathan H. Adler, "The Regulations from the Executive In Need of Scrutiny (REINS) Act," *The Federalist Society*, New Federal Initiatives Project, January 14, 2011, www.fed-soc. org/publications/pubid.2074/pub_detail.asp (accessed April 20, 2011).
21. Davis, interview.
22. Ibid.
23. Ibid.
24. Ibid.
25. U.S. Sen. Rand Paul, telephone interview by Phil Kerpen, March 14, 2011.
26. Ibid.
27. Ibid.
28. Ibid.
29. Ibid.
30. Ibid.
31. Davis, interview.
32. Paul, interview.

# Chapter 2—The Heat Is On

1.  Barack Obama, interview by San Francisco Chronicle Editorial Board, January 17, 2008. *San Francisco Chronicle* video, comment begins at 40:30, www.sfgate.com/cgi-bin/object/ article?f=/c/a/2008/01/19/EDIAUHASH.DTL (accessed November 20, 2010).
2.  Colin Sullivan, "Vow of Silence Key to White House-Calif. Fuel Economy Talks," *Greenwire*, May 20, 2009, www.nytimes.com/ gwire/2009/05/20/20greenwire-vow-of-silence-key-to-white-house-calif-fuel-e-12208.html (accessed November 20, 2010).
3.  Chip Knappenberger, "Climate Impacts of Waxman-Markey (the IPCC-Based Arithmetic of No Gain)," *MasterResource*, May 6, 2009, www.masterresource.org/2009/05/part-i-a-climate-analysis-of-the-waxman-markey-climate-bill—the-impacts-of-us-actions-alone/ (accessed April 20, 2011).
4.  Obama, interview with *San Francisco Chronicle* editorial board.
5.  Fiona Harvey, "Elevenses with the FT: Emission Statement," *Financial Times*, November 4, 2006, www.ft.com/cms/s/0/ daf6749a-6a41-11db-8ae5-0000779e2340.html (accessed November 20, 2010).

6. Doug Elmendorf to Henry Waxman, June 26, 2009, Congressional Budget Office, www.cbo.gov/ftpdocs/103xx/doc10376/hr2998WaxmanLtr.pdf (accessed November 20, 2010).

7. Statement of Douglas W. Elmendorf, Senate Committee on Finance, *Auctioning under Cap and Trade: Design, Participation and Distribution of Revenues*, 111th Cong., 1st sess., 2009, www.cbo.gov/ftpdocs/101xx/doc10115/Cap_and_Trade_Testimony.1.1.shtml (accessed November 23, 2010).

8. Mason Adams, "Coal Likely to Fuel Voters' Choice in 9th Congressional District Race," *Roanoke Times*, October 26, 2010, www.roanoke.com/politics/wb/265170 (accessed November 20, 2010).

9. Chris Cilizza, "The Best Campaign Ads of 2010," *WashingtonPost.com*, November 18, 2010, http://voices.washingtonpost.com/thefix/fix-notes/the-best-ads-of-2010.html (accessed November 20, 2010).

10. Office of Management and Budget, *Budget of the United States Government, Fiscal Year 2012* (Washington, DC, 2011), www.whitehouse.gov/sites/default/files/omb/budget/fy2012/assets/environmental.pdf (accessed May 16, 2011).

11. Marlo Lewis, "EPA's Greenhouse Power Grab: Baucus's Revenge, Democracy's Peril," *Pajamas Media*, March 21, 2011, http://pajamasmedia.com/blog/epa's-greenhouse-power-grab-baucus's-revenge-democracy's-peril/ (accessed May 5, 2011).

12. Environmental Protection Agency, RIN 2060-AP86, *Prevention of Significant Deterioration and Title V Greenhouse Gas Tailoring Rule*, April 13, 2010, www.epa.gov/nsr/documents/20100413final.pdf (accessed December 4, 2010).

13. House Committee on Energy and Commerce, Subcommittee on Energy and Air Quality, *Strengths and Weaknesses of Regulating Greenhouse Gas Emissions Using Existing Clean Air Act Authorities*, 110th Cong., 2d sess., April 10, 2008, http://frwebgate.access.gpo.gov/cgi-bin/getdoc.cgi?dbname=110_house_hearings&docid=f:51574.pdf (accessed November 20, 2010).

14. Barack Obama, November 3, 2010, press conference, www.whitehouse.gov/the-press-office/2010/11/03/press-conference-president (accessed November 20, 2010).

15. "Green Make Believe: Van Jones Admits Left is 'Pretending' Need for Regulations in Green Movement," *The Blaze*, December 21, 2010, www.theblaze.com/stories/green-make-believe-van-jones-admits-left-is-pretending-need-for-regulations-and-cap-trade-in-green-movement/ (accessed February 5, 2011).

16. John D. Podesta and Sarah Rosen Wartell, *The Power of the President: Recommendations to Advance Progressive Change*, Center for American Progress, November 16, 2010, www.americanprogress.org/issues/2010/11/pdf/executive_orders.pdf (accessed November 21, 2010).

17. National Mining Association, "EPA's Regulatory Train Wreck," http://actioncenter.nma.org/economic-impact/epatrainwreck (accessed April 20, 2011).

18. Obama, interview with *San Francisco Chronicle* editorial board, comment begins at 27:23.

19. Podesta and Wartell, *The Power of the President: Recommendations to Advance Progressive Change*.

20. Jon Basil Utley, "Job-Killing Environmentalists: How the EPA Cripples the American Economy," *Reason*, November 10, 2010, http://reason.com/archives/2010/11/10/job-killing-environmentalists (accessed November 21, 2010).

21. Podesta and Wartell, *The Power of the President: Recommendations to Advance Progressive Change*.

22. Environmental Protection Agency press release, "EPA Proposes First National Standard for Mercury Pollution from Power Plants...," March 16, 2011, http://yosemite.epa.gov/opa/admpress.nsf/d0cf6618525a9efb85257359003fb69d/55615df6595fbfa3852578550050942f!OpenDocument (accessed April 20, 2011).

23. Donald A. Norman, *Economic Implications of EPA's Proposed Ozone Standard (ER-707)*, Manufacturers Alliance/MAPI, September 15, 2010, www.mapi.net/MediaCenter/news/Lists/Posts/Post.aspx?ID=189 (accessed December 4, 2010).

24. Stephen Dinan, "Obama Climate Czar Has Socialist Ties," *The Washington Times*, January 12, 2009, www.washingtontimes.com/news/2009/jan/12/obama-climate-czar-has-socialist-ties/ (accessed November 20, 2010).

25. Although Browner was later scrubbed from the website, the Capital Research Center has preserved a snapshot from January 5, 2009 here: www.capitalresearch.org/blog/wp-content/uploads/2009/01/browner_si.pdf (accessed December 4, 2010).

26. Meeting of the Socialist International Commission on a Sustainable World Society, "Climate Change: Shared Goals and Responsibilities of the International Community," Santiago, Chile, March 24, 2008, www.socialistinternational.org/viewArticle.cfm?ArticleID=1917&ArticlePageID=1230&ModuleID=18 (accessed December 4, 2010).

27. St Petersburg Climate Change Seminar of the Socialist International Commission for a Sustainable World Society, July 14-15, 2008, www.socialistinternational.org/viewArticle.cfm?ArticleID=1935&ArticlePageID=1275&ModuleID=34 (accessed December 4, 2010).

28. Meeting of the Socialist International Commission on a Sustainable World Society in London, November 19, 2007, www.socialistinternational.org/viewArticle.cfm?ArticleID=1845&ArticlePageID=1078&ModuleID=18 (accessed December 4, 2010).

29. Carol M. Browner biography, EPA Office of Media Relations, February 1999, www.epa.gov/history/admin/agency/browner.htm, (accessed December 4, 2010).

30. Carol Browner biography, Center for American Progress website dated May 2008: "She is on the Board of the Directors of the Center for American Progress," www.americanprogress.org/events/2008/05/inf/BrownerCarol.html (accessed December 4, 2010).

31. "Carol M. Browner," *WhoRunsGov.com*, www.whorunsgov.com/Profiles/Carol_M._Browner (accessed December 5, 2010).

32. Memorandum, Jonathan Z. Cannon to Carol M. Browner, April 10, 1998. Included by Browner in testimony to Senate Environment and Public Works Committee, April 24, 2007, http://epw.senate.gov/public/index.cfm?FuseAction=Files.View&FileStore_id=7b2dffa6-a3ed-4e15-bcae-7a738541f9e9 (accessed November 20, 2010).

33. Colin Sullivan, "Vow of Silence Key to White House-Calif. Fuel Economy Talks," *Greenwire*, May 20, 2009, www.nytimes.com/gwire/2009/05/20/20greenwire-vow-of-silence-key-to-white-house-calif-fuel-e-12208.html (accessed November 20, 2010).

34. Pat Michaels, "The EPA's Odd View of 'Consumer Choice'," *Cato Institute*, October 17, 2010, www.cato.org/pub_display.php?pub_id=12480 (accessed November 20, 2010).

35. Environmental Protection Agency, *Advance Notice of Proposed Rulemaking: Regulating Greenhouse Gas Emissions under the Clean Air Act*, EPA-HQ-OAR-2008-0318, July 11 2008, www.epa.gov/climatechange/anpr.html (accessed November 23, 2010). This was a Bush administration release of the regulations sought by EPA career bureaucrats, with commentary on the devastating consequences.

36. In EPA-speak: "Performance benchmarking information, to the extent it is specific and relevant to the source in question, may provide useful information regarding energy efficient technologies and processes for consideration in the BACT as-

sessment." Environmental Protection Agency Office of Air and Radiation, *PSD and Title V Permitting Guidance For Greenhouse Gases*, November 2010, www.eenews.net/assets/2010/11/10/document_gw_04.pdf (accessed November 23, 2010).

37. Marc Ambinder, "3 Women to Watch in the New White House," *The Atlantic*, www.theatlantic.com/politics/archive/2010/10/three-women-to-watch-in-obama-20/64682/ (accessed March 4, 2011).

38. Kim Chipman and Jim Snyder, "Obama's Climate-Change Adviser Browner Leaves as Agenda Stalls," *Bloomberg*, January 25, 2011, www.bloomberg.com/news/2011-01-25/obama-energy-climate-adviser-browner-said-to-plan-leaving-administration.html (accessed May 5, 2011).

39. Gabriel Nelson, "Energy and Climate Czar Browner's Resignation Seen as the End of an Era," *Greenwire*, January 25, 2011, www.nytimes.com/gwire/2011/01/25/25greenwire-energy-and-climate-czar-browners-resignation-s-34804.html (accessed March 4, 2011).

40. Amy Harder, "Browner's Successor Says the Agenda Hasn't Changed," *National Journal*, March 2, 2011, www.national-journal.com/daily/browner-s-successor-says-the-agenda-hasn-t-changed-20110302 (accessed March 4, 2011).

41. Darren Goode, "Carol Browner Heads to Think Tank," *Politico*, April 19, 2011, http://dyn.politico.com/printstory.cfm?uuid=758BB41D-DBEF-4203-ACBF-4EE9D564155B (accessed April 20, 2011).

42. For a thorough discussion of this regulatory cascade, see George F. Allen and Marlo Lewis, "Finding the Proper Forum for Regulation of U.S. Greenhouse Gas Emissions: The Legal and Economic Implications of Massachusetts v. EPA, 44 *University of Richmond Law Review* 919 (2010), http://lawreview.richmond.edu/wp/wp-content/uploads/2010/03/Allen-AC.pdf (accessed December 4, 2010).

43. Simon Lomax, "EPA Studying Own Carbon-Trading System, Official Says," *Bloomberg*, March 15, 2010, www.bloomberg.com/apps/news?pid=newsarchive&sid=ammjHfzRpc9I (accessed November 20, 2010).

44. James Valvo, "Of Elephants and Mouseholes: How EPA Could Revive Cap-and-Trade" (working paper no. 1010, Americans for Prosperity, October 2010), http://www.americansforprosperity.org/files/Elephants_Mouseholes_1010_0.pdf (accessed May 16, 2011).

45. Kevin Bundy, Brendan Cummings, Vera Pardee, and Kassie Siegel, "Yes, He Can: President Obama's Power to Make an

International Climate Commitment Without Waiting for Congress" (working paper no. 2, Climate Law Institute, December 2009), www.biologicaldiversity.org/programs/climate_law_institute/pdfs/Yes_He_Can_120809.pdf (accessed November 20, 2010).

46. Marcelo Furtado, "Yes, He Can! How Obama Can Deliver Stronger Emissions Reductions," COP15 side event, Copenhagen, Denmark, video, comment begins at 0:39:33, December 8, 2009, http://cop15.meta-fusion.com/kongresse/cop15/templ/play.php?id_kongresssession=2338&theme=cop15 (accessed December 4, 2010).

47. Kassie Siegel, "Yes, He Can! How Obama Can Deliver Stronger Emissions Reductions," COP15 side event, Copenhagen, Denmark, video, exchange begins at 1:12:15, December 8, 2009, http://cop15.meta-fusion.com/kongresse/cop15/templ/play.php?id_kongresssession=2338&theme=cop15 (accessed December 4, 2010).

48. Lisa P. Jackson, question-and-answer session, U.S. Center, Copenhagen, Denmark, December 9, 2009, www.youtube.com/watch?v=tTh-sSx6HkU (accessed December 4, 2010).

49. Timothy Gardner, "US states sue EPA to stop greenhouse gas rules," *Reuters,* March 19, 2010, www.reuters.com/article/idUSN1916237120100319 (accessed December 4, 2010).

50. Brian W. Shaw and Greg Abbott to Lisa Jackson and Alfredo Armendariz, August 2, 2010, www.eenews.net/assets/2010/08/04/document_gw_01.pdf (accessed November 21, 2010).

51. Office of U.S. Sen. Jim Webb, "Sen. Webb Opposes Murkowski Amendment to Block EPA Action on Greenhouse Gases," news release, June 10, 2010, http://webb.senate.gov/newsroom/pressreleases/2010-06-10-03.cfm (accessed November 21, 2010).

52. U.S. Sen. Webb of Virginia, speaking on the Senate floor, June 10, 2010, against S.J. Res. 26, 111th Cong., 2d sess., www.c-spanvideo.org/videoLibrary/clip.php?appid=598291665 (accessed November 23, 2010).

53. Office of U.S. Sen. Jay Rockefeller, "Rockefeller Says Support for Murkowski Resolution Is a Vote For a Strong West Virginia Economy," news release, June 8, 2010, http://rockefeller.senate.gov/press/record.cfm?id=325532 (accessed November 21, 2010).

54. Energy Tax Prevention Act of 2011, HR 910, 112th Cong., 1st sess., *Congressional Record* 157 (April 7, 2011): H 2506,

http://clerk.house.gov/evs/2011/roll249.xml (accessed April 20, 2011).

55. S.Amdt. to S 493, 112th Cong., 1st sess., *Congressional Record* 157 (April 6, 2011): S 2179, http://www.senate.gov/legislative/LIS/roll_call_lists/roll_call_vote_cfm.cfm?congress=112&session=1&vote=00054 (accessed April 20, 2011).

56. Phil Kerpen, "No rubber stamp for EPA's agenda," *Politico*, March 29, 2011, www.politico.com/news/stories/0311/52111.html (accessed April 20, 2011).

## *Chapter 3—Hacking Our Online Rights*

1. Barack Obama speech at Google headquarters, November 14, 2007, www.freepress.net/obama_net_neutrality (accessed February 5, 2011).

2. Robert McChesney, interview, "Media Capitalism, the State and 21st Century Media Democracy Struggles," *The Bullet*, August 9, 2009, www.socialistproject.ca/bullet/246.php (accessed February 5, 2011).

3. Sara Jerome, "Every candidate supporting PCCC's net-neutrality pledge lost," *The Hill*, November 3, 2010, http://thehill.com/blogs/hillicon-valley/technology/127441-every-candidate-supporting-pcccs-net-neutrality-pledge-lost (accessed February 5, 2011).

4. Amy Schatz, "Court Backs Comcast Over FCC on 'Net Neutrality'," *The Wall Street Journal*, April 7, 2010, http://online.wsj.com/article/SB10001424052702303411604575167782845712768.html (accessed February 5, 2011).

5. Rasmussen Reports, "Just 21% Want FCC to Regulate Internet, Most Fear Regulation Would Promote Political Agenda," December 28, 2010.

6. Andrew Orlowski, "Father of Internet Warns Against Net Neutrality," *The Register*, January 18, 2007, www.theregister.co.uk/2007/01/18/kahn_net_neutrality_warning/ (accessed February 5, 2011).

7. David Farber, "ITIF Event: Designed for Change: End-to-End Arguments, Internet Innovation, and the Net Neutrality Debate" (speech, Information Technology and Innovation Foundation, September 25, 2009), comment at 1 hour, 7 min., 10 sec., www.itif.org/media/itif-event-designed-change-end-end-arguments-internet-innovation-and-net-neutrality-debate#video (accessed February 5, 2011).

8. Lawrence Lessig, "The Fiction Zone that DC Has Become," *Lessig*, January 13, 2006, http://lessig.org/blog/2006/01/the_fiction_zone_that_dc_has_b.html (accessed February 5, 2011).

9. Vint Cerf, comment on post, "Cerf: Nationalize the Internet?" *The Technology Liberation Front*, June 27, 2008, http://techliberation.com/2008/06/27/cerf-nationalize-the-internet/#comment-1454808 (accessed February 5, 2011).

10. Megan Tady, "Million-Dollar Ad Blitz to Kill Net Neutrality," *The Huffington Post*, May 13, 2010, www.huffingtonpost.com/megan-tady/million-dollar-ad-blitz-t_b_574917.html (accessed February 5, 2011).

11. Michael J. Copps, "Remarks To The Joint Center For Political And Economic Studies Media And Technology Policy Forum" (speech, National Press Club, Washington, DC, March 3, 2010), http://hraunfoss.fcc.gov/edocs_public/attachmatch/DOC-296655A1.pdf (accessed February 5, 2011).

12. Alex Lockwood, "Seeding Doubt: How Sceptics Use New Media to Delay Action on Climate Change," paper delivered to the Association for Journalism Education annual conference, "New Media, New Democracy?" Sheffield University, September 12, 2008, http://www.alexlockwood.net/wp-content/uploads/2009/02/20080912-aje-alex-lockwood.pdf (accessed February 5, 2011).

13. Robert McChesney, "The Monthly Review Story: 1949-1984," *MR Zine*, June 5, 2007, http://mrzine.monthlyreview.org/2007/mcchesney060507.html (accessed February 5, 2011).

14. John Fund, "The Net Neutrality Coup," *The Wall Street Journal*, December 21, 2010, http://online.wsj.com/article/SB10001424052748703886904576031512110086694.html (accessed February 5, 2011).

15. McChesney, "Media Capitalism."

16. Ibid.

17. Foster and McChesney, "A New New Deal under Obama?" *Monthly Review*, February 2009, www.monthlyreview.org/090201foster-mcchesney.php (accessed February 5, 2011).

18. Robert McChesney, "Nattering Networks: How Mass Media Fails Democracy," *LiP Magazine*, September 24, 2001, http://web.archive.org/web/20070927012245/http://www.lipmagazine.org/articles/featclark_138.shtml (accessed February 5, 2011).

19. Free Press, "Free Press Calls on Obama Administration to Resist Extremism in the Media; Defends Former Free Press Board Member Van Jones," news release, September 8, 2009, http://www.freepress.net/node/72459 (accessed February 5, 2011).

20. Free Press, "Prepared Remarks at the Free Press Summit," news release, May 11, 2010, www.freepress.net/press-release/2010/5/11/josh-silver-we-must-summon-courage-advance-smart-media-policy (accessed February 5, 2011).

21. Rasmussen Reports, poll.

22. Fund, "The Net Neutrality Coup."

23. Phil Kerpen, "FCC Official Spokeswoman Jen Howard Still Working for Radical Left-Wing Group 'Free Press'," *Americans for Prosperity*, October 21, 2009, www.americansforprosperity.org/102109-fcc-official-spokeswoman-jen-howard-still-working-radical-left-wing-group-"free-press" (accessed February 5, 2011).

24. Nicholas Thompson, "Obama's Geek Squad," *Wired*, June 18, 2009, www.wired.com/politics/onlinerights/magazine/17-07/mf_cio?currentPage=2 (accessed February 5, 2011).

25. Bill Collier, "Freedom Czar Alert—Expose the Internet Czar," *Freedomist.com*, October 8, 2009, freedomist.com/2009/10/08/freedom-czar-alert-expose-the-internet-czar-our-rt-campaign/ (accessed February 5, 2011).

26. OneWebDay website, http://onewebday.org/participating-organizations/ (accessed February 5, 2011).

27. "Our Story," http://onewebday.org/ourstory/ (accessed February 5, 2011).

28. OneWebDay website.

29. Barack Obama, speech at Google headquarters, 50 sec., November 14, 2007, http://www.freepress.net/obama_net_neutrality (accessed February 5, 2011).

30. "Explore Our Businesses," *IAC*, www.iac.com/Our-Businesses/ (accessed February 5, 2011).

31. Free Press, "Free Press Welcomes News of Next FCC Chair," news release, January 12, 2009, www.freepress.net/node/47145 (accessed February 5, 2011).

32. Cited in Pejman Yousefzadeh, "The Obama Way: Nationalizing The Internet," *RedState*, May 3, 2009, www.redstate.com/pejman_yousefzadeh/2009/05/03/the-obama-way-nationalizing-the-internet/ (accessed February 5, 2011).

33. Phil Kerpen, "Grassroots Awaken to Threat of Internet Regulation," *National Review Online*, April 29, 2010, www.nationalreview.com/corner/198634/grassroots-awaken-threat-internet-regulation/phil-kerpen (accessed February 5, 2011).

34. Washington Prowler, "Showdown Alarms," *American Spectator*, November 2, 2009, http://spectator.org/archives/2009/11/02/for-petes-sake/ (accessed February 5, 2011).

35. Sara Jerome, "Telecom Gurus Discuss Competition, Reform at Free Press Conference," *The Hill*, April 10, 2011, http://thehill.com/blogs/hillicon-valley/technology/155087-telecom-gurus-discuss-competition-reform-at-free-press-conference (accessed April 20, 2011).

36. *Comcast Corporation* v. FCC, No. 08-1291 (D.C. Cir. April 6, 2010). Available at www.scribd.com/doc/29489974/Full-Text-Comcast-vs-FCC-Federal-Court-Ruling (accessed February 5, 2011).

37. Free Press, "Industry Front Group Plans Campaign of Lies: AT&T-Funded Attack Dog Stooping to New Lows," news release, May 12, 2010, www.freepress.net/press-release/2010/5/12/industry-front-group-plans-campaign-lies (accessed February 5, 2011).

38. Eric Savitz, "Will FCC Choose 'The Nuclear Option' In Net Neutrality Fight?" *Barron's*, April 6, 2010, http://blogs.barrons.com/techtraderdaily/2010/04/06/will-fcc-choose-the-nuclear-option-in-net-neutrality-fight/ (accessed February 5, 2011).

39. Federal Communications Commission, *Report to Congress in the Matter of Federal-State Joint Board on Universal Service*, 105th Cong., 2d sess., CC Docket No. 96-45 (Washington, DC, April 10, 1998).

40. Free Press, "Free Press Cheers FCC Decision to Take Steps to Protect Consumers, Cautions that 'the Devil Is in the Details'," news release, May 5, 2010, www.freepress.net/press-release/2010/5/5/free-press-cheers-fcc-decision-take-steps-protect-consumers (accessed February 5, 2011).

41. Foster and McChesney, "A New New Deal under Obama?"

42. Seton Motley, "Net Neutrality Power Grab Is Worse than Obamacare," January 19, 2011, *BigGovernment*, http://biggovernment.com/smotley/2011/01/19/net-neutrality-power-grab-is-worse-than-obamacare/ (accessed February 5, 2011).

43. Phil Kerpen, "Silencing Voices of Internet Dissent: FCC's 'Net Neutrality' Puts New Congress to the Test," *The Washington Times*, December 14, 2010, www.washingtontimes.com/news/2010/dec/14/silencing-voices-of-internet-dissent/ (accessed February 5, 2011).

44. White House Office of the Press Secretary, "Statement by the President on Today's FCC Vote on Net Neutrality," news release, December 21, 2010, www.whitehouse.gov/the-press-office/2010/12/21/statement-president-today-s-fcc-vote-net-neutrality (accessed February 5, 2011).

45. John Eggerton, "FCC's Net Neutrality Proceeding Means More Work For State Department," *Broadcasting & Cable*, March 17, 2010, www.broadcastingcable.com/article/450391-FCC_s_Net_Neutrality_Proceeding_Means_More_Work_For_State_Department.php (accessed February 5, 2011).

46. Eggerton, "FCC's Net Neutrality Proceeding Means More Work For State Department."

47. John Eggerton, "Free Press' Ben Scott Exits For State Department Post," *Broadcasting & Cable*, May 27, 2010, www.broadcastingcable.com/article/453116-Free_Press_Ben_Scott_Exits_For_State_Department_Post.php (accessed February 5, 2011).

48. Ben Scott, "The Communicators: Reactions to FCC's Net Neutrality Proposal" (C-SPAN, September 27, 2009), comment begins at 24 min., 50 sec., www.youtube.com/watch?v=b8LrJL0Z3cg (accessed February 5, 2011).

49. Robert McDowell, "The U.N. Threat to Internet Freedom," *The Wall Street Journal*, July 22, 2010, http://online.wsj.com/article/SB10001424052748704684604575381571670766774.html (accessed February 5, 2011).

50. "So Chavez Hears Us Now?" *TechBytes*, Institute for Policy Innovation, January 27, 2011, http://www.ipi.org/IPI/IPIPressReleases.nsf/70218ef1ad92c4ad86256ee5005965f6/a480240b8731983c8625782500692035?OpenDocument (accessed February 5, 2011).

51. Robert McChesney and Mark Weisbrot, "Venezuela and the Media: Fact and Fiction," *Common Dreams*, June 1, 2007, www.commondreams.org/archive/2007/06/01/1607 (accessed February 5, 2011).

52. HJ Res 37, 112th Cong., 1st sess., *Congressional Record* 157 (April 8, 2011): H 2564-5.

53. Josh Smith, "Pelosi: Anti-Net Neutrality Bill Isn't Going Any where," *National Journal*, April 9, 2011, www.nationaljournal.com/tech/pelosi-anti-net-neutrality-bill-isn-t-going-anywhere-20110409 (accessed May 3, 2011).

54. Lloyd Rogers, telephone interview by Phil Kerpen, February 8, 2011.

55. Spencer E. Ante and Thomas Catan, "Columbia Law's Tim Wu to Advise FTC," *The Wall Street Journal*, February 8, 2011, http://online.wsj.com/article/SB10001424052748703313304576132310943386724.html (accessed February 8, 2011).

## *Chapter 4—On the Waterfront*

1. Marc Ambinder, "At SEIU, Obama Rocked The House," *The Atlantic*, September 17, 2007, www.theatlantic.com/politics/archive/2007/09/at-seiu-obama-rocked-the-house/50398/ (accessed December 29, 2010).
2. Craig Becker, "Democracy in the Workplace: Union Representation Elections and Federal Labor Law," *Minnesota Law Review* 77 (1993): 500.
3. William Tate, "Obama, the PAC-Man," *American Thinker*, July 10, 2008, http://www.americanthinker.com/2008/07/obama_the_pacman.html (accessed December 29, 2010).
4. Ambinder, "At SEIU, Obama Rocked The House."
5. Michael Misak, "Unplugged: The SEIU Chief on the Labor Movement and the Card Check," *Las Vegas Sun*, May 10, 2009, www.lasvegassun.com/news/2009/may/10/stern-unplugged-seiu-chief-labor-movement-and-card/ (accessed December 29, 2010).
6. Vadim Rizov, "*Labor Day*, a Crappy Infomercial Partly Funded by Its Subject," *The Village Voice*, October 27, 2009, www.villagevoice.com/2009-10-27/film/labor-day-a-crappy-infomercial-partly-funded-by-its-subject/ (accessed May 3, 2011).
7. Linda Staulcup, "How to Spend $53 Million," *National Right to Work Committee*, June 27, 2008, www.nrtwc.org/how-to-spend-53-million/ (accessed December 29, 2010).
8. James Sherk, "Declining Unionization Calls for Re-Envisioning Workplace Relations," *The Heritage Foundation*, January 21, 2011, www.heritage.org/Research/Reports/2011/01/Declining-Unionization-Calls-for-Re-Envisioning-Workplace-Relations (accessed February 2, 2011).
9. Arthur Laffer and Stephen Moore, "The (Tax) War Between the States," *The Wall Street Journal*, December 10, 2007, http://online.wsj.com/article/SB119724619828518802.html (accessed February 3, 2011).
10. George S. McGovern, "The End of 'More'," *Los Angeles Times*, May 22, 2006, http://articles.latimes.com/2006/may/22/opinion/oe-mcgovern22 (accessed December 29, 2010).
11. "The 30-50 Myth," *Labor Pains*, August 19, 2008, http://labor-pains.org/2008/08/19/the-30-50-myth/ (accessed March 4, 2011).
12. "Cards Are Not Votes," *Center for Union Facts*, www.unionfacts.com/cardcheck/cardsAreNotVotes.cfm (accessed March 4, 2011).

13. Letter to Junta Local de Conciliacion y Arbitraje del Estado de Puebla, August 29, 2001, http://myprivateballot.com/wp-content/uploads/2011/01/xeteq0j27r501e-.pdf (accessed May 3, 2011).

14. F. Vincent Vernuccio, "When Mexicans Have More Rights than U.S.," *The Washington Times*, February 13, 2009, www.washingtontimes.com/news/2009/feb/13/when-mexicans-have-more-rights-than-us/ (accessed February 3, 2011).

15. Patrick O'Connor, "Waxman Dethrones Dingell as Chairman," *Politico*, November 20, 2008, www.politico.com/news/stories/1108/15822.html (accessed March 4, 2011).

16. Howard McKeon, "Secret Ballot Hypocrisy," *Town Hall*, January 9, 2009, http://townhall.com/columnists/howardmckeon/2009/01/09/secret_ballot_hypocrisy (accessed March 4, 2011).

17. "Americans for Prosperity Exposes the Left's 'Secret Plan' to Use Forced Unionization to Take Over the Country," *Americans for Prosperity*, August 14, 2009, www.americansforprosperity.org/081409-americans-prosperity-exposes-lefts-%E2%80%9Csecret-plan%E2%80%9D-use-forced-unionization-take-over-country (accessed February 2, 2011).

18. Barack Obama, speech in Dubuque, IA, November 13, 2007, http://my.barackobama.com/page/content/laborissues (accessed December 29, 2010).

19. "Hobbs Act—Extortion By Force, Violence, or Fear," *United States Attorneys' Manual*, Title 9 Criminal Resource Manual 2403, www.justice.gov/usao/eousa/foia_reading_room/usam/title9/crm02403.htm (accessed December 29, 2010).

20. McLaughlin & Associates, "American Voters Reject the Employee Free Choice Act," poll, January 2009, http://myprivateballot.com/wp-content/uploads/2011/01/voters_reject_EFCA.pdf (accessed March 4, 2011).

21. Joseph Lehman, "Union Members' Attitudes Towards Their Unions' Performance," *Mackinac Center for Public Policy Policy Brief* S2004-05 (September 1, 2004): 4, www.mackinac.org/archives/2004/s2004-05.pdf (accessed December 29, 2010).

22. Sam Stein, "Specter's EFCA Move Helps Him With Primary: Norquist," *The Huffington Post*, April 25, 2009, www.huffingtonpost.com/2009/03/25/specters-efca-move-helps_n_179074.html (accessed December 29, 2010).

23. White House Office of the Press Secretary, "Readout of the President's Meeting with Labor Leaders," news release, July 13, 2009, www.whitehouse.gov/the_press_office/Readouts-of-the-

Presidents-meetings-with-labor-leaders-and-leaders-from-the-Jewish-community-today/ (accessed December 29, 2010).

24. Ben Smith, "White House official: 'Organized Labor Just Flushed $10 Million Down the Toilet'," *Politico*, June 8, 2010, www.politico.com/blogs/bensmith/0610/White_House_official_Organized_labor_just_flushed_10_million_of_their_members_money_down_the_toilet_.html (accessed February 2, 2011).

25. Misak, "Unplugged."

26. Sam Stein, "Patrick Gaspard: Obama's Glue Man," *The Huffington Post*, December 4, 2008, www.huffingtonpost.com/2008/12/04/obamas-glue-man-the-best_n_148415.html (accessed February 2, 2011).

27. Jason Horowitz, "Patrick Gaspard Writes Poems, Collects Comics, Kills for Obama," *The New York Observer*, June 29, 2009, www.observer.com/4185/patrick-gaspard-writes-poems-collects-comics-kills-obama (accessed February 2, 2011).

28. House Committee on Oversight and Government Reform, staff report, *Follow the Money: ACORN, SEIU and Their Political Allies*, 111th Cong., 2d sess., February 18, 2010.

29. Matthew Vadum, "ACORN's Man in the White House," *The American Spectator*, September 28, 2009, www.spectator.org/archives/2009/09/28/acorns-man-in-the-white-house (accessed February 2, 2011).

30. Matthew Vadum, "Becker Lied to McCain," *The American Spectator*, February 10, 2010, http://spectator.org/archives/2010/02/04/becker-lied-to-mccain (accessed February 3, 2011).

31. Wade Rathke, "Becker to the NLRB," *Chief Organizer Blog*, April 30, 2009, http://chieforganizer.org/2009/04/30/becker-to-the-nlrb/ (accessed February 3, 2011).

32. William E. Forbath, "Craig Becker Should Be Confirmed," *Politico*, February 16, 2010, www.politico.com/news/stories/0210/33015_Page2.html (accessed February 2, 2011).

33. Stewart Acuff, "Restoring the Right to Form Unions and Bargain Collectively," *The Huffington Post*, February 3, 2010, www.huffingtonpost.com/stewart-acuff/restoring-to-form-unions_b_447714.

34. Becker, Democracy in the Workplace, 500.

35. Ibid., 585.

36. Ibid., 587.

37. Office of U.S. Sen. Ben Nelson, "Senator Nelson Will Oppose Nominee with Personal Agenda," news release, February 8, 2010,

http://bennelson.senate.gov/press/press_releases/020810-02.cfm (accessed February 2, 2011).

38. "Obama to Make 15 Recess Appointments," CNN, March 27, 2010, http://news.blogs.cnn.com/2010/03/27/obama-to-make-15-recess-appointments/ (accessed February 2, 2011.

39. U.S. Senate, letter from 36 U.S. Senators to President Bush, 109th Cong., 1st sess., July 29, 2005. www.talkingpointsmemo. com/docs/senate.bolton.letter.pdf (accessed February 2, 2011).

40. F. Vincent Vernuccio, "Critics Say NLRB Pursuing Card Check Outside Legislative Process," The Daily Caller, January 21, 2011, http://dailycaller.com/2011/01/21/critics-say-nlrb-pursuing-card-check-outside-legislative-process/ (accessed February 2, 2011).

41. Ivan Osorio and F. Vincent Vernuccio, "Big Labor May Still Reap Benefits Despite Election Losses," Forbes, November 5, 2010, www.forbes.com/2010/11/05/labor-elections-unions-opinions-contributors-ivan-osotio-f-vincent-vernuccio.html (accessed February 2, 2011).

42. "Legal Aid Foundation Files Comments Opposing NLRB 'Electronic Voting' Scheme for Union Organizing Drives," National Right to Work Foundation, news release, June 23, 2010, www.nrtw.org/en/press/2010/06/legal-aid-foundation-files-comments- (accessed February 2, 2011).

43. Brett McMahon, "Now It's Unions Vs. Girl Scouts," Halt the Assault, January 7, 2011, http://halttheassault.com/2011/01/07/now-its-unions-vs-girl-scouts/ (accessed February 2, 2011).

44. Matthew Boyle, "National Labor Relations Board to Decide Whether Labor Organizers Can Use 'Micro Union' Targets," The Daily Caller, February 16, 2011, http://dailycaller.com/2011/02/16/national-labor-relations-board-to-decide-whether-labor-organizers-can-use-micro-union-targets/ (accessed March 4, 2011).

45. Peter Schaumber, "Quickie Elections: Rigging the Rules to Favor Big Labor," National Review Online, June 13, 2011, www.nationalreview.com/corner/269494/quickie-elections-rigging-rules-favor-big-labor-peter-schaumber (accessed July 5, 2011).

46. Susanna Ray, "Boeing Must Add 787 Line After Union Retaliation, U.S. Says," Bloomberg, April 20, 2011, www.bloomberg.com/news/2011-04-20/boeing-should-move-2nd-787-line-to-washington-u-s-board-says.html (accessed April 20, 2011).

47. "Worker Advocate Asks Attorney General Holder to Investigate Apparent Violations of Obama Ethics Pledge by Labor Board Member," news release, National Right to Work Committee, August

9, 2010, www.nrtw.org/en/press/2010/08/worker-advocate-asks-attorney-genera (accessed February 3, 2011).

48. Executive Order no. 13490, "Ethics Commitments by Executive Branch Personnel," *Federal Register* 74, no. 15 (January 26, 2009): 4673-8.

49. "Union Card Checkmate," *The Wall Street Journal*, November 9, 2010, http://online.wsj.com/article/SB10001424052748704353504575596790376536822.html?mod=googlenews_wsj (accessed February 2, 2011).

50. Michael O'Brien, "Harkin Hints 'card-check' Bill Could Move during Lame-Duck Session of Congress," *The Hill*, June 24, 2010, http://thehill.com/blogs/blog-briefing-room/news/105223-harkin-hints-card-check-could-move-during-lame-duck-congress (accessed February 2, 2011).

51. Public Safety Employer-Employee Cooperation Act of 2010, S 3991, 111th Cong., 2d sess., *Congressional Record* 156 (December 8, 2010): S 8626-7.

52. Sam Hananel, "Feds Threaten to Sue States over Union Laws," *The Associated Press*, January 14, 2011.

53. Sam Hananel, "States Rebuff Federal Threat over Union Laws." *The Associated Press*, January 27, 2011.

54. James Sherk, "Declining Unionization Calls for Re-Envisioning Workplace Relations," *The Heritage Foundation*, January 21, 2011, www.heritage.org/Research/Reports/2011/01/Declining-Unionization-Calls-for-Re-Envisioning-Workplace-Relations (accessed February 2, 2011).

55. "Representation Election Procedure: A Proposed Rule by the National Mediation Board on 11/03/2009," *Federal Register*, www.federalregister.gov/articles/2009/11/03/E9-26437/representation-election-procedure (accessed February 28, 2011).

56. Office of U.S. Sen. Johnny Isakson, "Isakson Files 'Disapproval Resolution' to Stop Rule Designed to Ease Path to Unionization," news release, May 11, 2010, http://isakson.senate.gov/press/2010/051110nmb.htm (accessed February 28, 2011).

57. SJ Res 30, Vote Number: 239, 111th Cong., 2d sess., *Congressional Record* 156 (September 23, 2010): S 7383.

58. Barbara Comstock, "When Unions Refuse To Take 'No' for an Answer," *Labor Watch*, Capital Research Center, February 2011, www.capitalresearch.org/pubs/pdf/v1296610380.pdf (accessed February 28, 2011).

## Chapter 5—Ill-Advised

1. Nancy Pelosi, speech to the 2010 Legislative Conference for National Association of Counties, March 20, 2010, *SayAnythingBlog.com*, http://sayanythingblog.com/entry/pelosi_we_must_pass_the_health_care_bill_so_that_we_can_find_out_whats_in_i/ (accessed February 7, 2011).
2. Phil Kerpen, "Memo to 219 House Democrats—November Is Coming," *FOXNews.com*, March 22, 2010, www.foxnews.com/opinion/2010/03/22/phil-kerpen-health-care-obama-democrats-congress-november (accessed April 20, 2011).
3. Austan Goolsbee, testimony before the House Committee on Ways and Means, *Hearing on the Health Care Law's Impact on Jobs, Employers, and the Economy*, 112th Cong., 1st sess., January 26, 2011, www.youtube.com/watch?v=VYDTPIkzOGg (accessed February 7, 2011).
4. "Negotiate Health Care Reform in Public Sessions Televised on C-SPAN," *PolitiFact*, July 10, 2009, www.politifact.com/truth-o-meter/promises/obameter/promise/517/health-care-reform-public-sessions-C-SPAN (accessed February 7, 2011).
5. Ibid.
6. "The world's largest employers," Rediff.com, December 13, 2010, www.rediff.com/business/slide-show/slide-show-1-the-worlds-biggest-employers/20101207.htm (accessed February 7, 2011).
7. Ryan Grim, "Internal Memo Confirms Big Giveaways In White House Deal With Big Pharma," *The Huffington Post*, September 13, 2009, www.huffingtonpost.com/2009/08/13/internal-memo-confirms-bi_n_258285.html (accessed February 7, 2011).
8. "Who we are," *Health Care for America Now*, http://healthcareforamericanow.org/site/content/who_we_are/(accessed February 7, 2011).
9. Michelle Malkin, "Who's Funding the Obamacare Astroturf Campaign?" *MichelleMalkin.com*, June 24, 2009, http://michelle-malkin.com/2009/08/04/flashback-who%E2%80%99s-funding-the-obamacare-astroturf-campaign/(accessed February 7, 2011).
10. Mimi Hall, "Biden Announces White House Deal with Hospitals," *USA Today*, July 8, 2009, www.usatoday.com/news/washington/2009-07-08-biden-health-care_N.htm (accessed February 7, 2011).
11. Memorandum, John D. Shatto and M. Kent Clemens, "Projected Medicare Expenditures under an Illustrative Scenario with

Alternative Payment Updates to Medicare Providers," Centers for Medicare and Medicaid Services, August 5, 2010.

12. Scott Gottlieb, "Accountable Care Organizations: The End of Innovation in Medicine?" *American Enterprise Institute*, February 2011, http://www.aei.org/outlook/101027 (accessed March 10, 2011).

13. Hall, "Biden Announces White House Deal."

14. Rasmussen Reports, "41% Favor Health Care Reform Plan—Demographic Crosstabs," National Survey of 1,000 Likely Voters Conducted March 19-20, 2010, www.rasmussenreports.com/platinum/political_tracking_crosstabs/march_2010/crosstabs_health_care_reform_march_19_20_2010 (accessed May 2, 2011).

15. Larry Hunter, "AARP's Payoff for Betraying Seniors," *Social Security Institute*, January 4, 2011, http://socialsecurityinstitute.com/blog_post/show/652 (accessed May 2, 2011).

16. Wally Herger and Dave Reichert, "Behind the Veil: The AARP America Doesn't Know," March 2011, http://waysandmeans.house.gov/UploadedFiles/AARP_REPORT_FINAL_PDF_3_29_11.pdf (accessed May 2, 2011).

17. Phil Kerpen, "Don't Be Distracted by the Public Option Debate," *FoxNews.com*, August 24, 2009, www.philkerpen.com/?q=node/284 (accessed February 7, 2011).

18. John Fund, "Somebody Up There Doesn't Like ObamaCare," *The Wall Street Journal*, March 12, 2010, http://online.wsj.com/article/SB10001424052748704131404575117943656230542.html (accessed February 7, 2011).

19. Leanne Gendreau, "UConn Health Center Denied $100M Federal Grant," *NBC Connecticut*, December 30, 2010, www.nbcconnecticut.com/news/local/UConn-Hospital-Denied-100M-Federal-Grant-112623029.html (accessed March 10, 2011).

20. Gail Russell Chaddock, "Mr. Brown Goes to Washington, Signs His Autograph '41'," *The Christian Science Monitor*, January 21, 2010, www.csmonitor.com/USA/Politics/2010/0121/Mr.-Brown-goes-to-Washington-signs-his-autograph-41 (accessed February 7, 2011).

21. "Barney Frank Concedes Health Care Approach 'No Longer Appropriate' After Brown Beats Coakley," *The Huffington Post*, January 19, 2010, www.huffingtonpost.com/2010/01/19/barney-frank-concedes-hea_n_429128.html (accessed February 7, 2011).

22. Carrie Budoff Brown and Patrick O'Connor, "No easy rescue plan for health care," *Politico*, January 18, 2010, www.politico. com/news/stories/0110/31635.html (accessed May 3, 2011).

23. Larry Hunter, "Obstruct, Obstruct, Obstruct," *Social Security Institute*, December 14, 2009, http://socialsecurityinstitute. com/blog_post/show/387 (accessed February 7, 2011).

24. David Brody, "Senator DeMint: The Problem in the Republican Party is That the Leadership Has Gone to the Left," *CBN News*, December 10, 2009, http://blogs.cbn.com/thebrodyfile/ archive/2009/12/10/senator-demint-the-problem-in-the-republican-party-is-that.aspx (accessed February 7, 2011).

25. Nancy Pelosi, speech, March 20, 2010.

26. Curtis W. Copeland, *New Entities Created Pursuant to the Patient Protection and Affordable Care Act*, report for Congress, Congressional Research Service 7-5700: R41315 (Washington, DC, July 8, 2010).

27. Philip Klein, "The Empress of ObamaCare," *The American Spectator*, June 2010, http://spectator.org/archives/2010/06/04/ the-empress-of-obamacare (accessed February 7, 2011).

28. Kathleen Sebelius to Karen Ignagni, March 29, 2010, Department of Health and Human Services, http:/ www.health reform.gov/newsroom/children_preexisting.html (accessed February 7, 2011).

29. Office of U.S. Sen. Mike Enzi, "Senator Enzi Proposes to Overturn Job Killing Provision in Health Care Law," news release, September 22, 2010, http://help.senate.gov/newsroom/ press/release/?id=04612b7b-4766-4106-bd9d-ce7153e90bb1 (accessed February 7, 2011).

30. David Hogberg and Sean Higgins, "ObamaCare: Unions Get Better Grandfathers," *Investors Business Daily*, June 14, 2010, http://blogs.investors.com/capitalhill/index.php/home/35-politicsinvesting/1834-obamacare-unions-get-better-grandfathers (accessed February 7, 2011).

31. S.J. Res. 39, 111th Cong., 2d sess., Congressional Record 156 (September 29, 2010): S 7693.

32. Michelle Malkin, "Waivers for Favors: Big Labor's Obamacare Escape Hatch," *MichelleMalkin.com*, January 28, 2011, http:// michellemalkin.com/2011/01/28/waivers-for-favors-big-labors-obamacare-escape-hatch/ (accessed February 7, 2011).

33. Department of Health and Human Services, "State-Mandated Policies: Approved Applications for Waiver of the Annual Limits Requirements," January 26, 2011, www.hhs.gov/ociio/ regulations/approved_applications_for_waiver.html (accessed February 24, 2011).

34. Donald Berwick, interview, "Rethinking Comparative Effectiveness Research," *Biotechnology Healthcare*, June 2009, www.ncbi.nlm.nih.gov/pmc/articles/PMC2799075/pdf/bth06_2p035.pdf (accessed February 7, 2011).

35. "Measuring effectiveness and cost effectiveness: the QALY," National Institute for Health and Clinical Excellence, April 20, 2010, www.nice.org.uk/newsroom/features/measuring effectivenessandcosteffectivenesstheqaly.jsp (accessed February 7, 2011).

36. Donald M. Berwick, "A Transatlantic Review of the NHS at 60," *NHS Live: Wembley*, July 1, 2008, www.pnhp.org/news/2010/may/a-transatlantic-review-of-the-nhs-at-60 (accessed February 7, 2011).

37. Charles Krauthammer, "Government by regulation. Shhh," *The Washington Post*, December 31, 2010, www.washingtonpost.com/wp-dyn/content/article/2010/12/30/AR2010123003047.html (accessed February 7, 2011).

38. Sally Pipes, "The Era Of Health Care Rationing Begins," *Investors Business Daily*, September 15, 2010, www.investors.com/NewsAndAnalysis/Article/547365/201009151817/The-Era-Of-Health-Care-Rationing-Begins.aspx (accessed February 8, 2011).

39. Rob Stein, "FDA considers revoking approval of Avastin for advanced breast cancer," *The Washington Post*, August 16, 2010, www.washingtonpost.com/wp-dyn/content/article/2010/08/15/AR2010081503466.html (accessed February 8, 2011).

40. See, generally, Serious Medicine Strategy, http://serious medicinestrategy.blogspot.com.

41. Office of U.S. Sen. David Vitter, "Vitter Raises Concerns about Cancer Treatment Rationing Practices at FDA," news release, July 28, 2010, http://vitter.senate.gov/public/index.cfm?FuseAction=PressRoom.PressReleases&ContentRecord_id=902ac27b-f5a3-3781-e25f-a8d2e60ca40c&Region_id=&Issue_id=4af88f02-caf5-45a2-aa81-fd00521903c5 (accessed February 8, 2011).

42. Food and Drug Administration, "FDA begins process to remove breast cancer indication from Avastin label," news release, December 16, 2010, http://www.fda.gov/newsevents/newsroom/pressannouncements/ucm237172.htm (accessed February 8, 2011).

43. Andrew Pollack, "Medicare Coverage for Breast Cancer Drug Ends in Some States," *The New York Times*, January 6, 2011, http://prescriptions.blogs.nytimes.com/2011/01/06/

medicare-coverage-for-breast-cancer-drug-ends-in-some-state s/?scp=2&sq=avastin&st=cse (accessed February 8, 2011).

44. Randy E. Barnett, "Is Health-Care Reform Constitutional?" *The Washington Post*, March 21, 2010, www.washingtonpost.com/ wp-dyn/content/article/2010/03/19/AR2010031901470.html (accessed February 8, 2011).

45. Jennifer Staman and Cynthia Brougher, "Requiring Individuals to Obtain Health Insurance: A Constitutional Analysis," *Congressional Research Service*, July 24, 2009, http://assets. opencrs.com/rpts/R40725_20090724.pdf (accessed March 10, 2011).

46. Memorandum, "The Budgetary Treatment of an Individual Mandate to Buy Health Insurance," *Congressional Budget Office*, August 1994, www.cbo.gov/ftpdocs/48xx/doc4816/doc38.pdf (accessed March 10, 2011).

47. Valerie Richardson, "South Dakota GOP Takes Aim at 'Obamacare' with a Gun Bill," *The Washington Times*, February 7, 2011, www.washingtontimes.com/news/2011/feb/7/south-dakota-gop-takes-aim-obamacare-gun-bill/ (accessed February 8, 2011).

48. HR 4, 112th Cong., 1st sess., Congressional Record 157 (March 3, 2011): H 1553.

49. HR 4, 112th Cong., 1st sess., Congressional Record 157 (April 5, 2011): S 2107-8.

50. "Interstate Competition in the Individual Health Insurance Marketplace," *National Center for Policy Analysis*, www.ncpa. org/healthcare/interstate-competition-in-the-individual-health-insurance-marketplace (accessed February 8, 2011).

## *Chapter 6—The New Golden Rules*

1. David Cho, Jia Lynn Yang and Brady Dennis, "Lawmakers Guide Dodd-Frank Bill for Wall Street Reform into Homestretch," *The Washington Post*, June 26, 2010; www.washingtonpost. com/wp-dyn/content/article/2010/06/25/AR2010062500675_ pf.html (accessed February 10, 2011).

2. Binyamin Applebaum, "On Finance Bill, Lobbying Shifts to Regulations," *The New York Times*, June 26, 2010, www.ny-times.com/2010/06/27/business/27regulate.html (accessed February 10, 2011).

3. Rick Green, "No Mortgage Break for Non-VIPs," *The Hartford Courant*, June 20, 2008, http://articles.courant.com/2008-06-

20/news/rgreen0620.art_1_vip-dodd-angelo-mozilo-chris-dodd (accessed February 13, 2011).

4. Larry Margasak, "Dodd, Conrad Told Deals Were Sweetened," *The Associated Press,* July 27, 2009.

5. Eric Kleefeld, "Dodd's Retirement Could Improve Dem Chances To Hold Seat," *Talking Points Memo,* January 6, 2010, http://tpmdc.talkingpointsmemo.com/2010/01/dodds-retirement-could-improve-dem-chances-to-hold-seat.php (accessed February 13, 2011).

6. "Friend of Chris," *The Wall Street Journal,* February 20, 2009, http://online.wsj.com/article/SB123508724716027847.html (accessed February 13, 2011).

7. "Barney Frank: Front Door Single Payer Suicidal," *Single Payer Action,* July 27, 2009, www.singlepayeraction.org/blog/?p=1257 (accessed February 27, 2011).

8. Bill Sammon, "Lawmaker Accused of Fannie Mae Conflict of Interest," *FoxNews.com,* October 3, 2008, www.foxnews.com/story/0,2933,432501,00.html (accessed February 27, 2011).

9. Ibid.

10. "Washington's 'Ten Most Wanted Corrupt Politicians'," *Judicial Watch,* www.judicialwatch.org/washingtons-ten-most-wanted-corrupt-politicians (accessed February 27, 2011).

11. "Judicial Watch Announces List of Washington's 'Ten Most Wanted Corrupt Politicians' for 2010," *Judicial Watch,* www.judicialwatch.org/news/2010/dec/judicial-watch-announces-list-washingtons-ten-most-wanted-corrupt-politicians-2010 (accessed February 27, 2011).

12. Donovan Slack, "Stance on Fannie and Freddie dogs Frank," *The Boston Globe,* October 14, 2010, www.boston.com/news/politics/articles/2010/10/14/frank_haunted_by_stance_on_fannie_freddie/ (accessed February 27, 2011).

13. Ibid.

14. Lloyd Rogers, telephone interview by Phil Kerpen, February 8, 2011.

15. "AFR to Senator Dodd: Support Strong Reforms," February 3, 2010, http://ourfinancialsecurity.org/2010/02/afr-to-senator-dodd-support-strong-reforms/ (accessed February 13, 2011).

16. Victoria McGrane, "Subprime Guru Drives Debate," *Politico,* January 16, 2008, www.politico.com/news/stories/0108/7946.html (accessed February 13, 2011.

17. Ibid.

18. Peter Roff, "Who's REALLY to Blame for the Subprime Mess?" *FoxNews.com,* April 10, 2009, www.foxnews.com/opin-

ion/2009/04/10/whos-really-blame-subprime-mess/ (accessed February 13, 2011).

19. Liberty Chick (pseudonymous), "Goldman Figure John Paulson Gives $15 Million to Non-Profit; Non-Profit Ramps Up Lobbying," *Big Government*, April 20, 2010, http:// biggovernment.com/libertychick/2010/04/20/helping-thyself-at-self-help-the-paulson-connection/ (accessed February 13, 2011).

20. "Securities & Investment: Long-Term Contribution Trends," Center for Responsive Politics, www.opensecrets.org/industries/totals.php?cycle=2010&ind=F07 (accessed February 13, 2011).

21. Neil M. Barofsky, *Extraordinary Financial Assistance Provided to Citigroup, Inc.*, special audit report, SIGTARP 11-002 (Washington, DC, January 13, 2011).

22. Kevin Drawbaugh, "Is Too Big to Fail Too Big for Dodd-Frank?" *Reuters*, February 28, 2011, www.reuters.com/article/2011/02/28/us-finance-summit-liquidate-idUS-TRE71O6ED20110228 (accessed February, 28, 2011).

23. Matt Viser, "Brown Will Back Financial Overhaul," *The Boston Globe*, July 13, 2010, www.boston.com/business/articles/2010/07/13/brown_will_back_financial_overhaul/ (accessed February 13, 2011).

24. "ALG Says Unlimited Bank Tax Still in Bill, Urges Brown to Vote 'No'," *Americans for Limited Government*, June 30, 2010, www.getliberty.org/content.asp?pl=10&sl=5&contentid=492 (accessed March 6, 2011.)

25. Kent Conrad, 111th Cong., 2d sess., *Congressional Record* 156, no. 105 (July 15, 2010): S 5893.

26. Cho, Yang, and Dennis, "Lawmakers Guide Dodd."

27. "The Uncertainty Principle," *The Wall Street Journal*, July 14, 2010, http://online.wsj.com/article/SB10001424052748704288204575363162664835780.html (accessed February 10, 2011).

28. "Financial Regulations: The Line Up," U.S. Chamber of Commerce, www.uschamber.com/regulations/finance (accessed February 13, 2011).

29. Statistic attributed to Noreen M. Culhane by James J. Cramer, "Behind the Euronext Deal," *The Wall Street Journal*, May 26, 2006.

30. Committee on Capital Markets Regulation, "Interim Report Summary," December 5, 2006, www.capmktsreg.org/pdfs/Summary_11.30interimreport.pdf (accessed February 13, 2011).

31. Josh Gerstein, "Friedman, 93, Set To Unleash Power of Choice," *The New York Sun*, March 22, 2006, www.nysun.com/pf.php?id=29551 (accessed February 13, 2011).

32. White House Office of the Press Secretary, "Remarks by the President at Signing of Dodd-Frank Wall Street Reform and Consumer Protection Act," news release, July 21, 2010, www.whitehouse.gov/the-press-office/remarks-president-signing-dodd-frank-wall-street-reform-and-consumer-protection-act (accessed February 10, 2011).

33. Thomas F. Cooley, "Elizabeth Warren's Holy Crusade," *Forbes.com*, April 22, 2009, www.forbes.com/2009/04/21/congressional-oversight-panel-tarp-opinions-columnists-elizabeth-warren.html (accessed February 13, 2011).

34. "We Need Elizabeth Warren at the CFPB!" *MoveOn.org Political Action*, http://pol.moveon.org/warren/ (accessed February 13, 2011).

35. Jerome Karabel, "Robert Gibbs, Elizabeth Warren, and the 2010 Election," *The Huffington Post*, August 13, 2010, www.huffingtonpost.com/jerome-karabel/robert-gibbs-elizabeth-wa_b_681858.html (accessed February 13, 2011).

36. Jim Puzzanghera and Peter Nicholas, "Obama Decision to Avoid Confirmation Battle for Elizabeth Warren Is Hailed and Criticized," *Los Angeles Times*, September 17, 2010, http://articles.latimes.com/2010/sep/17/business/la-fi-elizabeth-warren-20100917 (accessed February 13, 2011).

37. Meredith Shiner, "Chris Dodd warns White House on Elizabeth Warren move," Politico, September 16, 2010, http://www.politico.com/news/stories/0910/42278.html (accessed February 13, 2011).

38. Puzzanghera and Nicholas, "Obama decision to avoid confirmation battle."

39. Juliana Gruenwald, "Personnel Changes For 2011," *National Journal*, January 4, 2011, http://techdailydose.nationaljournal.com/2011/01/personnel-changes-for-2011.php (accessed February 15, 2011).

40. Curtis W. Copeland, "The Dodd-Frank Wall Street Reform and Consumer Protection Act: Regulations to be Issued by the Consumer Financial Protection Bureau," *Congressional Research Service*, August 25, 2010, www.fas.org/sgp/crs/misc/R41380.pdf (accessed February 13, 2011).

41. "Debit Card Interchange Fees and Routing," proposed rule by the Federal Reserve System, *Federal Register* 75, no. 248 (December 28, 2010): 81722-63.

42. John Berlau, "The Free Checking Restoration Act," *The Wall Street Journal*, October 26, 2010, http://online.wsj.com/article/ SB10001424052702303467004575574123982225624.html (accessed February 13, 2011).

43. Phil Kerpen, "If You Like Your Debit Card and Free Checking Account, Here's an Important Vote to Watch," *FoxNews.com*, May 23, 2011, www.foxnews.com/opinion/2011/05/23/like- debit-card-free-checking-account-heres-important-vote-watch (accessed June 9, 2011).

44. S.Amdt to S.782, 112th Cong., 1st sess., Congressional Record 157 (June 8, 2011): S 3984, www.senate.gov/legislative/LIS/ roll_call_lists/roll_call_vote_cfm.cfm?congress=112&session= 1&vote=00086 (accessed June 9, 2011).

45. Horace Cooper, "Racial quotas as financial services reform?" *The Washington Times*, July 15, 2010, www.washingtontimes. com/blog/watercooler/2010/jul/15/racial-quotas-financial- services-reform/ (accessed February 13, 2011).

46. Jean Eaglesham, "Firms Assail Whistleblower Plan by SEC," *The Wall Street Journal*, December 15, 2010, http://online.wsj. com/article/SB1000142405274870373420457602003263914 9392.html (accessed February 13, 2011).

47. Phil Kerpen, "An Under-the-Radar Threat to Capitalism," *National Review Online*, January 16, 2007, www.nationalreview. com/articles/219732/under-radar-threat-capitalism/phil- kerpen (accessed February 13, 2011).

48. Paul Atkins, "The SEC's Sop to Unions," *The Wall Street Journal*, August 27, 2010, http://online.wsj.com/article/SB1000142 405274870363230457545134342958522.html (accessed February 13, 2011.

49. Saul Alinsky, *Rules for Radicals* (New York City: Random House, 1989), 181.

50. Pat Garofalo, "What Happens to Financial Reform Funding If a Continuing Resolution Passes?" *Think Progress*, December 20, 2010, http://wonkroom.thinkprogress.org/2010/12/20/cr- finreg/ (accessed February 13, 2011).

51. David Dayen, "Continuing Resolutions Make Implementation of Dodd-Frank Nearly Impossible," *Fire Dog Lake*, December 20, 2010, http://news.firedoglake.com/2010/12/20/continuing- resolutions-make-implementation-of-dodd-frank-nearly- impossible/ (accessed February 13, 2011).

## Chapter 7—Drilling Down

1. John Holdren, Anne Ehrlich, and Paul Ehrlich, Human Ecology: Problems and Solutions (San Francisco: W.H. Freeman and Company, 1973), 279, cited by Robert Bradley, "The Heated Energy Debate Assessing John Holdren's Attack on Bjørn Lomborg's The Skeptical Environmentalist," Competitive Enterprise Institute, June 25, 2003, http://cei.org/studies-issue-analysis/heated-energy-debate (accessed February 16, 2011).

2. Joseph R. Biden Jr. and Sarah Palin, debate transcript, Washington University, St. Louis, October 2, 2008, http://debate.wustl.edu/transcript.pdf (accessed February 19, 2011).

3. "Drill Here, Drill Now, Pay Less Petition," American Solutions, www.americansolutions.com/drill (accessed February 17, 2011).

4. Jim Harger, "GOP election promoter urges handlers to unleash Sarah Palin," The Grand Rapids Press, October 2, 2008, www.mlive.com/news/grpress/index.ssf?/base/news-44/1222953355216000.xml&coll=6 (accessed February 17, 2011).

5. Biden and Palin debate, October 2, 2008.

6. Michael C. Bender, "Obama Would Consider Off-Shore Drilling as Part of Comprehensive Energy Plan," The Palm Beach Post, August 1, 2008, www.palmbeachpost.com/localnews/content/state/epaper/2008/08/01/0801obama1.html (accessed February 19, 2011).

7. Phil Kerpen, "A Stunning Pro-Drilling Victory," National Review Online, September 24, 2008, www.nationalreview.com/articles/225770/stunning-pro-drilling-victory/phil-kerpen (accessed February 19, 2011).

8. Ben Lieberman, "Congressional Moratorium on Offshore Drilling in the OuterContinental Shelf Should Be Allowed to Expire," The Heritage Foundation, August 8, 2008, www.heritage.org/research/reports/2008/08/congressional-moratorium-on-offshore-drilling-in-the-outer-continental-shelf-should-be-allowed-to-expire (accessed February 19, 2011).

9. U.S. Department of the Interior, "Secretary of the Interior Ken Salazar's Statement on Offshore Energy Strategy," news release, February 10, 2009, www.doi.gov/news/speeches/2009_02_10_speech.cfm (accessed February 19, 2011).

10. Vince Haley, "Drillgate: Cover Up at Interior, Internal Emails Show," American Solutions, February 4, 2010, www.american-

solutions.com/drill/2010/02/internal-emails-show-cover-up-at-interior.php (accessed February 20, 2011).

11. This e-mail is posted on the American Solutions website here: www.americansolutions.com/dhdn/2010/03/interior-touts-transparency-while-concealing-public-comments.php (accessed May 6, 2011).

12. Export-Import Bank Of The United States, "Summary Of Minutes Of Meeting Of Board Of Directors," April 14, 2009, www.exim.gov/article.cfm/69B39F09-A182-B668-8A5588CC8A0D64ED/<Query (accessed February 20, 2011.

13. *The Wall Street Journal*, "Obama Underwrites Offshore Drilling," August 18, 2009, http://online.wsj.com/article/SB1000142 4052970203863204574346610120524166.html (accessed February 20, 2011).

14. "Strengthening Our Economy: The Untapped US Oil and Gas Resources," *ICF International*, December 8, 2008, www.api.org/aboutoilgas/upload/ICF_Study_Summary_12_8_08.pdf (accessed February 20, 2011).

15. John M. Broder, "Obama to Open Offshore Areas to Oil Drilling for First Time," *The New York Times*, March 31, 2009, www.ny-times.com/2010/03/31/science/earth/31energy.html (accessed February 19, 2011).

16. Ibid.

17. Office of the Governor of Virginia, "Statement of Governor Bob McDonnell on President's Offshore Energy Plan," news release, March 31, 2010, www.governor.virginia.gov/news/viewRelease.cfm?id=99 (accessed February 20, 2011).

18. "Kerpen on Drilling: 'Obama Is Talking about Lifting a Nonexistent Ban'," *Americans for Prosperity*, March 31,2010, www.americansforprosperity.org/033110-kerpen-drilling-obama-talking-about-lifting-nonexistent-ban (accessed February 20, 2011).

19. William M. Welch and Chris Joyner, "Memorial service honors 11 dead oil rig workers," *USA Today*, May 25, 2010, www.usatoday.com/news/nation/2010-05-25-oil-spill-victims-memorial_N.htm (accessed February 20, 2011).

20. "BP Leak the World's Worst Accidental Oil Spill," *The Telegraph*, August 3, 2010, www.telegraph.co.uk/finance/newsbysector/energy/oilandgas/7924009/BP-leak-the-worlds-worst-accidental-oil-spill.html (accessed February 20, 2011).

21. Jake Tapper and Huma Khan, "'Political Stupidity': Democrat James Carville Slams Obama's Response to BP Oil Spill," *ABC News*, May 26, 2010, http://abcnews.go.com/GMA/Politics/

bp-oil-spill-political-headache-obama-democrats-slam/
story?id=10746519 (accessed February 20, 2011).

22. Rasmussen Reports, "Toplines—Oil Leak and Obama—
September 12-13, 2010," September 13, 2010.

23. James Carville on *Good Morning America*, quoted in Glynnis
MacNicol, "James Carville: Obama Needs To Lift Drilling
Moratorium ASAP," *Mediaite*, June 14th, 2010, www.
mediaite.com/tv/james-carville-obama-needs-to-lift-drilling-
moratorium-asap/ (accessed February 20, 2011).

24. E. Arnold to Gov. Bobby Jindal, U.S. Sen. Mary Landrieu,
and U.S. Sen. David Vitter, www.instituteforenergyresearch.
org/pdf/Fax_to_Governor_Jindal,_Senator_Landrieu_and_
Senator_Vitter.pdf (accessed February 20, 2011).

25. Kenneth E. Arnold, et al, "The Primary Recommendation
in the May 27, 2010 report, 'Increased Safety Measures for
Energy Development on the Outer Continental Shelf' Given by
Secretary Salazar to the President Misrepresents our Position,"
www.instituteforenergyresearch.org/pdf/Our_Views_Are_
Not_Appropriately_Represented-_Rev_1.pdf (accessed
February 20, 2011).

26. Office of the Inspector General, U.S. Department of the Interior,
*Investigative Report of Federal Moratorium on Deepwater Drilling*,
(Washington, DC, November 8, 2010).

27. Stephen Power and Leslie Eaton, "U.S. Saw Drill Ban Killing
Many Jobs," *The Wall Street Journal*, August 21, 2010, http://
online.wsj.com/article/SB100014240527487044884045 7544
1760384563880.html (accessed February 20, 2011).

28. Shane Cohn, "Industry officials say Pacific drilling different
than Gulf, threat of a leak not as big a concern," *Ventura County
Reporter*, July 29, 2010, www.vcreporter.com/cms/story/detail/
new_offshore_drilling_moratorium_lays_off_dozens_of_
local_workers/8107/ (accessed February 20, 2011).

29. Amy Asman, "Santa Barbara County supes address the energy
crisis," *Santa Maria Sun*, August 27, 2008, www.santamaria-
sun.com/news/518/santa-barbara-county-supes-address-the-
energy-crisis/ (accessed February 20, 2011).

30. *Hornbeck Offshore Services L.L.C et al., v. Kenneth Lee "Ken"
Salazar et al*, case 2:10-cv-01663 (U.S. District Court, Eastern
District Of Louisiana June 22, 2010).

31. Margaret Cronin Fisk and Laurel Brubaker Calkins, "Appeals
Court Rejects Bid to Delay U.S. Drilling Ban Order," *Bloomberg*,
July 9, 2010, www.bloomberg.com/news/2010-07-08/u-s-
appeals-court-denies-request-to-reinstate-deep-water-oil-
drilling-ban.html (accessed February 20, 2011).

32. Josh Voorhees, "Interior not ready to lift offshore drilling ban," *Politico*, September 30, 2009, www.politico.com/news/stories/0910/42947.html (accessed February 20, 2011).

33. Stephen Power and Ann Zimmerman, "Gulf Drilling Ban Is Lifted," *The Wall Street Journal*, October 13, 2010, http://online.wsj.com/article/SB100014240527487034400045755479804255525408.html (accessed February 20, 2011).

34. Connie Hair, "Obama's Stealth Moratorium on Shallow-Water Drilling," *Human Events*, July 2, 2010, www.humanevents.com/article.php?id=37894 (accessed February 20, 2011).

35. Rob Bluey, "Permitorium: 103 Gulf of Mexico Drilling Plans Await Government Approval," *The Heritage Foundation*, February 4, 2011, http://blog.heritage.org/2011/02/04/permitorium-103-gulf-of-mexico-drilling-plans-await-government-approval/ (accessed February 20, 2011).

36. Greater New Orleans Inc., "GPI—Gulf Permit Index—as of February 1," February 3, 2011, http://gnoinc.org/press-releases/gpi-gulf-permit-index-as-of-february-1 (accessed February 20, 2011).

37. "Seahawk Drilling seeks bankruptcy, to sell assets," *The Associated Press*, February 12, 2011, www.usatoday.com/money/companies/2011-02-12-seahawk-drilling_N.htm (accessed February 24, 2011).

38. Phil Taylor, "Shell Cancels 2011 Arctic Drilling Plans," *Greenwire*, February 3, 2011, www.nytimes.com/gwire/2011/02/03/03greenwire-shell-cancels-2011-arctic-drilling-plans-18881.html (accessed February 20, 2011).

39. Kristen Hays, "Exxon says Gulf oil spill response system ready," *Reuters*, February 17, 2011, www.reuters.com/article/2011/02/17/us-usa-offshore-containment-idUSTRE71G69W20110217 (accessed March 6, 2011).

40. Office of Science and Technology Policy, "About OSTP," www.whitehouse.gov/administration/eop/ostp/about (accessed February 20, 2011).

41. Chris Horner, "Dr. Doom," *The American Spectator*, February 12, 2009, http://spectator.org/blog/2009/02/12/dr-doom (accessed February 20, 2011).

42. Bradley, "The Heated Energy Debate."

43. John Holdren and Paul Ehrlich, "Introduction," in Holdren and Ehrlich, eds., *Global Ecology* (New York: Harcourt Brace Jovanovich, 1971), 3, cited in Robert Bradley, "The Heated Energy Debate: Assessing John Holdren's Attack on Bjørn Lomborg's The Skeptical Environmentalist," *Competitive*

*Enterprise Institute*, June 25, 2003, http://cei.org/studies-issue-analysis/heated-energy-debate (accessed February 16, 2011).

44. John Holdren, "Memorandum to the President: The Energy-Climate Challenge," in Donald Kennedy and John Riggs, eds., *U.S. Policy and the Global Environment: Memos to the President* (Washington, DC: The Aspen Institute, 2000), 21, cited in Robert Bradley, "The Heated Energy Debate: Assessing John Holdren's Attack on Bjørn Lomborg's The Skeptical Environmentalist," Competitive Enterprise Institute, June 25, 2003, http://cei.org/studies-issue-analysis/heated-energy-debate (accessed February 16, 2011).

45. Rasmussen Reports, "National Survey of 1,000 Likely Voters Conducted December 3-4, 2010," December 4, 2010.

46. Office of the Governor of Virginia, "Statement of Governor Bob McDonnell on Obama Administration Decision to Block Offshore Energy Development Efforts in Virginia," news release, December 1, 2010, www.governor.virginia.gov/news/viewRelease.cfm?id=490 (accessed February 20, 2011).

# Chapter 8—*Property in Peril*

1. R.J. Smith, "Federal Land-Grabs Are Destroying American Dream," *Human Events*, October 8, 2008, www.humanevents.com/article.php?id=28917 (accessed February 23, 2011).

2. For a complete analysis of the legislative history, see John Broomes, "Navigating in Isolated Waters: Section 404 of the Clean Water Act Revisited," *Washburn Law Journal* 41 (2001), 209-30. http://washburnlaw.edu/wlj/41-1/articles/broomes-john.pdf (accessed February 22, 2011).

3. Felicity Barringer, "Michigan Landowner Who Filled Wetlands Faces Prison," *The New York Times*, May 18, 2004, www.nytimes.com/2004/05/18/national/18enviro.html (accessed February 22, 2011).

4. Ibid.

5. David Shepardson, "Man Avoids Prison in Land Feud; Judge Rejects Efforts to Sentence Midland Developer to 10 Months for Filling in Wetlands," *The Detroit News*, March 16, 2005.

6. Statement by M. Reed Hopper, U.S. House Committee on Transportation and Infrastructure Subcommittee on Water Resources and Environment, *Hearing on Status of the Nation's Waters, including Wetlands, under the Jurisdiction of the Federal Water Pollution Control Act*, July 17, 2007.

7. Brad Swenson, "Landowners Oppose Oberstar, Clean Water Act," *Bemidji Pioneer*, September 25, 2010.
8. Ibid. The word "about" was deleted with permission.
9. Bonner R. Cohen and D. Brady Nelson, "Voters Rebuke Environmental Extremism in Oberstar Defeat," *Environment & Climate News*, January 2011, www.heartland.org/environmentandclimate-news.org/article/28872/Voters_Rebuke_Environmental_Extremism_in_Oberstar_Defeat_.html (accessed February 23, 2011).
10. Paul Quinlan, "Regulation Haters Join Chorus Urging New Clean Water Act Rules," *Greenwire*, February 17, 2011, www.nytimes.com/gwire/2011/02/17/17greenwire-regulation-haters-join-chorus-urging-new-clean-66183.html (accessed February 23, 2011).
11. "EPA Seeks to Increase Water Act's Scope," *Western Farm Press*, February 21, 2011, http://westernfarmpress.com/government/epa-seeks-increase-water-acts-scope (accessed February 23, 2011).
12. EPA Clean Water Protection Guidance, December 2010 draft, www.westernroundtable.com/Portals/0/Docs/lands/water/2011/draft_wous_guid_final_review.pdf (accessed February 23, 2011).
13. Quinlan, "Regulation Haters."
14. U.S. Rep. Bob Gibbs et al. to Lisa Jackson and Jo-Ellen Darcy, April 14, 2011, http://republicans.transportation.house.gov/Media/file/112th/Water/2011-04-14-EPA_Guidance_Letter.pdf (accessed May 6, 2011).
15. Office of U.S. Rep. Bob Gibbs, "Gibbs Leads Bipartisan Group of Lawmakers in Call for Administration to Halt 'Guidance' to Dramatically Expand Clean Water Act Jurisdiction," news release, April 18, 2011, http://gibbs.house.gov/press-release/gibbs-leads-bipartisan-group-lawmakers-call-administration-halt-%E2%80%9Cguidance%E2%80%9D (accessed May 6, 2011).
16. Robert Lawrence, "Can We Comment Yet? EPA and Corps Issue Proposed New Rapanos Guidance," May 2, 2011, *American College of Environmental Lawyers*, www.acoel.org/2011/05/articles/water/can-we-comment-yet-epa-and-corps-issue-proposed-new-rapanos-guidance/ (accessed May 6, 2011).
17. U.S. House Committee on Natural Resources, "Hastings Blasts Lame Duck Democrats' Attempt to Push Through Massive Omnibus Package," news release, December 2, 2010, http://naturalresources.house.gov/News/DocumentSingle.aspx?DocumentID=216632 (accessed February 23, 2011).

18. R.J. Smith, "Federal Land-Grabs Are Destroying American Dream."

19. Ibid.

20. U.S. Department of the Interior, "Salazar, Abbey Restore Protections for America's Wild Lands," news release, December 23, 2010, www.interior.gov/news/pressreleases/Salazar-Abbey-Restore-Protections-for-Americas-Wild-Lands.cfm (accessed February 23, 2011).

21. Alston Chase, *Playing God in Yellowstone* (San Diego: Harcourt Brace & Company, 1987), 309.

22. Holly Fretwell and Shawn Regan, "Make Good On Tea Party Rhetoric By Selling Federal Lands," *Forbes.com*, November 18, 2010, www.perc.org/articles/article1321.php (accessed February 24, 2011).

23. Office of U.S. Rep. Mike Simpson, "Simpson Defunds 'Wild Lands' Initiative in Final Budget Bill," news release, April 12, 2011, http://simpson.house.gov/News/DocumentSingle. aspx?DocumentID=235285 (accessed April 20, 2011).

24. See www.ProjectNoProject.com.

25. David Ehrenfeld, *The Arrogance of Humanism* (New York: Oxford University Press, 1978), 116-18. He was discussing fusion power, but the point is applicable to any energy source. The true environmental concern is the powering of modern civilization.

26. Juliet Eilperin, "Salazar Voids Drilling Leases On Public Lands in Utah," *The Washington Post*, February 5, 2009, www. washingtonpost.com/wp-dyn/content/article/2009/02/04/ AR2009020401785.html (accessed February 24, 2011).

27. Mark Jaffe, "Salazar Halts Oil-Shale Leases," *Denver Post*, February 26, 2009, www.denverpost.com/ci_11786821 (accessed February 24, 2011).

28. "Western Energy Alliance Releases 'Dashboard' Showing Trends in Western Oil and Natural Gas Development," *Western Energy Alliance*, December 9, 2010, http://westernenergyalliance. org/wp-content/uploads/2009/05/News-Release-%E2%80%9CDashboard%E2%80%9D-Showing-Trends-in-Western-Oil-and-Natural-Gas-Development.pdf (accessed February 24, 2011).

29. Margasak, "Darrell Issa Out Front Of Obama On Regulations."

30. David A. Fahrenthold, "Environmental Regulations to Curtail Mountaintop Mining," *The Washington Post*, April 2, 2010, www. washingtonpost.com/wp-dyn/content/article/2010/04/01/ AR2010040102312.html (accessed March 3, 2011).

31. Bonner Cohen, "Salazar's Wild Lands Policy Sends Shockwaves Across the West," *CFACT*, January 18, 2011, www.cfact. org/a/1869/Salazars-wild-lands-policy-sends-shockwaves-across-the-West (accessed February 24, 2011).

32. H. Sterling Bernett, "ESA Listing Not Needed for Polar Bears," *Environment & Climate News*, March 2007, www.heartland. org/policybot/results/20631/ESA_Listing_Not_Needed_for_Polar_Bears.html (accessed May 16, 2011).

33. Joel Whitley and Teresa Imm, "Polar Bear Critical Habitat Poses Threat to North Slope Residents and Alaska's Economy," *Resource Development Council*, December 2010, http://akrdc. org/newsletters/2010/december/polarbearch.html (accessed February 24, 2011).

34. Ibid.

35. Lou Dolinar, "Killing Owls to Save Owls," *National Review*, February 22, 2010, www.nationalreview.com/articles/260150/killing-owls-save-owls-lou-dolinar (accessed March 3, 2011).

36. Ibid.

37. Eric Mortenson, "Make This Call in the Wild: Should Oregon Shoot Barred Owls to Save Spotted Owls?" *The Oregonian*, February 5, 2011, www.oregonlive.com/environment/index. ssf/2011/02/make_this_call_in_the_wild_sho.html (accessed March 3, 2011).

38. *Investors Business Daily*, "Will A Lizard Stop West Texas Oil?" April 27, 2011, www.investors.com/NewsAndAnalysis/Article/570339/201104271827/Will-A-Lizard-Stop-West-Texas-Oil-.aspx (accessed May 16, 2011).

39. National Park Service, "Antiquities Act of 1906," http://www. cr.nps.gov/history/hisnps/npshistory/antiq.htm (accessed February 24, 2011).

40. Utah Geologic Survey, "A Preliminary Assessment of Energy and Mineral Resources within the Grand Staircase-Escalante National Monument," January 1997, http://geology.utah.gov/online/c/c-93/index.htm (accessed February 24, 2011).

41. Amy Seigel, "Ten Years Later: Grand Staircase-Escalante Still Elicits Both Cheers and Jeers from Utahns," *New West Development*, September 20, 2006, www.newwest.net/index. php/topic/article/ten_years_later_grand_staircase_escalante_still_elicits_both_cheers_and_jee/C57/L35/ (accessed February 24, 2011).

42. William La Jeunesse, "Exclusive: Obama Eyes Western Land for National Monuments, Angering," *FOXNews.com*, February 18, 2010, http://www.foxnews.com/politics/2010/02/18/obama-

eyeing-millions-wild-acres-national-monuments (accessed February 24, 2011).

43. Office of U.S. Rep. Denny Rehberg, documents posted on Rehberg's official Website, http://rehberg.house.gov/index.cf m?sectionid=89&sectiontree=2,89 (accessed February 24, 2011).

44. La Jeunesse, "Exclusive."

45. Ibid.

46. Bruce Babbitt, *Cities in the Wilderness* (Washington: Island Press, 2005), 169.

47. Heller is now a U.S. senator, appointed April 27, 2011, by Nevada Gov. Brian Sandoval to finish the term of former U.S. Sen. John Ensign, who resigned.

48. H.R. 1, February 19, 2011, 112th Cong., 1st sess., *Congressional Record* 157 (February 19, 2011): H 1338-9.

49. Roger Pilon, *Property Rights and the Constitution*, in the Cato Handbook for Policymakers, 7th edition 2009: 361.

# Chapter 9—The Back Door to the Back Door

1. Stephan Holmes and Cass R. Sunstein, "Why We Should Celebrate Paying Taxes," *Chicago Tribune*, April 14, 1999, http://home.uchicago.edu/~csunstei/celebrate.html (accessed February 26, 2011).

2. Barack Obama, "Toward a 21st-Century Regulatory System," *The Wall Street Journal*, January 18, 2011, http://online.wsj. com/article/SB1000142405274870339660457608827211211 03698.html (accessed February 26, 2011).

3. U.S. Sen. Rand Paul, telephone interview by Phil Kerpen, March 14, 2011.

4. Obama, "Toward a 21st-Century Regulatory System."

5. Ibid.

6. Ibid.

7. U.S. House Select Committee on Energy Independence & Global Warming, "Sensenbrenner, Issa Seek Joint Probe on Carbon Emissions 'Vow of Silence'," press release, June 9, 2009, https://republicanglobalwarmingforms.house.gov/press/ PRArticle.aspx?NewsID=2619 (accessed February 26, 2011).

8. Andrew Restuccia, "EPA 'Confident' Obama Reg Policy Won't Affect New Climate Rules," *The Hill*, January 18, 2011, http://thehill.com/blogs/e2-wire/677-e2-wire/138627-epa-

confident-new-obama-reg-policy-wont-alter-climate-rules (accessed February 26, 2011).

9.  White House Office of the Press Secretary, "Remarks by the President to the Chamber of Commerce," news release, February 7, 2011, www.whitehouse.gov/the-press-office/2011/02/07/remarks-president-chamber-commerce (accessed February 26, 2011).

10. Executive Order no. 13563, "Improving Regulation and Regulatory Review," *Federal Register* 76, no. 14 (January 21, 2011) 3821-23.

11. Wayne Crews, "Obama Needs To Confront Regulation," *Forbes.com*, January 28, 2011, www.forbes.com/2011/01/18/barack-obama-executive-order-regulation-opinions-contributors-wayne-crews.html (accessed February 26, 2011).

12. Executive Order no. 13563.

13. Ibid.

14. Stephan Holmes and Cass R. Sunstein, "Why We Should Celebrate Paying Taxes," *Chicago Tribune*, April 14, 1999, http://home.uchicago.edu/~csunstei/celebrate.html (accessed February 26, 2011).

15. Cass R. Sunstein and Richard H. Thaler, "Libertarian Paternalism Is Not an Oxymoron," University of Chicago Law Review (working paper no. 03-2, AEI-Brookings Joint Center for Regulatory Studies, May 2003), http://ssrn.com/abstract_id=405940 (accessed February 26, 2011).

16. Josh Stephens, "Green Nudges: An Interview with Obama Regulatory Czar Cass Sunstein," *Grist*, April 6, 2009, www.grist.org/article/2009-green-nudges-an-interview-with-obama-re (accessed February 26, 2011).

17. Ibid.

18. Cass R. Sunstein and Adrian Vermeule, "Conspiracy Theories," Harvard Public Law Working Paper No. 08-03; University of Chicago, Public Law Working Paper No. 199; University of Chicago Law & Economics, Olin Working Paper No. 387, January 15, 2008, http://ssrn.com/abstract=1084585 (accessed February 26, 2011).

19. For a good recap and criticism of the episode from the left, see Jane Hamsher, "How the White House Used Gruber's Work to Create Appearance of Broad Consensus," *The Huffington Post*, January 13, 2010, www.huffingtonpost.com/jane-hamsher/how-the-white-house-used_b_421549.html (accessed February 26, 2011).

20. Cass Sunstein, interview, WBEZ-FM, February 2001, available from *Naked Emperor News*, http://blip.tv/file/3633495 (accessed February 26, 2011).

21. Cass R. Sunstein, *On Rumors* (New York: Farrar, Straus and Giroux, 2010), 78.

22. Cass R. Sunstein, *Democracy and the Problem of Free Speech* (New York: Simon & Schuster, 1993), 92.

23. According to former FEC commissioner Hans A. von Spakovsky. See "Leaked: Obama Executive Order Intends to Implement Portions of DISCLOSE Act," *Pajamas Media*, April 19, 2011, http://pajamasmedia.com/blog/leaked-obama-executive-order-intends-to-implement-portions-of-disclose-act (accessed April 20, 2011).

24. "Washington Journal: Cass Sunstein, Professor, University of Chicago Law School" (C-SPAN, November 13, 2005), www.c-span.org/Events/Cass-Sunstein-Professor-Univ-of-Chicago-Law-School/3904/ (accessed February 26, 2011).

25. Phil Kerpen, "Regulatory state needs more than a trim," *The Washington Times*, January 21, 2011, www.washingtontimes.com/news/2011/jan/21/regulatory-state-needs-more-than-a-trim/ (accessed February 26, 2011).

26. Larry Margasak, "Darrell Issa Out Front Of Obama On Regulations," *The Associated Press*, February 7, 2011, www.kpbs.org/news/2011/feb/07/darrell-issa-out-front-obama-regulations/ (accessed February 26, 2011).

27. Ibid.

28. Ibid.

29. Susan Dudley, "Why I support regulatory pay-go," *The Daily Caller*, February 7, 2001, http://dailycaller.com/2011/02/07/why-i-support-regulatory-pay-go/ (accessed February 26, 2011).

30. Susan Dudley, "Regulation in a 21st Century Economy" (remarks, Mercatus Center conference, Washington, DC, March 3, 2011), http://mercatus.org/events/regulation-21st-century-economy (accessed March 6, 2011).

31. Office of U.S. Rep. Kevin Brady, "Office of Congressman Kevin Brady Federal Sunset Act Executive Summary," news release, www.house.gov/brady/sunset_executive_summary.html (accessed February 26, 2011).

32. U.S. Rep. Geoff Davis, interview by Phil Kerpen, Washington, DC, February 28, 2011.

# Conclusion—Restoring the Republic

1. See, for instance: Engels to Franz Mehring, *Marx and Engels Correspondence*, July 14, 1893, www.marxists.org/archive/marx/works/1893/letters/93_07_14.htm (accessed March 3, 2011).

2. White House Office of the Press Secretary, "Remarks by the President at DSCC Fundraiser De La Torre Residence, Boston, Massachusetts," news release, October 16, 2010, www.whitehouse.gov/the-press-office/2010/10/16/remarks-president-dscc-fundraiser (accessed March 3, 2011).

3. White House Office of the Press Secretary, "Press Conference by the President," news release, November 3, 2010, www.whitehouse.gov/the-press-office/2010/11/03/press-conference-president. Retrieved (accessed March 3, 2011).

4. F. A. Hayek, *The Fatal Conceit* (Chicago: University of Chicago Press, 1988), 85.

5. Lloyd Rogers, telephone interview with Phil Kerpen, February 8, 2011.

6. Nicole Crain and Mark Crain, "The Impact of Regulatory Costs on Small Firms," for the U.S. Small Business Administration Office of Advocacy under contract number SBAHQ-08-M-0466, September 2010, http://archive.sba.gov/advo/research/rs371tot.pdf (accessed March 3, 2011).

7. T. Randolph Beard, George S. Ford, Hyeongwoo Kim, and Lawrence J. Spiwak, *Regulatory Expenditures, Economic Growth and Jobs: An Empirical Study*, Phoenix Center Policy Bulletin 28 (April 2011), www.phoenix-center.org/PolicyBulletin/PCPB28Final.pdf (accessed April 20, 2011).

8. Andy Cohen, "Maneuvering Room On Signing Statements," *CBS News*, March 9, 2009, www.cbsnews.com/8301-503544_162-4854750-503544.html (accessed March 3, 2011).

9. Robert Higgs, *Crisis and Leviathan* (New York: Oxford University Press, 1987), 262.

# INDEX

# ACKNOWLEDGMENTS

This book would not have been possible without the remarkable patience and support of my wife, Joanna, who put up with me writing this book on top of other work responsibilities while she was pregnant, and then after we had our first baby. Joanna: you deserved more of my time. I love you.

My Americans for Prosperity colleagues, especially James Valvo and Erik Telford, have been key collaborators on many of the book's underlying ideas, and have been critical in helping carry these ideas to our more than 1.8 million members. Tommy Downs deserves special thanks for creating the ObamaChart graphic. I thank Mike Harinstein for the title *Democracy Denied*, which he came up with for an early version of the chart, and Justin Dugyon for assisting with interviews.

I thank the board of directors for giving me the platform I have at AFP, and all of our staff and volunteer activists for being the finest leaders in the free-market movement.

Lloyd Rogers, Geoff Davis, and Rand Paul were generous with their time for interviews, and deserve special thanks for developing and supporting the REINS Act—legislation that may actually save us from the threats highlighted in this book.

Seton Motley, Vinnie Vernuccio, Matthew Vadum, Bill Collier, Paul Collier, and Eric Novack were kind enough to review the material in their areas of expertise to help me get my facts straight. Any errors that remain are exclusively mine.

I thank the endorsers who offered such kind words, and all of my professional mentors who have influenced me as a writer and a thinker, especially Steve Moore, Ralph Benko, and Peter Roff. I also thank Peter, as well as Stephen Manfredi, for connecting me with my agent, Scott Hoffman.

Thanks to Scott and to the team at BenBella—Glenn Yeffeth, Debbie Harmsen, Lisa Miller, and Adrienne Lang—for helping me through the process.

Finally, I thank President Obama for his constant attacks on Americans for Prosperity that have credentialed me as an opponent of his policies, and for being so extreme that, just maybe, we can get Congress to stop the galloping growth of federal regulatory power.

# ABOUT THE AUTHOR

**PHIL KERPEN** is vice president for policy at Americans for Prosperity (AFP), a national grassroots organization committed to educating Americans about economic policy and returning the federal government to its constitutional limits.

Also a columnist on FoxNews.com and chairman of the Internet Freedom Coalition, Kerpen is a sought-after television and radio commentator regarding economic growth issues. His op-eds have run in newspapers ranging from *The Wall Street Journal*, *The Washington Post*, *Boston Globe*, and *New York Post* to the *Los Angeles Times*, *San Jose Mercury News*, and *San Diego Union-Tribune*.

Prior to joining AFP, Kerpen served as policy director and executive director for the Free Enterprise Fund, an organization he co-founded in 2005. Kerpen also worked as an analyst and researcher for the Club for Growth, the Woodhill Foundation, and the Cato Institute.

A native of Brooklyn, New York, Kerpen currently resides in Washington, D.C., with his wife, Joanna, and their daughter, Lilly.

His website is **PhilKerpen.com**.